PARALLEL AND DISTRIBUTED REAL-TIME SYSTEMS

PARALLEL AND DISTRIBUTED REAL-TIME SYSTEMS

JAN VAN KATWIJK
JANUSZ ZALEWSKI
EDITORS

Nova Science Publishers, Inc.
Huntington, New York

Senior Editors: Susan Boriotti and Donna Dennis
Coordinating Editor: Tatiana Shohov
Office Manager: Annette Hellinger
Graphics: Wanda Serrano
Book Production: Matthew Kozlowski, Jonathan Rose and Jennifer Vogt
Circulation: Cathy DeGregory, Ave Maria Gonzalez

Library of Congress Cataloging-in-Publication Data
p. cm.
Includes bibliographical references and index.
ISBN 1-59033-115-X

227 Main Street, Suite 100
Huntington, New York 11743
Tele. 631-424-6682 Fax 631-424-4666
e-mail: Novascience@earthlink.net
Web Site: http://www.nexusworld.com/nova

Printed in the United States of America

Contents

PARALLEL AND DISTRIBUTED REAL-TIME SYSTEMS: AN INTRODUCTION

JAN VAN KATWIJK* AND JANUSZ ZALEWSKI†

Abstract. In this Special Issue we collected nine contributions on "Parallel and Distributed Real-Time Systems." Below, we overview all nine papers included, which deal with problems and challenges in this rapidly growing domain. The particular papers tackle different issues related to developing applications. The topics covered in the first two groups of papers vary from off-the-shelf components using CORBA, to scheduling mechanisms in parallel real-time systems and load balancing in this kind of systems, to real-time communication protocols based on multicasting and providing fault tolerance, as well as standard protocols, such as Resource ReSerVation Protocol (RSVP). Another group of papers deals with verification principles in an environment supporting a radio broadcast paradigm and with two most challenging application domains for real-time distributed systems: on-board embedded systems for satellites and control of large high-energy physics experiments. Finally, we make some predictions on the most important aspects of the research practice in the near future, which we believe will have focused on system architectures and the verification process.

Key words. CORBA, parallel real-time computing, real-time computing, distributed real-time computations, real-time scheduling, load balancing, verification and validation, radio broadcast paradigm, on-board systems, experiment control

1. Motivation. Development of real-time systems gets an ever increasing attention within the fields of computer science and engineering. This is no surprise, since the computerization of our society has intensified enormously in the last decade. Computerization and automation causes our lives to be surrounded by computerized products and services. On one hand, there are simple examples we meet in our daily lives: the washing machine, our wristwatch and the central heater are classical examples of computer controlled devices. On the other hand, our existence is surrounded by far more complex systems.

In our direct living environment, we are confronted with things like a telephone, home computer and television, all fairly complex devices nowadays. Outside the house, we encounter all kinds of systems influencing our behavior there: traffic lights are controlled by complex distributed control systems, shopping centers are controlled via security cameras, our air flights could not take place if the control did not grow to the level it has today, and so on. These systems distinguish themselves by their enormous growth in the last decade, from relatively simple single computer systems a couple of decades ago, to vast distributed control systems nowadays.

The enormous impact of the area, and its growing importance in our daily lives makes it worthwhile to give an overview of current issues in the domain of parallel and distributed real-time software and systems. In this special issue of *Parallel and Distributed Computing Practices*, we therefore address this problem

*Department of Mathematics and Informatics, Delft University of Technology, P.O. Box 356, 2600 AJ Delft, The Netherlands. E-mail: J.vanKatwijk@twi.tudelft.nl

†Department of Electrical & Computer Engineering, University of Central Florida, Orlando, FL 32816-2450, USA. E-mail: jza@ece.engr.ucf.edu

by giving an overview of the domain. Since such an overview should provide a certain balance in treatment, we have chosen to include selected contributions from most subareas of the real-time software and systems discipline.

2. Real-Time Issues in Parallel and Distributed Computing. The easiest way to develop and run a parallel/distributed real-time system seems to take existing software, with proven operational record in a parallel or distributed environment, and run it for real time. This approach, however, raises the obvious question, how contemporary tools, suitable for traditional distributed applications, would perform in real time? In order to find an answer to this question, we invited researchers we knew would address exactly this problem.

Polze, Malek, Wallnau and Plakosh discuss in their invited contribution the use of off-the-shelf components based on CORBA, in the construction of distributed real-time software systems. They pinpoint several problems that arise with an intuitive simplistic approach, and develop their own solution to most of them. Their solution is based on what they call Composite Objects. The main idea of composite objects is to leave programming on the high level of abstraction with CORBA and to concentrate all issues related to the detailed knowledge of the objects' timing behavior with the special extension mechanisms. The invited paper titled *Real-Time Computing with Off-the-Shelf Components: The Case for CORBA* serves as a good background to the rest of this issue, because it outlines a number of problems that need fundamental solutions, not just quick fixes.

What is crucial in presenting challenges of the discipline and how they are addressed, is to focus on new problems which emerge with the evolution of requirements for parallel and distributed real-time systems and overview the attempts for their solutions. The distinctive features of parallelism and distribution versus traditional, mostly uniprocessor systems, are primarily those, which deal with the multiplicity of processors. That is, in the first place, the issue is how to schedule multiple tasks on these processors, to let them perform optimally in real time, and secondly, how to balance the load to minimize idle cycles, a different face of the same problem.

In the contribution of Fouad, Narahari and Hahn, the imprecise computation model is used as a framework for developing a real-time parallel scheduler and incorporating the effects of and possibilities for graceful degradation in soft real-time applications. In their contribution, *A Real-Time Parallel Scheduler for the Imprecise Computation Model*, the authors address this issue by establishing a set of constraints that must be adhered to in utilizing dynamic load balancing for a parallel real-time system such that schedules are not invalidated and the computational error is not increased.

Imprecision and uncertainty, when formalized, are also the basis for a novel real-time load balancing scheme discussed in the paper on *Distributed Computations in Real Time Based on a Rough Grammar Principle*, by Wójcik and Zalewski. The concept of a rough grammar is based on that of a rough set. More specifically, the paper shows that using the rough grammar concept one can sequence dynamically all tasks in a processor net in a pipeline fashion. The duration of each pipeline is normalized to the duration of one of the shortest tasks, by which a reduction of the idle and wait times is brought to a minimum.

3. Real-Time Communication Protocols. The issues of scheduling and load balancing can never be fully resolved without thorough knowledge of communication protocols, which allow participating parties to exchange information. Real-time communication is particularly tricky due to uncertainties in the network, such as loss of messages or node failures, so that guaranteeing message delivery is difficult unless special measures are taken.

In this view, Tunali, Erciyeş and Soysert discuss in their contribution, *A Hierarchical Fault Tolerant Ring Protocol for Distributed Real-Time Systems*, an approach to solve a communication problem in distributed real-time systems via the use of a synchronous communication protocol operating on hierarchical rings. The fault-tolerant algorithm developed allows the protocol to maintain communication in case of crash failures and is easily usable for real-time applications.

Gannod and Bhattacharya, in their paper titled *Real-Time Multicast in Wireless Communication*, present a new way to resolve multicast communication in wireless/mobile networks. In particular, they define a new performance metric for real-time multicast networks: delay of reconstruction of the multicast tree at the instance of node migration. This issue is important, because nodes in a mobile network tend to migrate from cell to cell causing the necessity to rebuild their descriptive patterns. In their paper, the authors give some simulation results of measuring performance metrics as a function of different system configurations when node migration occurs.

The third contribution addressing the development and application of communication protocols in the real-time domain, by Benzekri and Sarafoglou, is titled *Protocols for Real-Time Network Applications Programming*. The authors discuss the entire hierarchy of protocols (protocol stack) usable in real-time communication, in particular, IP Multicast, RTP/RTCP (Real-Time Protocol and Real-Time Control Protocol), and RSVP (Resource ReSerVation Protocol) and present related work on a video server application in a campus-wide network.

4. Real-Time System Development. One could think that having resolved the issues with real-time scheduling, load balancing, and real-time communication, would let the researchers and practitioners sleep quietly, but that is not so. Knowing what algorithms and protocols to use is just a tip of an iceberg – one needs to apply these concepts in real circumstances. In other words, intensive development and verification procedures are needed to prove that at least some of these concepts work.

In their contribution, *Software Development and Verification of Dynamic Real-Time Distributed Systems Based on the Radio Broadcast Paradigm*, van Katwijk, de Rooij, Stuurman and Toetenel address the use of an architectural style, defined as the Radio Broadcast Paradigm as a basis for software development. They develop formal verification techniques to analyze the required behavior of an underlying distributed system built according to this paradigm. Their principle relies on subsequent use of experimentation, abstraction and verification, and is labeled "bottom-up" as opposed to traditionally used top-down methodologies. They discuss the application of their verification approach to determining the timing constraints of an implemented communication protocol.

All theoretical methods are only as good as they get into practical use. Therefore we gave a very serious thought as to what particular parallel or distributed applications we would like to see covered in this issue. From practical research work we knew that there may exist only a few more challenging applications, in the development of parallel or distributed real-time systems, than those used in space research and high-energy physics. We were lucky enough to participate recently on Ph.D. defense committees of two practitioners who agreed to make invited contributions based on their dissertation work.

In the space domain, we welcome the contribution of Vardanega, who discusses issues in the development of software for multiple processors on-board satellite systems. In a paper titled *On the Distribution of Control in New Generation On-board Embedded Real-Time Systems*, he presents a sound engineering approach to distributing control functions onto multiple processing nodes in such systems. In the high-energy physics domain, the contribution of Gaspar, Franek and Schwarz titled *Architecture of a Distributed Real-Time System to Control Large High-Energy Physics Experiments*, discusses the generic architecture and framework capable of handling the control and monitoring of all aspects of a high-energy physics experiment. In particular, they outline the tools they developed to support design and implementation of such architecture with respect to two main issues: control and communication.

5. Summary. When we compare this issue on "Parallel and Distributed Real-Time Systems" to the previous one we have done for *Informatica* four years ago [1], a few thoughts on the evolution of the field come up. This time, we structured the papers into three major categories, encompassing the following topics:

- timing problems, including parallel scheduling and load balancing
- real-time communication protocols
- system development strategies.

Papers in each of these categories were present in the previous edition, only in different numbers. The number of contributions on real-time communication protocols has increased, at the cost of papers on real-time scheduling algorithms. Furthermore, design issues were made more explicit here than in the previous edition. These facts reflect the actual tendency of intensified research in communication protocols that are crucial to the reliable operation of parallel and distributed real-time systems and achieving their high performance.

However, the key aspect of dealing with these systems is in their development procedures, where assessing directions of progress is the most important from both the research and practical standpoint. In this view, we can distinguish two crucial factors of development strategies for parallel and distributed real-time systems:

- Having up-front a well defined *system architecture*, perhaps in a form of design patterns, would significantly facilitate the development process by allowing designers to focus on more specific aspects of the application.
- Following a well-established *verification process* for real-time system development would be of tremendous advantage to developers, not only in the area of parallel and distributed real-time systems.

In both respects, we are glad to observe some notable attempts to respond to these issues. Papers by Polze et al., and by Gaspar et al. clearly identify certain fundamental characteristics of system architectures that are indispensable for proper design of real-time distributed systems. These contributions acknowledge the need for further research on system and software architectures as a basis for the development of parallel and distributed real-time systems. Papers by van Katwijk et al., and Vardanega emphasize the need to start with a solid architectural style, and address the need for providing feedback information as a necessary component of the development process. Indeed, it is only through feedback analysis that design and implementation can be adapted in order to meet the requirements. Improving the verification process is easier said than done, but both papers provide practical examples how to incorporate sound and formalized verification methods into the development process and how to be successful in it.

So, in summary, can we answer the question: *Where is this technology heading, where does it evolve?* It is our opinion, based not only on beliefs and experience but primarily on hard facts, such as the contents and results of some of the above mentioned papers, that in the foreseeable future, the crucial aspects of parallel and distributed real-time systems will relate to necessary enhancements in their development methodologies, focusing on the system architecture and the verification process. This is where the most advanced research will be heading. And all of us have to watch the progress, because it is clear that sooner or later all computer systems (with very few exceptions) will become real-time systems. This is for the simple reason that real-time systems have much better performance characteristics.

One uncertain point, we see at the moment, is the role of the Unified Modeling Language (UML) in system development. Despite some claims, UML is not ready yet to play any major role or even prove its usefulness in parallel or distributed real-time applications. But its time may come very soon, once its semantics are formalized, it is better standardized and appropriate software tools are built. This is because UML is, in principle, compatible with the major factors that, as we believe, will determine progress in this area. First, any well defined system architecture can be easily expressed in the UML notation. Second, the verification process can be substantially enhanced by a strict graphical notation (such as statecharts), which UML is hoped to provide.

REFERENCES

[1] M. PAPRZYCKI, J. ZALEWSKI, Eds., *Special Issue on Parallel and Distributed Real-Time Systems*, **Informatica**, Vol. 19, No. 1, February 1995, ISSN 0350-5596

REAL-TIME COMPUTING WITH OFF-THE-SHELF COMPONENTS: THE CASE FOR CORBA

ANDREAS POLZE†, KURT WALLNAU‡, DAN PLAKOSH‡, AND MIROSLAW MALEK†

Abstract. The Common Object Request Broker Architecture (CORBA) is a successful standardized system integration framework based on distributed object technology. The key feature of CORBA is that users can create application systems by integrating existing heterogeneous hardware and software components. CORBA abstracts from implementation details like object's locations, hardware and operating systems.

Correctness of real-time computing depends not only on output values generated by a computation but also on the times at which outputs are generated. Therefore, locations, hardware speeds, workloads, and the schedulers used by the operating systems can affect timing and the correctness of real-time computing.

The real-time extension of CORBA is not a simple refinement of the existing CORBA model. Rather, it is at the heart of CORBA specifications: what should and should not be abstracted away and how to do it. In this paper, we study the application of principles from the real-time computing domain within a CORBA-based framework. We have investigated the Simplex system's coordinated inverted pendulum demo developed at the SEI, CMU, and a real-time manufacturing system developed at NIST (National Institute of Standards and Technology). We view those applications as model problems that are present in numerous application domains (telecom, manufacturing, etc.).

Based on our experiences, we have developed Composite Objects as a methodology for predictable integration of real-time and distributed (non-real-time) computing. We discuss our implementation of Composite Objects and present results of an experimental evaluation.

Key words. CORBA, distributed computations, real-time computing, COTS

1. Introduction. The notion of real-time computing is often associated with special purpose systems which are vendor-specific, expensive, hard to maintain and difficult to upgrade. Examples include embedded computer systems in today's airplanes, cars and automated factories. With the need of integrating multiples of those real-time control systems into a bigger whole, requirements arise to integrate the real-time system into standard (non-real-time) distributed computing environments. This way, non-real-time components like graphical user interfaces and databases can be connected to the system.

Distributed computing using commercial-off-the-shelf (COTS) components is appealing because of its cost-effectiveness. A number of standards have evolved over the past few years, which ensure interoperability among heterogeneous hardware platforms from different vendors. Object technology has been used to describe interfaces and interaction patterns for such distributed applications. The Common Object Request Broker Architecture (CORBA) [6][17] is the most successful representative for an object-based distributed computing architecture.

†Department of Computer Science, Humboldt University of Berlin, Rudower Chaussee 5, 10099 Berlin, Germany, {apolze,malek}@informatik.hu-berlin.de

‡Software Engineering Institute, Carnegie Mellon University, 4500 Fifth Avenue, Pittsburgh, PA, 15213, USA, {kcw,dplakosh}@sei.cmu.edu

In this paper, we investigate how fundamental principles from the real-time computing domain can be applied within a CORBA-based framework. We use the Simplex architecture [13] as the basis for a model problem that allows us to explore the use a CORBA implementation as an interconnection mechanism *between* hard real-time systems. We view Simplex applications as model problems that arise in numerous application domains (telecom, manufacturing, etc.).

We evaluate a version of the "synchronized inverted pendulum" demo application, where CORBA communication is used to exchange position information between a graphical user interface and two lower-level Simplex subsystems. This way, we create a layered architecture where CORBA serves as an interprocess communication vehicle with soft real-time characteristics, for communication between applications having more stringent real-time requirements.

We use the NIST Real-time Control System (RCS) [5] architecture as the basis for a second model problem that allows us to explore the use of available CORBA implementations as a communication mechanism *within* a real-time system. The RCS application is the NIST Motion Controller, a simulation of a device that receives NC instructions and mills an appropriate surface. In contrast to the pendulum example, we have used CORBA inside the motion controller's inner control loop.

We present the Composite Objects approach as a technique for predictable integration of CORBA with real-time requirements. Composite Objects rely on the principle of "separation of concerns". The concept of a scheduling server [9] is used to restrict CORBA in its processor utilization — thus leaving the real-time application a predetermined share of CPU cycles. Replicated data and weakly consistent memory protocols are used to decouple CORBA communication latency and the application's timing behavior. By making the tradeoff between an application's predictability and CORBA's communication latency explicit, Composite Objects allow the programmer to use CORBA for real-time computing.

The rest of the paper is organized as follows. In Section 2 we briefly describe CORBA and two top-level approaches for integrating CORBA with the Simplex and NIST RCS real-time system architectures. Section 3 discusses the coordinated inverted pendulum model problem, while Section 4 presents a closer look at the NIST motion controller model problem. In Section 5 we outline the key concepts underlying Composite Objects, whereas Section 6 presents implementation issues and gives an experimental evaluation of Composite Objects. Section 7 provides an outline of related work. Finally, we present our conclusions in Section 8.

2. Background.

2.1. CORBA in Real Time. CORBA (Common Object Request Broker Architecture) is an object-based environment for distributed programming using off-the-shelf components. CORBA has been standardized by the *Object Management Group* (OMG). The current version 2.2 [6] has been specified in 1998.

CORBA provides transparent distribution for objects, efficiency and openness. Components of a CORBA program can be implemented in different programming languages on a variety of operating systems and hardware platforms. CORBA enables client programs to invoke a server object's methods regardless whether the server object is in the client's address space or located on a remote node in a distributed system. CORBA defines services that: locate a server object implementation; prepare the server object for receiving a client's request; and finally communicate data making up a request.

CORBA Interface Definition Language (IDL) is a declarative language that describes the interfaces to server object implementations, including the signatures of all server object methods that are callable by clients. The surface syntax of IDL is similar to that of C++, but IDL is language-independent. Mappings from IDL to C, C++, Ada, and Smalltalk have been specified. However, IDL does not provide syntax for object implementations. Today, a number of CORBA-compliant *Object Request Broker* (ORB) implementations are commercially available.

An ongoing effort within the OMG concerns real-time CORBA (RT-CORBA). RT-CORBA is a future extension to the OMG Object Management Architecture to support a wide spectrum of distributed, real-time, fault-tolerant systems. The requirement specification for RT-CORBA is under development by the OMG Real-Time SIG. The Request for Proposal (RFP) for the fixed priority version of Realtime CORBA 1.0 [7] has been announced in September 1997.

By extending a real-time system with a CORBA interface, a real-time application can interact with other components in a distributed environment. For instance, an administration and monitoring component could be connected to the real-time application.

In contrast to a real-time system's internal communication mechanisms, the notion of real-time has to be revisited for the CORBA-based communication channels. It has to be ensured that CORBA-based interactions cannot break real-time scheduling assumptions. Before stepping into detail and presenting our experiences with using CORBA in real-time context, we enumerate a number of critical issues here:

1. Assignment of priorities. The CORBA gateway should be executed with a priority lower than every component included in the inner control loop (the controller, device I/O manager, etc.).

2. Management of shared resources (memory, I/O channels). Real time applications often assume that memory for all components of an application is allocated up front and is locked against paging during runtime. It has to be investigated, how CORBA server objects (depending on ORB/OA implementation) can be forced to follow this rule.

3. Priority inversion problems. At least a safety controller has to be implemented in a fashion that it can work completely independently from any CORBA interactions. Otherwise, a blocking CORBA interaction may violate the system assumptions.

4. Predictable performance. To implement the concept of an outer control

loop, performance of the CORBA gateway should be predictable with respect to method execution time and communication latency. This is highly dependent on the ORB (preferable multithreaded) implementation.

2.2. The SIMPLEX Architecture and CORBA. Current real-time computer software architectures do not support the safe and reliable insertion of new components and technologies into existing systems. The Simplex architecture [13] has been developed to support safe and reliable online upgrade of hardware and software components in spite of errors in new modules. This is important when introducing changes, such as new COTS components, into running systems.

To mitigate the risks in a system upgrade, the Simplex architecture has been designed to tolerate timing faults such as overrun, programming system faults such as illegal addressing, and semantic faults due to modeling, algorithm design or implementation errors. Simplex handles timing faults and programming system faults by temporal and spatial encapsulations. Software semantic faults are handled by the use of analytic redundancy [14].

The Simplex architecture is based on the generalized rate monotonic scheduling theory. Furthermore, the Simplex architecture assumes that the underlying operating system supports either the priority inheritance protocol or the priority ceiling protocol to circumvent priority inversion problems during the management of shared resources. A number of demonstration applications have been implemented using Simplex on top of the LynxOS commercial real-time operating system.

The Simplex architecture has been successfully used to solve a number of control problems. These solutions demonstrate how real-time software can be altered and tested without making the controlled device unsafe. A number of controllers (Replacement Units) can be interchanged. In case of faults the system implements graceful degradation and the safety controller finally implements fail-operational behavior.

The basic building block in the Simplex architecture is the *Replacement Unit*, containing one or more processes with a communication template. Replacement units are designed in such a way that they can be added, deleted, merged or split online by a set of standardized upgrade transactions. In the Simplex architecture, autonomous subsystems like those found in typical industrial systems, will be implemented as an application module. The application module implements software fault-tolerance mechanisms.

An application module is made of specialized replacement units: application units (controllers), a module management unit (decision module) and a safety unit. The safety unit implements a safety controller when the physical subsystem is not fail-safe. The application units implement the application-specific functionality of a given subsystem. The application module acts as software fault-containment unit and its components run in their own address spaces. Fig. 2.1 shows the basic architecture of a Simplex-based application extended by a CORBA gateway. Two application-specific replacement units (complex

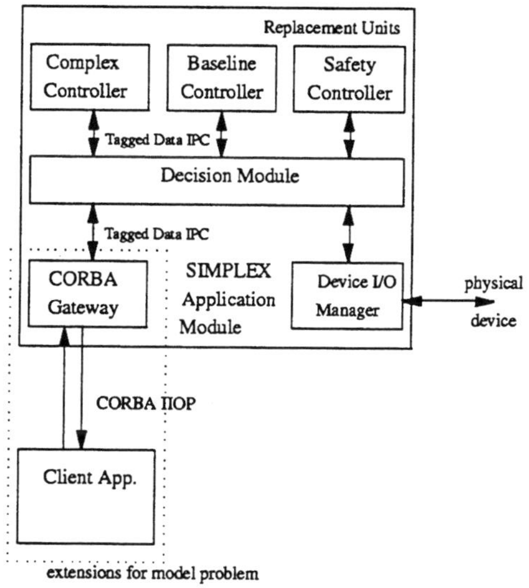

FIG. 2.1. *CORBA gateway to Simplex*

and baseline controller) are shown as well as the safety controller and the device I/O manager. We propose insertion of the CORBA gateway as just another, specialized replacement unit into the Simplex architecture.

Communication between the components of an application module is realized following the real-time publisher/subscriber model. The current implementation, called *tagged data interprocess communication*, is based on POSIX message queues as available in LynxOS.

2.3. Real-Time Control System Architecture (RCS) and CORBA. The NIST Real-time Control System (RCS) is a reference model architecture for manufacturing applications. The RCS architecture attempts to abstract from implementation-dependent details of real-time control software as well as its underlying computing platform. RCS provides to the application developer a unified interface to operating systems and hardware devices. Code using this interface can be ported between different platforms and applications. The NIST motion controller investigated within this paper is an example for a RCS application representing a manufacturing model problem.

The Real-Time Control System (RCS) library [5] is a C++ class library intended for multi-platform real-time distributed applications. RCSlib provides synchronization and communication constructs.

The Communication Management System (CMS) provides access to a fixed-size buffer of general data to multiple reader or writer processes on the same processor, across a backplane, or over a network. The Neutral Manufacturing Language (NML) provides a higher level interface to CMS. It provides a mechanism for handling multiple types of messages in the same buffer as well as simplifying the interface for encoding and decoding buffers in neutral format

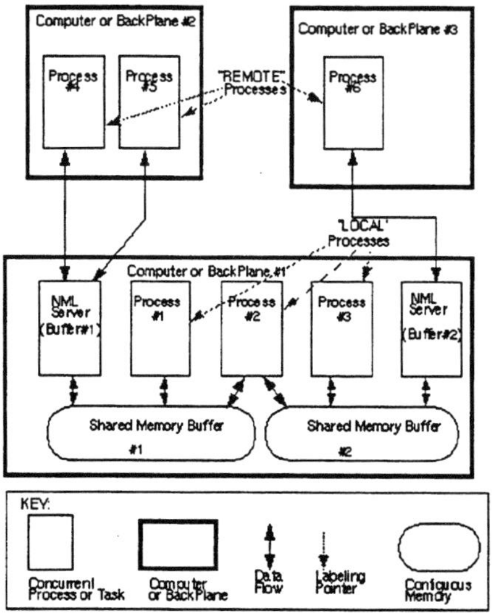

FIG. 2.2. *Structure of an application using RCSlib*

and the configuration mechanism.

Fig. 2.2 illustrates the structure of a typical RCS application using NML. The application is distributed across three computers. Processes 1, 2, and 3 are able to write directly into the shared memory buffers they use because they are located in the same computer or backplane. Processes 4, 5 and 6 can only access the buffers through an NML Server (labeled "REMOTE").

The original motion controller demo uses the RCSlib's timers and shared memory communication mechanisms. In this paper, we study how changing the communication style to CORBA remote method invocations may change the behavior of the motion controller application. The usage of CORBA inside a real-time application would offer the advantages of object technology — like encapsulation, data abstraction and structuring — to the real-time programmer.

Because there was no commercial CORBA implementation for LynxOS available in Spring 1997 we use the ILU CORBA implementation as platform for our experiments. ILU (Inter Language Unification) is available in source form from XEROX Palo Alto Research Center (PARC). We have ported the ILU ORB (version 2.0alpha9) to the LynxOS 2.4 real-time operating system.

3. The Synchronized Inverted Pendulum. The "inverted pendulum" is a Simplex demonstration application, where a physical device is controlled through fault-tolerant software. The rod of the pendulum is attached to a cart by a freely swinging hinge, but is not powered. The cart can move horizontally under computer control. The pendulum is instrumented to provide the rod angle and cart position on the track as signals to the controlling computer.

Three different controllers in the Simplex system implement more or less

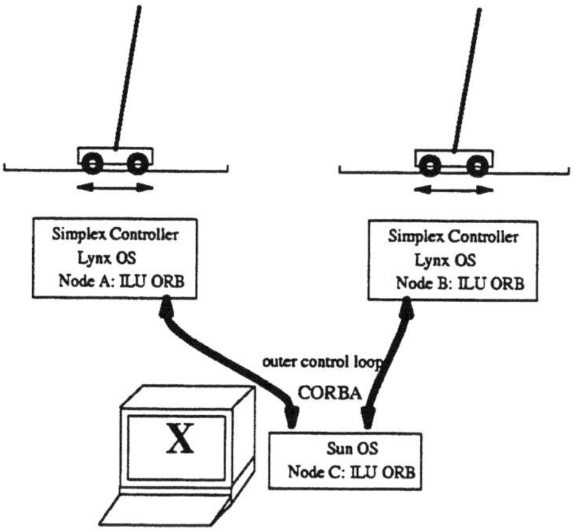

FIG. 3.1. *Synchronized inverted pendulum scenario*

```
INTERFACE Pendulum;
CONSTANT
   serverId : ilu.CString = "Pendulum-Server" ;
TYPE T = OBJECT METHODS
   getPosition(OUT position: REAL,
          OUT angle: REAL, OUT refpoint: REAL),
   setReference(IN refpoint: REAL),
   startComputation()
END;
```

FIG. 3.2. *Interface Definitions for GUI-Pendulum Communication*

sophisticated algorithms for keeping the rod upright. Every controller tries to position the cart close to a given point on the track (the set-point). By changing the value for the set-point, the cart can be moved along the track. However, keeping the pendulum balanced has a higher priority than approaching the position given by the set-point.

3.1. Architecture. We consider the more complex scenario shown in Fig. 3.1, where two Simplex inverted pendulum applications are controlled via CORBA communication links. Both Simplex applications are extended by a CORBA gateway object. The X window-based graphical user interface acts as a CORBA client and polls position data (track position, angle of the rod) from the two Simplex applications. Furthermore, in response to user actions, the GUI component calls a method at the Simplex gateway objects to change the value of the set-points. Thus, the user can interactively move the inverted pendulums.

Fig. 3.2 shows the ILU ISL specifications for the methods implemented in the Simplex gateway objects (the ILU Interface Specification Language - ISL - is similar although not identical to CORBA's IDL).

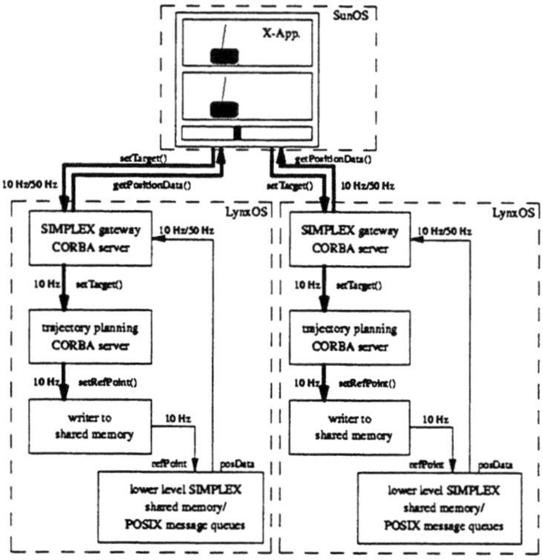

FIG. 3.3. *Communication structure for the synchronized inverted pendulum*

Besides methods for getting pendulum status information and for changing the set-point, Fig. 3.2 contains a method `startComputation()`. The implementation of this method simulates a compute-intensive task and makes use of `malloc()` to stress the real-time system's resource management. Changing the frequency with which data is polled from the Simplex applications is another way to change the load of the real-time system. We have changed this value between 10Hz and 100Hz. Separate measurements have shown, that communication latency with ILU CORBA is around 10ms for client/server communication between a Sun Sparc II and a 586 PC running LynxOS 2.4.

We have implemented the CORBA communication using a multithreaded version of ILU. Therefore, in the Pendulum-gateway object a separate thread per method and per client is created. This allows us to combine the creation of communication- and computation-intensive tasks on the Simplex system and to study the impact ILU CORBA has on the performance of the real-time system. All ILU-method invocations are executed by low-priority threads on the LynxOS system. Other components of the lower-level Simplex run as high-priority processes.

Besides the Simplex gateway, we have introduced another CORBA object to the scenario shown in Fig. 3.3. This component performs trajectory planning and translates abrupt changes in the set-point's value into a series of smaller changes which are performed with a frequency of 10Hz. Fig. 3.3 also shows the default frequencies of the several communication steps in the synchronized pendulum scenario. As mentioned earlier, the graphical user interface allows user-initiated changes in the polling rate. Shared memory is used for interactions between the Simplex gateway and the other components of the lower-level Simplex system.

3.2. Experiences. The synchronized pendulum demo allows us to study several aspects of interaction between ILU CORBA and the LynxOS real-time system:

1. Changes to the rate with which data is polled from the Simplex gateways increase network- and CPU-load on the real-time systems.
2. Execution of the `startComputation()` method increases the CPU load and usage of virtual memory on the real-time system.
3. Variation of the number of simultaneously active CORBA clients (the GUI component) may flood the real-time computer's network interface.

In our specific application scenario, ILU CORBA proved to be very usable to connect the graphical user interface to the synchronized pendulum demo. Although measurements show a substantial variation of communication latency when using ILU, those variations are not immediately visible to the user. One reason is, that the Simplex control loop — although running with a 20 ms period — needs more than 100 ms to re-establish balance, once the pendulum has been disturbed. Therefore, Simplex always takes some time to react on changes to the cart's position — and the varying CORBA communication latency just adds to that time.

On the other hand, it is hardly noticeable for the user, whether updates to the pendulum's image on the screen occur exactly every 100 ms. Therefore, we draw the conclusion that today's CORBA can be used in real-time settings for monitoring and obtaining status information. Occasional CORBA method invocations on the real-time computer to change the system's state also work well.

However, we have noticed, that untamed execution of CORBA methods may disturb the real-time system's behavior. CORBA has no idea about concepts like call admission. Therefore, by just invoking enough methods, the ORB on the real-time system may put unacceptable load onto the system. Indeed, we could show that with a sufficiently high number of pendulum-GUIs connected to the same Simplex application, the networking load on the LynxOS 2.4 system increases so much, that real-time tasks get delayed and miss their deadlines and the pendulum finally falls down. We therefore argue, that some firewall has to be build between CORBA and the real-time application. We propose the concept of Composite Objects which is briefly outlined in Section 5. The Composite Object approach allows for predictable integration of CORBA and real-time programming without having to build an own Object Request Broker.

4. The NIST Motion Controller Demo. The motion controller demo represents a model problem from the manufacturing domain. The demo simulates control of a machine tool. This machine tool has three axes, therefore all components deal with 3-tuples to specify the tools motion. The application consists of three interacting components:

1. **`testmotsrv`**, a user interface which reads control commands
2. **`traj`**, a trajectory generator which is driven by the user's commands

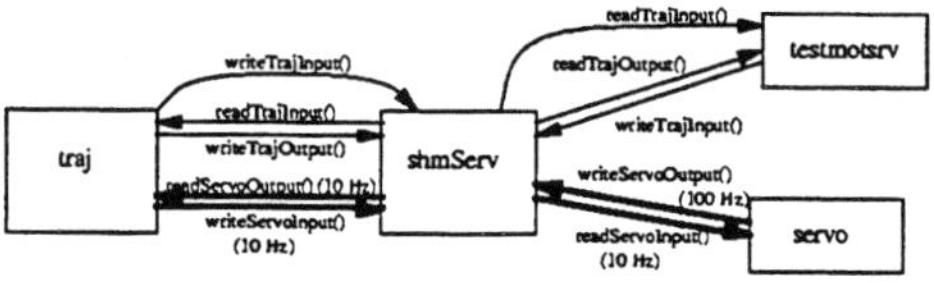

FIG. 4.1. *The CORBA-based motion controller's communication structure*

3. **servo**, a simulated electro motor which represents the actual machine tool.

The `traj` and `servo` components are implemented as periodic tasks: `servo` runs with a period of 10 ms, `traj` period is 100 ms. The `servo` component reads fresh trajectory information every tenth cycle. In the initial version of the demo, both components access the same shared memory locations. The RCSlib implementation provides an own, independent clock to each client process. Therefore, and since `servo` and `traj` are not explicitly synchronized, `servo` may occasionally get out of synchronization with `traj`. This results in abrupt changes in the simulated motor's behavior. `servo` records the motor control data. The control data can be plotted. Jumps in the plotted curves indicate changes in the latency of communication between `traj` and `servo`.

We have used the motion controller demo to investigate applicability of a CORBA implementation (ILU) in a manufacturing scenario. We have replaced motion controller's shared memory communication by communication through a CORBA shared memory object. This way we gain location transparency of all the components, however, we have to deal with CORBA's communication latency problems. In our experiments, we have seen, that ILU's performance varies substantially between machine architectures. However, on fast machines, like Sparc 5 and Pentium P166, we were able to create a CORBA-based version of the motion controller demo, which behaves pretty similar to the original, shared memory-based version.

4.1. Communication Structure. Fig. 4.1 shows the communication structure of the CORBA-based motion controller demo. We have introduced `shmServ`, a CORBA object, which implements four shared memory structures. Read and write methods allow access to those data structures. One may notice, that we have changed the semantics of the motion controller demo somewhat by just introducing `shmServ`. In contrast to the original implementation, where concurrent accesses to shared memory have been synchronized based on word-entities, the CORBA `shmServ` synchronizes accesses on a per-method basis. Therefore, we have created a tighter coupling between `traj` and `servo`.

However, resolving concurrent accesses based on the application-specific data structures seems to be more correct than the initial approach. With the shared memory-based implementation of the motion controller demo, when trying to get a 3-tuple describing the tool's next position, `servo` might read one old and two new data components — which certainly is incorrect. To evaluate the effect of the extra synchronization introduced by `shmServ`, we have implemented

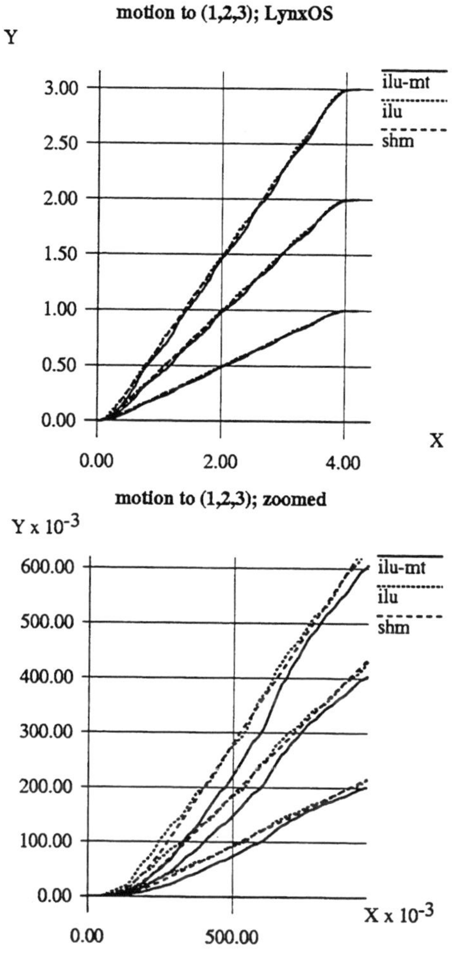

FIG. 4.2. *Servo motion to position (1, 2, 3)*

that component in a singlethreaded and a multithreaded version.

4.2. Experiences. Fig. 4.2 shows, that there are some differences in the behavior of the CORBA-based motion controller demo (curves ilu and ilu-mt) compared to the shared memory-based one (curve shm in Fig. 4.2). The different curves in Fig. 4.2 indicate, that varying communication latency is the biggest problem with the CORBA-based version of our demo. Those variations cause `servo` to occasionally read the same trajectory point twice, which results in slowdown of the motor. Later, the `servo` component skips one trajectory point. As a results, the motor accelerates for a short period of time. This results in curves which are not as smooth as the curve produced by `servo` in the shared memory-based version of our demo application. Furthermore, variation

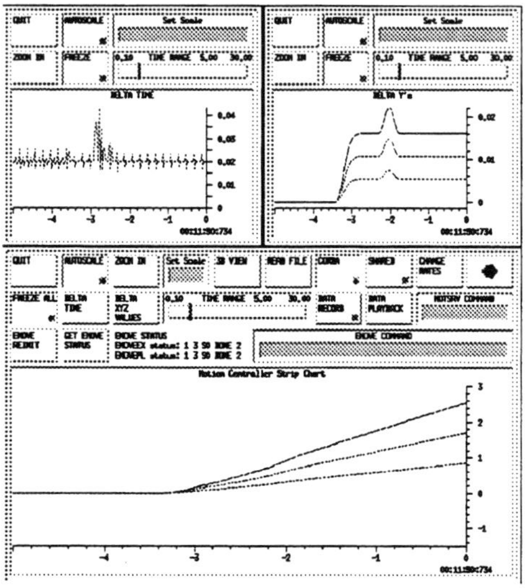

FIG. 4.3. *Simulation tool - strip chart*

in CORBA communication latency can cause changes to the cycle time of `traj` and `servo`. All the data shown in Fig. 4.2 results from experiments on the LynxOS 2.4 real-time operating system.

To further investigate the effects of different communication approaches in our manufacturing scenario, we have extended the motion controller into a simulation tool which allows to visualize timing behavior and process interaction.

One set of tools is centered on a strip chart. Fig. 4.3 shows a record of the x, y, and z coordinates of the servo plotted against time. Associated with the strip-chart view are windows that depict communication latency (the delta-time view) and servo acceleration (the delta y's view). The software also supports switching between shared memory and CORBA interprocess communication, modification of timing parameters, capture and playback of sessions, viewing data at different scales (time and distance), and so forth.

Our conclusions from the CORBA-based motion controller experiment are not as pleasant as the ones obtained from the synchronized pendulum demo. In our case, CORBA seems to interfere with the real-time application. Replacement of shared memory communication — which is implemented with predictable performance on the LynxOS — by CORBA communication significantly disturbs the motion controller's behavior. We therefore conclude, that just porting an ORB (ILU) to the real-time platform (LynxOS) is not sufficient to integrate CORBA and real-time programming. Rather, one has to think about firewalls and separation between CORBA communication and time-triggered real-time execution.

We propose the concept of Composite Objects for predictable integration of CORBA and real-time. In the case of the motion controller demo, `traj` and `servo` could be converted into time-triggered methods of two Composite Objects. A central clock event would synchronize execution of those methods. All communication would be handled by a different, non-real-time thread in the Composite Objects. This way varying latency of CORBA communication could be eliminated as a source for changes to the cycle time of the periodic execution in `traj` and `servo`.

5. The Composite Objects Approach. Our concept of Composite Objects [8] is an approach to integrate real-time and non-real-time computing into a single object-based framework. From our point of view, the real-time extension of CORBA is not a simple refinement of the existing CORBA model. Rather, it is at the heart of CORBA specifications: what should and should not be abstracted away and how to do it. We advocate a "co-existence and the-need-to-know" approach to address this problem. There are three design rules:

1. NONINTERFERENCE. We should create an environment in which general purpose computing and real-time computing will not burden each other.
2. INTEROPERABILITY. The services exported by general purpose computing objects and by real-time computing objects can be utilized by each other.
3. ADAPTIVE ABSTRACTION. Lower level information and scheduling actions needed by real-time computing are available for real-time objects but transparent to non-real-time objects.

Rule 1 is implemented by partitioning the system's computation and communication resources. Such partitions can be done physically or logically. Rules 2 and 3 are implemented by creating Composite Objects.

Composite Objects may provide a unified interface for interacting between real-time and non-real-time objects. This interface will be identical to the existing CORBA definitions from the viewpoint of non-real-time objects. Non-real-time clients can invoke the service of real-time objects via the standard CORBA interface. It is the task of the Composite Object to ensure that the service to non-real-time clients will be carried out in best effort without adversely affecting the real-time computation. This way, non-real-time components like graphical user interfaces and databases can be connected to existing real-time systems.

Real-time clients can obtain the service from standard CORBA facilities. In that case the Composite Object acts as the surrogate of the real-time object in getting the service and forwarding it to the real-time object, so that real-time clients will not wait for the unpredictable timing of non-real-time services. An important application of this service is to identify potential real-time servers registered with CORBA. Once real-time clients and servers are identified and their resources are reserved, execution of their methods and creation of data flow paths can be managed by sending commands to Simplex architecture servers.

Since Composite Objects provide functionality to react on CORBA method invocations, they can be seen as descendants of a class which implements Object Adaptor functionality (Basic Object Adaptor Implementation — `BOAImpl` in ORBIX jargon). On the other hand, Composite Objects have the capability to

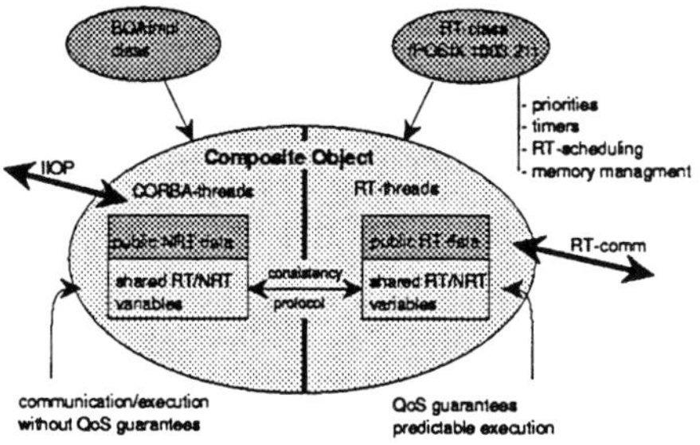

FIG. 5.1. *Structure of a Composite Object*

create real-time programming abstractions like prioritized threads and real-time communication channels. Thus, they can be seen as descendants of a class which implements real-time servers such as Simplex architecture servers. Fig. 5.1 shows the overall structure of a Composite Object.

Composite Objects consist of a real-time and a non-real-time part. Design time and runtime guarantees can be given for execution of "time triggered methods" and "real-time service methods", respectively. In contrast, methods in the non-real-time part of the Composite Object are executed following a best effort approach. Those non-real-time methods correspond to the well-known standard CORBA method invocations. The principle of ADAPTIVE ABSTRACTION as realized here allows to hide all implementation details from the CORBA user, whereas scheduling and timing information is accessible for the real-time part of a Composite Object.

A Composite Object's real-time services include:

1. *Time-triggered methods.* Those methods encapsulate time-triggered actions such as periodic sampling of a sensor device.

2. *Real-time service methods.* Those methods encapsulate data driven service at a given level of priority and with a worst case execution time, e.g., a particular filtering method in a filter object.

3. *Data flow service.* Those methods encapsulate real-time communication service such as the real-time publisher and subscriber [10].

The invocation of these methods can be either accepted or rejected, subject to the decision of the schedulability analysis provided by Simplex replacement transaction servers. If all the requested client objects, server objects and their data flow paths are schedulable, they will be created and a new real-time service will be created at runtime. Otherwise, the request will be rejected.

Composite Objects establish timing firewalls [9] between real-time and non-real-time (CORBA) computing, so that the non-real-time part cannot violate the real-time scheduling rules [15] that are needed by the real-time part. This approach allows us to implement the idea of NONINTERFERENCE. Additionally, Composite Objects allow for INTEROPERABILITY between real-time and non-real-time computing by providing data transfer mechanisms in such a way that real-time accesses to the data cannot be blocked by non-real-time functions.

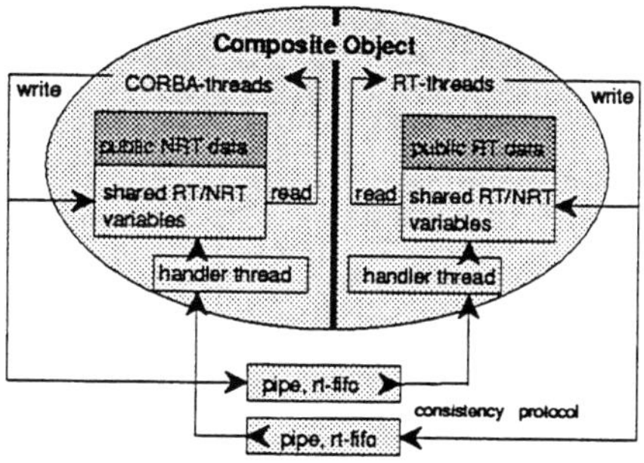

FIG. 6.1. *Consistency Protocol and Communication inside a Composite Object*

6. Implementation Issues. The implementation of the consistency protocol for shared real-time and non-real-time (RT/NRT) variables as well as implementation of resource allocation (CPU cycles, memory) and call admission for CORBA clients are crucial for bringing the concept of Composite Objects to life. We have used the Mach (NeXTSTEP 3.3) and rtLinux [2] operating systems for our implementations of Composite Objects. A version for LynxOS is under development. To realize the consistency protocols, we have used the operating system's concepts of pipes, shared buffers and message queues (Mach IPC). Fig. 6.1 shows the communication structure required by the consistency protocol inside a Composite Object.

Let us discuss the data flow during `read/write` accesses to a Composite Object's shared RT/NRT variables in some detail. As depicted in Fig. 6.1, `read` requests in both parts of the Composite Object are always satisfied by accessing the local copy of a replicated, shared RT/NRT variable. In contrast, `write` requests result not only in updating the local copy, but the value is also stored in an interprocess communication (IPC) data structure (pipes or rt-fifos in our case). On both sides of the Composite Object do exist handler threads, which periodically copy values out of the IPC data structures into the local replica of the shared RT/NRT variable. The update rate for those handler threads is programmable.

Alternatives to the implementation outlined here include usage of shared memory or message passing (Mach IPC) for the data transfer between CORBA part and real-time part of the Composite Object. In our experiments, we have evaluated Composite Objects implementations based on pipes and shared memory.

Another design alternative is an event-triggered consistency protocol in contrast to the time-triggered, periodical protocol described above. In that case, a `write` operation would include signaling arrival of a new data value to the handler thread on the opposite side of the Composite Object. We have implemented consistency protocols following both schemes.

To measure the overhead introduced by Composite Objects, we have investigated a scenario where a CORBA client accesses a remote real-time data source via a Composite Object. We have measured CORBA's communication latency, the Composite Object's internal latency and real-time communication latency for the request sent out by the CORBA client, respectively. Our experiments indicate that the overhead introduced by the Composite Object is roughly 1ms or 10% of the CORBA communication's latency.

7. Related Work. So far, only little work concerning the integration of CORBA and real-time programming techniques and environments has been published.

The Object Management Group (OMG) has founded a "Realtime CORBA" special interest group (SIG) in 1996 [4]. The Request for Proposal (RFP) for the fixed priority version of Realtime CORBA 1.0 has been announced in September 1997 [7]. The RFP solicits technology for a Realtime Object Request Broker (ORB) comprising: fixed priority scheduling, control over ORB resources for end-to-end predictability, and flexible communications

ANSA (Advanced Networked Systems Architecture) [1] is an open, collaborative research program managed by the British company APM Limited. The initial programming interface supported by ANSA follows "Open Distributed Processing" (ODP) standards. However, the current project "Jet" was started to provide a CORBA API to the previously released ANSA/ODP API. Jet provides an own CORBA IDL compiler and a subset of the CORBA 2.0 C++ mapping. The project's objective is to extend CORBA with real-time multimedia functionality, such as streams, signals, explicit binding and Quality of Service (QoS). Jet seeks to provide interoperability with CORBA platforms. It shall be possible to run management applications to control real-time applications from remote CORBA platforms.

Work at the University of Rhode Island and the MITRE Corporation deals with syntactical extensions to CORBA IDL to express timing constraints [19][20]. "Timed distributed method invocations" are identified as one necessary feature in a real-time distributed computing environment, as well as a "Global Time Service", "Real-Time Scheduling of Services", a "Global Priority Service" and "Bounded Message Latency". The "Affected Set Priority Ceiling Protocol" as a combination of semantic locking and priority ceiling techniques has been proposed for concurrency control in real-time object-oriented systems [18].

A new endsystem architecture for CORBA systems called TAO is discussed in [11][12]. Main goal of this work is to provide end-to-end Quality-of-Service qualities for CORBA-based applications. A list of requirements for Object Request Broker implementations is presented, among them are resource reservation protocols, optimized real-time communication protocols and a real-time object adapter. However, in contrast to the Composite Objects idea of interfacing an existing real-time system with CORBA, the TAO approach focuses on completely new, CORBA-based real-time systems.

Besides description of an object system's runtime behavior, the RTO.k model [3] focuses on design-time guarantees for timely service capabilities of encapsulated object-subsystems. Based on an active object approach, time-triggered (spontaneous) methods with design-time guarantees and service methods without those guarantees are distinguished. A basic concurrency constraint rule restricts the execution of service methods in a way, that no time-triggered methods are disturbed. The Distributed Real-time Ever Available Microcomputing (DREAM) kernel implements an execution engine for RTO.k objects. A prototypical implementation is based on PCs and Ethernet. Ongoing research considers application of the RTO.k concepts to middleware platforms such as CORBA [16].

8. Conclusions. CORBA is a widely accepted COTS-platform for object-based distributed computing in open, heterogeneous environments. We have discussed the integration of CORBA and real-time programming techniques and environments. Two different approaches have been described: Simplex and RCS.

By providing gateways to existing real-time systems, a layered architecture can be created. CORBA can be used to interconnect multiple, hard real-time applications with, for example, management components. This approach seems to be well suited for a number of industrial applications like factory shop-floor automation and transport systems. Within this context, CORBA has to fulfill soft-real-time requirements. We have discussed, how the Simplex inverted pendulum demo can be extended by a CORBA gateway. Our experiences show, that CORBA works well as soft-real-time interconnect in this case. Key issue is the clean separation between CORBA and the Simplex real-time computing.

Using CORBA as communication vehicle inside a real-time application is a different approach. With the NIST motion controller demo we have experienced that varying CORBA communication latency can significantly disturb the real-time application's behavior. Implementation of firewalls between CORBA and time-triggered real-time execution allows to solve above problems.

We have briefly introduced our concept of Composite Objects which provides a methodology for predictable integration of CORBA and real-time programming. Composite Objects allow for separation of concerns: CORBA-based distributed programming on a high level of abstraction and real-time computing and analysis based on detailed knowledge of the object's timing behavior. We have implemented the Composite Objects concept and have demonstrated its efficiency by experimental evaluation.

REFERENCES

[1] `http://www.ansa.co.uk/ANSA/index.html`

[2] M.Barabanov, V.Yodaiken, *Introducing Real-Time Linux*, Linux Journal, Issue 34, February 1997 (see also: `http://www.ssc.com/ lj/issue34/0232.html`).

[3] K.H.Kim , *Toward New-Generation Real-Time Object-Oriented Computing*, Proceedings of Fifth IEEE Workshop on Future Trends of Distributed Computing Systems, pp. 520-529, Cheju Island, South Korea, 1995.

[4] J. McGoogan (ed.), *Realtime CORBA - A White Paper - Issue 1.0*, OMG Realtime Platform SIG, Initial Review Draft, November 1996.

[5] NATIONAL INSTITUTE OF STANDARDS AND TECHNOLOGY, *RCSlib – Intelligent Controller Systems Development*, http://isd.cme.nist.gov/brochure/SoftwareSystems.html
[6] OMG, *The Common Object Request Broker: Architecture and Specification*, Object Management Group, Inc., Framingham, Mass., 1998.
[7] OMG, *Realtime CORBA 1.0 RFP*, Document orbos/97-06-01, http://www.omg.org.
[8] A.POLZE, L.SHA, *Composite Objects: Real-Time Programming with CORBA*, Proceedings of 24th Euromicro Conference, Network Computing Workshop, Vol. II, pp. 997-1004, Vaesteras, Sweden, August 1998.
[9] A.POLZE, G.FOHLER, M.WERNER, *Predictable Network Computing*, in Proceedings of International Conference on Distributed Computing Systems (ICDCS'97), Baltimore, Maryland, May 1997.
[10] R.RAJKUMAR, M.GAGLIARDI, AND L.SHA, *The Real-Time Publisher/Subscriber Inter-Process Communication Model for Distributed Real-Time Systems: Design and Implementation*, Proceedings of First IEEE Real-Time Technology and Applications Symposium, May 1995.
[11] D.C.SCHMIDT, A.GOKHALE, T.H.HARRISON, D.LEVINE, AND C.CLEELAND, *TAO: A High-Performance Endsystem Architecture for Real-Time CORBA*, RFI response to the OMG Special Interest Group on Real-Time CORBA, 1997.
[12] D.C.SCHMIDT, A.GOKHALE, T.H.HARRISON, G.PARULKAR, *A High-Performance Endsystem Architecture for Real-Time CORBA*, IEEE Communications Magazine, Vol. 14, No. 2, February 1997.
[13] L.SHA, R.RAJKUMAR, M.GAGLIARDI, *Evolving Dependable Real-Time Systems*, Proceedings of 1996 IEEE Aerospace Applications Conference, Vol. 1, pp. 335-346, Aspen, Colo., February 1996.
[14] L.SHA, M.GAGLIARDI, R.RAJKUMAR, *Analytic Redundancy: A Foundation for Evolvable Dependable Systems*, Proceedings of 2nd ISSAT International Conference on Reliability, and Quality of Design, March 1995.
[15] L.SHA, R.RAJKUMAR, S.S.SATHAYE, *Generalized Rate-Monotonic Scheduling Theory: A Framework for Developing Real-Time Systems*, Proceedings of the IEEE, Vol. 82, No. 1, January 1994.
[16] E.SHOKRI, K.KIM , *An Implementation Model for the Time-Triggered Message-Triggered Object Support Mechanisms in CORBA-Compliant COTS Platforms*, Proceedings of First IEEE International Symposium on Object-Oriented Real-Time Distributed Computing (ISORC), pp. 12-21, Kyoto, Japan, April 1998.
[17] R.M.SOLEY (ED.), *Object Management Architecture Guide*, Third Edition, John Wiley and Sons, New York, 1995.
[18] M.SQUADRITO, L.ESIBOV, L.C.DIPIPPO, V.F.WOLFE, G.COOPER, B.THURAISINGHAM, P.KRUPP, M.MILLIGAN, R.JOHNSTON, *Concurrency Control in Real-Time Object-Oriented Systems: The Affected Set Priority Ceiling Protocols*, Proceedings of First IEEE International Symposium on Object-Oriented Real-Time Distributed Computing (ISORC), pp. 96-105, Kyoto, Japan, April 1998.
[19] B.THURAISINGHAM, P.KRUPP, AND V.WOLFE, *Position Paper: On Real-Time Extensions to Object Request Brokers*, Proceedings of Second Workshop on Object-Oriented Real-Time Dependable Systems (WORDS), Laguna Beach, Calif., February 1996.
[20] V.F.WOLFE, J.K.BLACK, B.THURAISINGHAM, P.KRUPP, *Real-Time Method Invocations in Distributed Environments*, Proceedings of the International High Performance Computing Conference, December, 1995.

A REAL-TIME PARALLEL SCHEDULER FOR THE IMPRECISE COMPUTATION MODEL*

HESHAM FOUAD†, BHAGIRATH NARAHARI‡, AND JAMES K. HAHN§

Abstract. This paper considers the problem of scheduling hard real-time, periodic jobs on a multiprocessor while allowing imprecise computations. A highly dynamic job set is assumed, where limited *a priori* knowledge of a job set's behavior is available. The use of static partitioning schemes for such a job set is shown to lead to load imbalances and unecessary error. Instead, a dynamic load balancing approach is used. A set of constraints are established so that balancing the load does not invalidate established schedules or increase the error. Finally a scheduling algorithm, based on these constraints is presented.

Key words. real-time systems, multiprocessors, scheduling algorithms, imprecise computations.

1. Introduction. The Imprecise Computation model [2] provides a framework for incorporating graceful degradation in real-time applications. The technique is based on the premise that, in some cases, producing less-that-perfect results on time is better than producing no results at all. This premise is particularly useful for interactive multimedia applications. A degraded image or sound may go unnoticed by users while a discontinuity in the media will most probably not. Devising scheduling algorithms that can effectively manage the real-time generation of synthetic images and sounds in such applications is particularly challenging. Interactive multimedia applications are compute intensive and exhibit a highly dynamic and non-deterministic behavior because of the user's interaction with the application.

Generating high quality synthetic media often requires the use of multiprocessor architectures in order to achieve interactive rates. While parallel real-time scheduling algorithms have been devised for the imprecise computation model, they are not very well suited to this task because they assume a static job set with *a priori* knowledge of the job set's behavior. Partitioning techniques are used where jobs are initially distributed among the processors and uniprocessor scheduling algorithms are then used to schedule each processor independently. Given a highly dynamic job set where the behavior of the jobs is not known *a priori*, these techniques lead to load imbalances and unnecessary degradation.

In this paper we describe a real-time parallel scheduler developed for use in a sound generation server for Virtual Environment (VE) applications. The Virtual

*This work was supported by the Naval Research Laboratory under contract N00173-97-P-5529.

†The Naval Research Laboratory, Code 5707, 4400 Overlook Drive, Washington DC, 20375 (hesham@acm.org).

‡The George Washington University, Department of Electrical Engineering and Computer Science, Washington DC, 20052 (narahari@seas.gwu.edu)

§The George Washington University, Department of Electrical Engineering and Computer Science, Washington DC, 20052 (hahn@seas.gwu.edu)

Audio Server (VAS) provides three dimensional audio cues for VEs. One of the distinguishing features of VAS is that it supports procedurally defined synthetic sounds. A procedural representation is advantageous because it affords users the maximum flexibility in shaping the sound and, through parameterization of the procedures, sounds can be mapped to motion parameters in the VE.

VAS was developed on a Silicon Graphics Onyx^{tm} machine with eight MIPS^{tm} R10000 processors. The Onyx^{tm} utilizes a shared memory architecture that is preferable in this application due the high data bandwidth required. Upon execution, the VAS system commandeers a user-specified number of processors that are isolated and subsequently scheduled by VAS.

2. A Real-Time Sound Server Application. Synthetic sounds are generated by evaluating their procedural representation, once for each sample produced in the output. Given that high quality audio requires sampling rates of 44100 Hz or 48000Hz, this places a significant computational burden on the system. The problem however is compounded because the sound server must effectively create a complete sonic environment composed of many sound sources. Each sound source must be generated and further processed in order to account for propagation effects from source to listener and also for localization effects in real-time.

In order to ensure the real-time response of the sound server given an arbitrary number of active sound sources, the system incorporates a real-time parallel scheduler that manages the sound generation processes. The scheduler creates an instance of a sound evaluation routine for each sound source. An execution of a sound evaluation routine entails generating a sample block of fixed size and processing the samples to simulate propagation and localization effects. A graceful degradation scheme is utilized whereby sounds in the environment are prioritized based on their characteristics and on the position and orientation of the listener. During overload conditions, less important sounds are degraded by under-sampling their representation. In [4] we present a multi-resolution representation of a synthetic sound. Using this technique, a sound generation routine evaluates the sound over a series of ten iterations. Each iteration improves the resolution and hence the quality of the resultant sound. The evaluation process can be stopped at any point past the first iteration and interpolation techniques are used to generate the missing samples.

3. A Real-Time Parallel Scheduler for Generating Sound. The sound generation process can be expressed in terms of the hard real-time, periodic workload model. The job set, $J = J_k$, consists of the set of sounds each making periodic requests for the same execution. Each task $T_{k,j}$ consists of a request for the evaluation of a block of samples. The size of this sample block is fixed across all jobs and thus occupies the same playback time in the output device. If the evaluation routine does not produce a new sample block before the current one has completed playback, silent gaps will appear in the output. The deadline for each of the requests is thus the time for a sample block to playback at the output device. Because the period of a job is defined as the time between two consecutive deadlines, all the jobs will have the same period, namely $\alpha_{k,j+1} - \alpha_{k,j}$ where $\alpha_{k,j}$ is the start time of task $T_{k,j}$.

3.1. The Imprecise Computation Model. In a seminal paper, Chung et al. [2] describe a technique for evaluating monotonic processes using a model for imprecise computations. A monotonic process is one that is guaranteed to produce increasingly accurate results as it is allowed to execute longer. The Imprecise Computation model partitions a task into a mandatory part and an optional part. The mandatory part is that required to produce results at the minimum acceptable precision. The mandatory task set is scheduled as a hard real-time task set and a precise schedule is obtained. Any remaining time is used to schedule the optional parts of the task set. The resultant schedule is termed a feasible schedule.

The scheduling strategy for the Imprecise Computation model requires that each task be executed for a minimum time of m_k and that any remaining time in the schedule be assigned to tasks such that some error metric is minimized. The characteristics of the job set determine the error metric used and thus the scheduling strategy. Jobs are classified according to their characteristics as type N or type C jobs. Type N jobs are those where the error incurred due to a task not completing its execution does not accumulate over time. For type C jobs, on the other hand, errors do accumulate and therefore require that periodically some task be allowed to execute to completion. The sound generation problem fits the characteristics of a type N job. The error incurred due to under-sampling one block of samples does not accumulate to subsequent blocks. We will therefore only consider the scheduling strategies developed for those types of jobs.

The evaluation of a sample block is a monotonic process because the sound's representation can be sampled at successively higher resolutions. We therefore define the minimum execution time m_k for each job to be the time required for the sound generation routine to perform one iteration. The optional job consists of the other nine iterations required to fully evaluate the sound. This, in effect, provides the graceful degradation that we sought to incorporate in the sound server.

Scheduling type N jobs requires two scheduling strategies, one to precisely schedule the mandatory jobs $M_k(p_k, m_k)$, and another to schedule the optional jobs $O_k(p_k, \alpha_k - m_k)$ so that some error metric is minimized. A good error metric for measuring the performance of a scheduling strategy for type N jobs is the average error of all results. An average error formulation for a type N job as described in [2] is

$$E_k = \frac{p_k}{p} \sum_{j=l-\frac{p}{p_k}+1}^{l} \epsilon_k(\alpha_k, j) \tag{3.1a}$$

where p is the least common multiple of the repetition periods of the jobs in J, p_k is the repetition period of job J_k, l is the period in which the error is being calculated, and α_k is the assigned execution time of task j. $\epsilon_k(\alpha_k, j)$ is the error in task j of job k given by

$$\epsilon_k(\alpha_k, j) = 1 - \frac{\alpha_{k,j} - m_k}{\tau_k - m_k} \tag{3.1b}$$

where m_k is the minimum acceptable execution time of job J_k, and τ_k is the total execution time of that job.

The total error for the system is expressed as

$$E = \sum_{k=1}^{K} w_k E_k \tag{3.2}$$

where w_k is a normalized, nonnegative constant weight signifying the relative importance of each job. The above general expressions can be simplified to

$$E = 1 - \frac{1}{p} \sum_{k=1}^{K} \frac{w_k}{v_k} \alpha_k(O) \tag{3.3a}$$

where v_k is the utilization factor of optional job O_k and is given by $v_k = \frac{(\tau_k - m_k)}{p_k}$. τ is the total processor time assigned to tasks in O_k over the time in which the error is measured $\frac{p}{p_k}$ and is given by

$$\alpha_k(O) = \sum_{j=l-\frac{p}{p_k}+1}^{l} \alpha_{k,j} - \frac{pm_k}{p_k} \tag{3.3b}$$

In [2] a two tiered approach is suggested for scheduling type N jobs. The mandatory job set is scheduled using the Rate Monotonic algorithm. The Rate Monotonic algorithm is a priority driven, preemptive algorithm that has been shown to be optimal among fixed priority algorithms. While the optional job set is scheduled using the Least Utilization (LU) algorithm. When the jobs are ordered in a non-decreasing order in k according to their weighted utilization factor $\frac{v_k}{w_k}$, it is evident from equation 3.3 that E is minimized when the maximum processing time is allocated to O_1 which corresponds to the smallest weighed utilization factor. This observation leads to the Least Utilization algorithm. This algorithm statically assigns higher priorities to the jobs with the smaller weighted utilization factors $\frac{v_k}{w_k}$. It is shown that this algorithm minimizes the average error when the error function is linear and when all the jobs have the same repetition period.

3.2. Multiprocessor Scheduling. Unfortunately, extending the above strategy to the multiprocessor case is not straightforward. According to [3] algorithms for scheduling periodic, hard real-time tasks on multiprocessors have been shown to have unacceptably poor worst-case performance. Alternatively, a partitioning approach is used where jobs are first assigned to processors, each processor is then scheduled independently using uniprocessor scheduling algorithms. The partitioning is optimized so that the number of processors used is minimized. This problem is equivalent to the bin-packing problem and hence is NP hard requiring a heuristic approach.

The Rate-Monotonic Next-Fit (RMNF) (or First-Fit (RMFF)) algorithm [3] prioritizes jobs according to their periods, with shorter periods having higher priority. The jobs are assigned to processors in priority order based on a next-fit or alternatively a first-fit basis. In deciding whether or not a job fits a processor, only the mandatory job M_k of J_k is considered. The scheduling strategy for the mandatory job set is invoked to determine whether the inclusion of the newly assigned job to the existing job set on that processor can yield a feasible schedule.

A number of non-partitioning approaches to scheduling periodic hard real-time jobs have been suggested. In [9] the myopic algorithm is presented which can schedule a job set with resource constraints on a multiprocessor. The problem of finding a precise schedule is formulated as search tree and the branch and bound technique is used to search the tree for a precise schedule. The algorithm orders the set of tasks based on a heuristic function H. Possible heuristics for H include: minimum deadline first, minimum processing time first, earliest start time first, minimum laxity first, and finally some weighted combination of the above. Starting with an empty schedule the task with the smallest H value is added to the schedule and a determination is made whether or not the resultant schedule is strongly feasible. A partial schedule is strongly feasible if all the schedules obtained by extending this schedule with one of the remaining tasks are also feasible. When a partial schedule is reached which does not satisfy this constraint, backtracking is performed to traverse other possible branches.

Normally such an algorithm would have $O(n^2)$ complexity. However, as the name implies, the algorithm does not consider all the remaining tasks when evaluating the H value and when determining whether a partial schedule is strongly feasible. Instead the tasks are ordered in increasing deadlines and only the first k tasks are considered in the evaluation, where k is fixed. The resultant algorithm exhibits $O(n)$ complexity. Surprisingly, this algorithm performs as well as the original $O(n^2)$ version.

In [7] a heuristic based algorithm is presented which assigns m tasks to n processors directly. The SA1 algorithm segments time into blocks that are the GCD of the deadlines of all the tasks. Each task is assigned its average time requirement within each block. The average requirement of each task is $T * \frac{C_i}{D_i}$, where T is the GCD of the deadlines. D_i is the task's deadline and C_i is its required execution time. Assuming processors are numbered $1, \cdots, n$, tasks are assigned their average requirement on the processors sequentially starting with processor 1. When the average requirement for a task exceeds the available time on the current processor, the task is split such that it uses the remaining schedulable time on processor 1 and the remaining execution time required to meet its average requirement is scheduled on the next processor, processor 2. In determining whether a task set m is schedulable on n processors precisely, the condition $U \leq n$ was determined to be sufficient [7], were U is the multiprocessor utilization factor

$$U = \sum_{i=1}^{n} \frac{C_i}{D_i} \tag{3.4}$$

The SA1 algorithm exhibits $O(m)$ complexity where m is the number of tasks. For a dynamic system with tasks entering and leaving the system on-line, the SA1 algorithm can be run for a newly arrived task in $O(1)$ time if no tasks have left the system and time is available on one processor to schedule the task without partitioning it. Otherwise the full algorithm must be evaluated at $O(m)$ time.

In [6] the SA1 algorithm is extended to handle imprecise computations. The problem is formulated as a min-cost-max-flow network flow problem. While this approach yields a minimum error schedule, the complexity of the approach makes it impractical for any real use.

3.3. Dynamic Load Balancing. We now examine the suitability of a static partitioning scheme for the sound generation problem. Given the transient nature of sounds in an environment, the system exhibits a very dynamic behavior where jobs frequently enter and leave the scheduler. Due to the non-deterministic nature of a user's interactions within a VE, we cannot predict *a priori* the behavior of the sounds in the system. In other words, we cannot predict at any point what sounds may be active.

Utilizing a static partitioning algorithm such as RMNF for the sound evaluation problem has a number of pitfalls. The dynamic nature of the job set leads to load imbalances due to the static assignment of jobs to processors. Situations occur where some processors are idle while others are overloaded and must needlessly degrade sounds. In general, the non-deterministic nature of the job set means that any static partitioning of the job set can only consider the potential load on any processor. This will not reflect the actual load conditions at runtime.

The idea of optimizing the partitions so that the number of processors used is minimized is not realistic for this problem. We are generally assigned a fixed number of processors on which to operate. Our goal is therefore to minimize the error given a fixed number of processors. The RMNF algorithm does not consider the resultant error in the imprecise computation when assigning jobs to processors since only the mandatory job set is considered.

Finally, RMNF assigns jobs to processors based on their period. As was described earlier, all of the jobs in our workload model have the same period. These algorithms therefore lead to an arbitrary assignment of jobs to processors.

If static analysis of the job set will not lead to a good partitioning, then we must consider a dynamic approach. A dynamic load-balancing scheme is concerned with distributing jobs among the processors in a parallel or distributed system such that the load is evenly balanced. While it is generally agreed upon that maintaining a balanced load across processors is beneficial, in this model balancing the load can actually result in an increase in the average error. The following theorem relates processor load to the average error.

THEOREM 3.1. *When the total utilization factor of all jobs $U > 1$, a partitioning which assigns each of N processors a load of $\frac{U}{N}$ is optimal if and only if $U \leq N$. We refer to optimality here in the sense that no other assignment of load to processors will produce less error.*

Proof. In order to prove this theorem, we consider two cases of U.

Case $U \leq N$: Here a balanced partitioning will assign each processor a load of $\frac{U}{N} \leq 1$

It has been shown in [8] that $u \leq 1$, where u is the utilization factor of the jobs assigned to one processor, is sufficient to guarantee that the job set is precisely schedulable. Therefore under this partitioning all the optional jobs will be assigned their full execution time and there is no error. Clearly no other partitioning can produce less error.

Case $U > N$: The expressions for average error presented in equations 3.1 and 3.2 can be reformulated in terms of a job's unassigned execution time as follows

$$E = \frac{1}{p} \sum_{k=1}^{K} \frac{w_k}{v_k} \epsilon_k(O) \tag{3.5a}$$

where

$$\epsilon_k(O) = \sum_{j=l-\frac{p}{p_k}+1}^{l} (\tau_k - m_k) - (\alpha_{k,j} - m_k). \tag{3.5b}$$

and $\epsilon_k(O)$ is the portion of k's optional job that is not executed.

Suppose that we have an optimal partitioning of the job set that allocates a load of $\frac{U}{N}$ to each processor, we should expect that the average error be minimized. If this supposition is correct, then moving some job J_i from processor P_j to P_k will result in a load imbalance and hence an increase the average error. We can formulate the difference in average error resulting from moving job J_i from processor P_j to P_k as follows

$$\Delta E = \frac{1}{p} \left(\left(\frac{w_i}{v_i} \epsilon_i'(O) + \sum_{k=1}^{K} \frac{w_k}{v_k} \Delta T_k \right) - \left(\frac{w_i}{v_i} \epsilon_i(O) + \sum_{j=1}^{J} \frac{w_j}{v_j} \Delta T_j \right) \right) \tag{3.6}$$

where w_i is the weight of job J_i, v_i is the total utilization factor of O_i, $\epsilon_i(O)$ is the error due to J_i's assigned time on processor P_j (equation 3.5), $\epsilon_i'(O)$ is the error due to J_i's new assigned time on processor P_k (equation 3.5), ΔT_k is the difference in assigned time to job k after adding J_i to P_k, and finally ΔT_j is the difference in assigned time to job j after removing J_i from P_j. We now consider the following job sets assigned to two processors P_1 and P_2 respectively:

$J_1 = (2, .5, .2), (4, .2, .3), (5, .1, .1), (6, 2, .4)$

$J_2 = (2, .2, .8), (7, .1, .1), (8, .1, .1)$

Each job is specified as a tuple (τ, m, w), consisting of the job's total execution time, its minimum acceptable execution time, and its weight respectively. The total utilization factor on each processor is 1.7 and the load is ideally balanced. According to equation 3.6, moving job $j_2(4, .2, .3)$ from P_1 to P_2 results in a decrease in average error of the jobs assigned to P_1 of .20369. The corresponding increase in average error that results from adding j_2 to P_2's job set is .056314. The net change in error due to this migration is $\Delta E = .056314 - .20369 = -.14738$. The total average error was decreased due to the job migration and hence we have a contradiction. □

3.4. The Minimum Distance Algorithm. A heuristic load-balancing algorithm was devised and incorporated into our scheduler. Due to the shared memory architecture chosen for this problem, the algorithm is able to use global load information across all processors, and use a preemptive migration policy. The following policies were defined for task allocation and task migration. The task allocation policy is based on the random allocation presented in [1]. This is based on the observation that client applications typically allocate all sounds during an initialization stage. At runtime sounds are dynamically started and stopped, and finally before exiting, sounds are deallocated. At task allocation time, when new sounds are created, no sounds are yet active and hence no actual load information exists to base a task allocation on. The static load information is of little use since it does not reflect the actual load during runtime. Finally as was shown in [1], the random allocation policy does a good job of distributing the load for a uniform grain size. While the sound evaluation routines can differ in grain size based on the complexity of the sound, experience has shown that the amount of variation they exhibit is fairly limited.

The task migration policy chosen is a sender initiated preemptory policy that affords better response to overload conditions [5]. In order to determine when a processor is to be considered overloaded, we use the total utilization factor of the mandatory and optional jobs assigned to that processor. The threshold used for initiating the send procedure is $u_p > 1$ where up the total utilization factor assigned to processor P.

We have not yet considered when load balancing should be initiated. A static invocation policy is one that is synchronous; load balancing occurs at regular predetermined intervals. A dynamic invocation policy is asynchronous such that load balancing can occur at any time. A dynamic invocation policy is more responsive and can reduce scheduling overhead since load balancing is only initiated when needed. Unfortunately, a dynamic policy can lead to serious problems for a real-time scheduler. Once each processor's scheduler has determined an allocation of time to its assigned jobs for a given period, migrating a job during that period will invalidate the schedules. A dynamic invocation policy is therefore not appropriate for a real-time system. Instead a static invocation policy is used where load balancing is initiated at the start of each period. The overhead incurred due to this policy is actually minimal because in highly dynamic sonic environments load imbalances may occur frequently enough so that a dynamic policy would invoke load balancing as often as a static policy, in which case both algorithms would impose the same overhead. In other cases, the overhead is minimized by only initiating load balancing when at least one of the processors meets the task migration threshold.

The determination of where to send a job and which job to send is made as follows. The algorithm first finds the least utilized processor P_{least}. A job is migrated from processor P_{from} to processor P_{least} if there exists a job j on P_{from} that satisfies the following two constraints. In order to insure that the migration will reduce the difference in load between the two processors we have $u_j < u_p - u_{p_{least}}$. u_j is the total utilization factor of job j, and $u_{p_{least}}$ is the utilization factor of the least utilized processor. The second constraint is based on theorem 3.1, which shows that migrating jobs in order to balance load might increase the average error. In general, equation 3.6 gives the exact change in error, ΔE, due migrating a job between two processors. Ideally we would like to guarantee that a given job migration will not only result in a negative ΔE but also maximize $|\Delta E|$. Unfortunately an exact solution requires that for each job that is being considered for migration, the post-migration schedule on P_1 and P_2 be generated in order to evaluate ΔE. The resulting overhead makes that an unreasonable approach. Instead we must resort to using a heuristic to determine which job, if any, should be migrated.

In order to examine the effect that our choice of job has on ΔE, we reformulate equation 3.6 to the following

$$\Delta E = \frac{w_i}{v_i}(\alpha - \alpha') + \sum_{k=1}^{K} \frac{w_k}{v_k}\Delta T_k - \sum_{j=1}^{J} \frac{w_j}{v_j}\Delta T_j \tag{3.7}$$

Our choice of job will determine the value of $\frac{w_i}{v_i}$ and the value of α, the current execution time. In order to make $\frac{w_i}{v_i}(\alpha - \alpha')$ as negative as possible, we must choose a job such that $\frac{w_i}{v_i}$ is maximized, α is minimized, and α', the new execution time, is maximized. Based on how execution time is assigned to optional jobs in the LU algorithm, there exists an integer f of the following property. Assuming the job set is ordered by the weighted utilization factor $\frac{v_k}{w_k}$ such that it is non-decreasing in k, $J = j_1, j_2, \cdots, j_k$, an optimal assignment will allocate the first f optional jobs in O_k their full execution time. More formally, we have

$$\sum_{k=1}^{f} v_k \leq 1 - u < \sum_{k=1}^{f+1} v_k \tag{3.8}$$

where u is the utilization factor of the K mandatory jobs, and v_k is the full utilization factor of an optional job [2]. In choosing a candidate job on P_{from} to migrate, we find a job j_i such that $i > f_{from}$. In other words, we choose the job with the least weighted utilization factor that is not receiving its full execution time. In order to guarantee that job j_i will receive more execution time after migration, we must ensure that on the target processor $\frac{v_i}{w_i} < \frac{v_f}{w_f}$.

Based on these observations, our load balancing algorithm finds the first job j_i on P_{from} such that $i > f$ on the source processor and $u_i < u_{p\_from} - u_{p\_least}$. Job j_i is migrated if and only if $\frac{v_i}{w_i} < \frac{v_f}{w_f}$ on the target processor. Because the algorithm tries to minimize the difference in load between any two processors, we termed the algorithm the Minimum Difference (MD) algorithm. Pseudo-code for the MD algorithm is listed in Fig. 3.1.

```
MD()
begin
P = {p1, p2, ..., pN}                /* P is the set of N processors */
for i:= 1 to N do
   p := P(i)
   if p.utilization > 1 then
         pmin = FindMinUtilized(P)          /* Returns the least utilized processor */
         if pmin = p then next i
         else
                 u := p.utilization – pmin.utilization
                 /* GetJobByUtilization finds a job with the least v_i/w_i */
                 /* where i > f and with a total utilization ≤ u */
                 j := GetJobByUtilization(p, u)
                 if (j <> null) and (v_i/w_i < v_f/w_f) then
                          Migrate(j, p, pmin)    /* Migrates a job from p to pmin */
                 endif
         endif
   endif
endfor
end
```

FIG. 3.1. *The Minimum Distance algorithm*

The MD algorithm was incorporated into our scheduler and processor loads were measured during the evaluation of a test sonic environment on two processors. In Fig. 3.2 the load imposed by this test environment is plotted. In Fig. 3.3 the load assigned to each processor with the MD algorithm and a static allocation policy are depicted. The static strategy that was used simply allocates an incoming job to the processor with the least assigned load. Also plotted in Fig. 3.3 is the optimal load assignment of $\frac{U}{N}$.

In order to measure the effectiveness of these two strategies, the mean of the difference between the load assigned to the two processors was measured. Clearly a mean value of zero implies that both processors received identical load and hence we have the optimal assignment of $\frac{U}{N}$. The mean value for the static allocation policy was found to be 0.8. The corresponding mean value for the dynamic allocation was 0.2. The dynamic policy clearly balanced the load much more effectively than the static policy. This is also evident by examination of the plots in Fig. 3.3. The processor loads for the dynamic allocation policy were

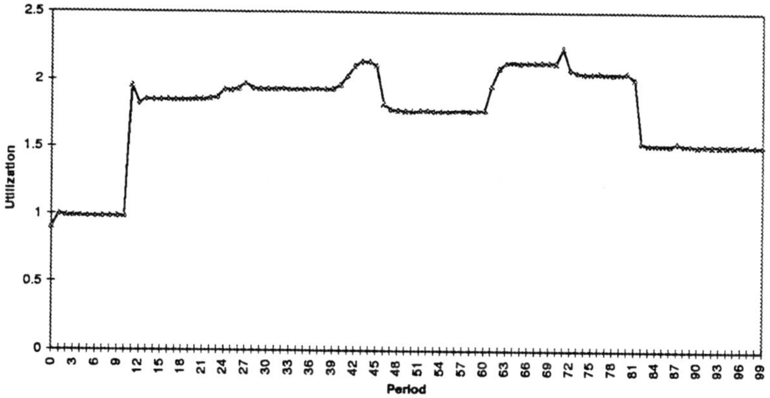

FIG. 3.2. *Processor utilization*

much closer to the optimal case than those for the static policy.

The effect of the load assignments on error was measured by calculating the total average error produced by both policies. The total average error was calculated simply as the sum of the average error produced on each processor over a time of 100 periods. The total average error produced by the static allocation strategy was 0.74046. The corresponding error generated using the dynamic task migration was 0.609861. As expected the MD algorithm balanced the load while significantly reducing the average error.

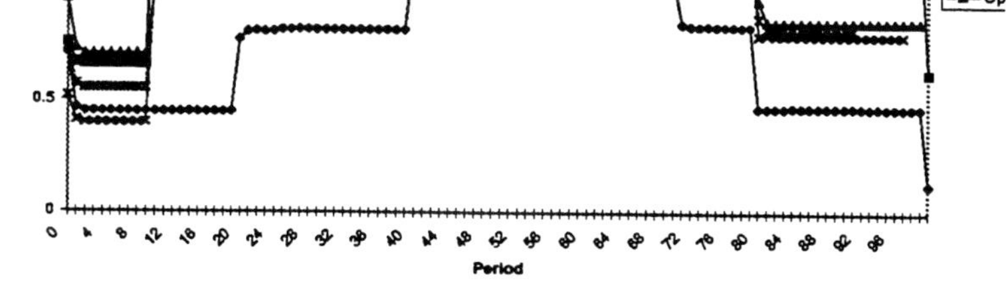

FIG. 3.3. *Processor loads with and without dynamic load balancing*

4. Conclusion. In this paper, we presented a parallel real-time scheduling algorithm for the Imprecise Computation model that utilizes dynamic load balancing. We have shown that for applications where the job set is dynamic and the behavior of jobs is not predictable, a static partitioning will lead to load imbalances and unnecessary degradation. We established a set of constraints that must be adhered to in utilizing dynamic load balancing for a real-time system such that schedules are not invalidated and the error is not increased. Finally we presented the MD algorithm which adheres to these constraints and was shown to balance the load among processors while decreasing the average error.

REFERENCES

[1] W.C. Athas and C.L. Seitz, *Multicomputers: Message-Passing Concurrent Computers*, IEEE Computer, 8 (1988), pp. 9–24.
[2] J.Y. Chung, J.W.S Liu, and K.J. Lin, *Scheduling Real-Time, Periodic Jobs Using Imprecise Results*, Proc. 1987 IEEE Real-Time Systems Symposium, pp. 252–260.
[3] S.K. Dhall and C.L. Liu, *On a Real-Time Scheduling Problem*, Oper. Res., 1 (1978), pp. 127–140.
[4] H. Fouad, J.K. Hahn, and J.A. Ballas, *Perceptually Based Scheduling Algorithms for Real-Time Synthesis of Complex Sonic Environments*, Proc. 1997 ICAD, pp. 77–81.
[5] D.L. Eager, E.D. Lazowska, and J. Zahorjan, *A Comparison of Receiver-Initiated and Sender-Initiated Adaptive Load Sharing*, Performance Evaluation, 1 (1986), pp. 53–68.
[6] A. Khemka, R. K. Shyamasundar, *Multiprocessor Scheduling for Imprecise Computations in a Hard Real-Time Environment*, Proc. 1993 IEEE Real-Time Systems Symposium, pp. 617–636.
[7] A. Khemka, R. K. Shyamasundar, *Multiprocessor Scheduling of Periodic Tasks in a Hard Real-Time Environment*, Int. Journal of High Speed Computing, 4 (1993), pp. 617–636.
[8] C. L. Liu, J. W. Layland, *Scheduling Algorithms for Multiprogramming in a Hard Real-Time Environment*, Journal of the ACM, 1 (1973), pp. 46–61.
[9] K. Ramamritham, J. A. Stankovic, and P. F. Shiah, *Efficient Scheduling Algorithms for Real-Time Multiprocessor Systems*, IEEE Trans. on Parallel and Distributed Sys., 2 (1990), pp. 184–194.

DISTRIBUTED COMPUTATIONS IN REAL TIME BASED ON A ROUGH GRAMMAR PRINCIPLE *

ZBIGNIEW M. WÓJCIK † AND JANUSZ ZALEWSKI ‡

Abstract. A novel methodology for high performance computing in real time is presented based on a rough grammar approach. Using the rough grammar we sequence dynamically all the tasks in a processor net in a pipeline fashion. The duration of each pipeline stage is normalized to the duration of one of the shorter tasks, by which a reduction of the idle and wait times of nodes to a minimum is achieved. The simulations show that the node busyness is almost one hundred percent at each node for an arbitrary algorithm and without knowing the task execution times in advance. Higher linear improvement is achieved by allocating the next nodes for a smaller quantum (e.g., at 10% of tasks completed) and passing all the tasks forward when the quantum expires.

Key words. distributed computations, real-time computing, rough sets, rough grammar

1. Introduction. Performing computations in real time means meeting the deadlines uncoditionally, if they are hard, or, at least, making computations predictable if the deadlines can be missed (in which case they are soft). In a variety of signal processing applications, such as image recognition, speech synthesis, deadlines are usually very short but not hard, that is, an occasionally missed deadline may degrade the quality of the result but does not cause more severe consequences. To perform this type of computations in real time, usually, the computational algorithm must take advantage of the natural structure of the problem to allow some sort of parallelization. If parallelization is possible, then several additional problems must be solved, such as parallel task allocation and scheduling, load balancing, etc.

A lot of solutions to both parallel task scheduling and load balancing has been proposed in the literature [1, 2]. Most of them work satisfactorily only in special cases and do not seem to be suitable for generalization. This paper presents a remedy to all such problems by exploiting a new principle of parallel computations, the rough grammar approach. The rest of the paper is organized as follows. In Section 2, a brief introduction to rough sets and rough grammars is presented. In Section 3, the principle of distributed computations based on a rough grammar is explained. This is followed by the discussion of experimental results in Section 4 and conclusions in Section 5.

2. Rough Sets and Rough Grammars.

2.1. Principles of Rough Sets Theory. Rough sets theory [3] is a mathematical technique developed to describe quantitatively uncertainty, imprecision, and vagueness. Below a brief outline is provided of the rough sets theory and

*Sponsored in part by the Army Research Office under the contract DAAH04-94-C-0019.

†Smart Machines, 13703 Morningbluff Drive, San Antonio, TX 78216, USA

‡Dept. of Electrical and Computer Engineering, University of Central Florida, Orlando, FL 32816-2450, USA, jza@ece.engr.ucf.edu.

how we deal with uncertainty concepts to make quantitative decisions. The simplest way to explain the nature of a rough set is to compare its membership function to the ordinary set and fuzzy set membership functions (see Fig. 1).

The ordinary set shown in Fig. 1a, describes a precise concept, which means that based on its membership function one can decide whether an element belongs to the set or not. A fuzzy set, shown in Fig. 1b, describes an imprecise concept, because based on its membership function one can tell only that elements $C \leq x \leq D$ belong to the set and elements $x \leq A$ or $x \geq B$ do not belong to the set. For elements $A < x < C$ and $D < x < B$ one can only tell that they belong to the set with a certain degree. For a rough set, shown in Fig. 1c, one does not define the degree of membership in the intervals $A < x < C$ and $D < x < B$, because of uncertainty. However, one defines the intervals of uncertainty and the level of uncertainty (roughness) for all elements in the vague intervals.

To deal with vagueness and uncertainty embedded in rough sets, as illustrated in Fig. 1c, the rough set is described by its two approximations: the lower approximation (interval $[C, D]$ in Fig. 1c) and the upper approximation (interval $[A, B]$ in Fig. 1c). In other words, a lower approximation of a set is the set of all elements belonging to it with certainty, while an upper approximation of a set is the set of all elements which cannot be excluded from it with certainty.

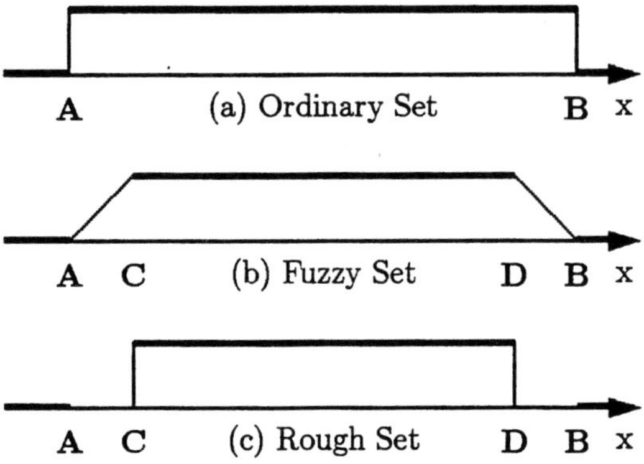

Fig. 1. Illustration of the Notion of a Rough Set.

Formally, the lower and upper approximations of a rough set, X, are defined as follows [3]:

(2.1) $$\underline{R}X = \cup\{Y \in U \mid R : Y \subseteq X\}$$

(2.2) $$\overline{R}X = \cup\{Y \in U \mid R : Y \cap X \neq \bigcirc\}$$

where U is the domain of discourse, R is the equivalence relation over U, representing the available knowledge, referred to as the knowledge base, $X \subseteq U$ is the rough set, and $\bigcirc$ is the empty set. The knowledge base (for simplicity, not depicted in Fig. 1c) provides *a priori* information on the structure of U via properties of its elements and can be interpreted as a collection of attribute values defined over U.

The lower approximation, $\underline{R}X$ represents the certainty that an object composed of the elements of U has a certain property. The upper approximation, $\overline{R}X$ refers to the possibility that an object composed of the elements of U has the referred property. Anything described by values from outside the upper approximation is considered with certainty not to have the relevant property.

The *boundary region*, B_R, of a rough set is the difference between an upper approximation and a lower approximation, formally defined as follows:

$$B_R = \overline{R}X - \underline{R}X \tag{2.3}$$

In other words, the boundary region is a set of elements which cannot be placed in the set with certainty and cannot be excluded from the set with certainty. The size of the boundary region can be used to measure the vagueness: the greater the boundary region the more vague is the concept represented by a rough set, and the smaller the boundary region the more precise the concept. This is expressed by the notion of accuracy, α, defined as follows:

$$\alpha_R(X) = \frac{size(\underline{R}X)}{size(\overline{R}X)} \tag{2.4}$$

2.2. Rough Grammars. We introduce the rough grammar [5, 6] as an extension of the rough sets [3]. Let U denote the entire space of data (operands), and R be the space of operators (i.e., the available software modules). The concept of the approximation space adopted from the rough sets [3] is used here as the pair (U, R). The equivalence relations defined for the rough sets are extended here to R, and the concept of the universe of discourse, U, is adopted in whole.

A token (elementary demand for software/data) is the pair $(X, r) \in U \times R$, consisting of:

a) Specification of operands (data), $X = \{x_1, \ldots, x_i, \ldots, x_N\}$, comprising their number, types, names, meanings, and specific metrics $m(X)$ (such as disk addresses and memory requirements);

b) Specification of an operator (a software module), r, involving its type, name, meaning and number of formal arguments, and metrics $m(r)$.

A token basically results in a transmission of the code of the operator to a destination node, then a request for actual parameters (data), and finally the execution and outputing of results. A result (called *object_approximation*) $a(X, r)$ of execution of r on X is composed of:

a) The lower approximation $\underline{A}(X, r)$ of the data X (i.e., meanings, types and number of operands). More specifically, the lower approximation defined for the rough sets [3, 4] must contain the greatest definable set of all possible results returned by r as far as meaning of the results, type and number of the output data is concerned;

b) The upper approximation $\overline{A}(X, r)$ (i.e., a specific symbolic representation $S(\overline{A}(X, r))$ and numerical values $V(\overline{A}(X, r)))$. More specifically, the upper approximation [3, 4] must be the least definable set of all possible output data during processing of X in its prespecified domain by appropriate operators (software) from R; and

c) Metrics $m(a(X, r))$ of data and software modules (e.g., addresses and memory requirements).

In this context, a rough set is any collection of approximations $a(X, r)$ in (U, R). If $(X, r_X) \equiv (Y, r_Y)$, which means that lower approximations, $\underline{A}(X, r_X)$ and $\underline{A}(Y, r_Y)$, of both sets are equal [5], then there exists a tolerance Tol such that $(X, r_X) \approx (Y, r_Y)$, which means that the sets are roughly equal. Here, Tol denotes some assumed admissible tolerances for the numerical values returned by r, and $\underline{A}(X, r)$ is the meaning or a type of the result returned by r. For instance, two software modules may give slightly different numerical results within the same meaning and a tolerance Tol, so they are roughly the same. This is applicable in finding out which operators can be used in place of others, and which intermediate results or their copies are equally useful during distributed computation.

The rough grammar, $G = \{N, T, P, S\}$, for distributed computation is composed of:

a) A set of start symbols, $S \subseteq U$, being input data (operands) for distributed computation;

b) A set of terminals, T, being approximations $\underline{A}(X, r)$ of some specific data $X \subseteq U$ to be returned as a result of some distributed computation in (U, R);

c) A set of nonterminals, N, composed of all the operators, R, intermediate results of processing, and the start symbols, S;

d) Production rules, P, executable on a distributed system, involving both operands $x \in U$ and operators, r_i, $\otimes \in R$ (usually different than concatenation).

Typical production rules are of the single form for a two place operation $\otimes$:

$$a(x_1 \otimes x_2) \longrightarrow object\_approximation \tag{2.5}$$

where $a \in \{\underline{A}, \overline{A}\}$; $x_1, x_2 \in U$. The operator $\otimes$ may have one or more operands.

3. Principle of Computing Based on Rough Grammars. High performance distributed computation is composed of transmissions of software modules and data, and then executions, all arranged and controlled by the rough grammar. A typical production rule of the rough grammar delivers some output as a result of execution for a given input composed of:

a) Data (of a rough nature within prespecified types, ranges, domains and/or meanings);

b) Operation (procedure or function) assumed by an algorithm. This operation is not necessarily a concatenation of input data (or symbols) in N.

The exact output of the operation is not easily predictable, this is why computer processing is necessary. The rough grammar production rule (token) predicts only a rough structure of the output as a type, range, domain and/or meaning of the results of processing using an operation. The productions of the rough grammar drive executions of the modules (procedures or functions) at the nodes where they are delivered.

This is a new principle of computing. We pass tokens as does the dataflow machine, but our tokens contain not only data, but also the operations. The operations are coarse-grained (such as procedures). To facilitate fast transmission of data and operations, we transmit first information of the distributed computation as the production rules of the rough grammar. Using these productions, each node can request both the actual values and executable code for processing.

3.1. Example. A sample illustration of the principle of a rough grammar is presented in Fig. 2. It shows a rough table to control distributed computations. Rows represent operators (such as *add*) and operands (such as a_0, a_1, ...). Operators with prespecified operands producing expected outcomes (being column pointers) are marked with 1's in the outcome column. Some of the rows (operators) can be the branch conditions (e.g., $c_1 < 0$). Elements filled with blanks are irrelevant.

The root of the distributed computation is the entire rough table. The root dependants are the start symbols of the rough grammar (assuming bottom-up processing). The start symbols are the operands pointing to a row but not pointing to a column (i.e., elements a_i). The terminal symbols are the column pointers not specified as row pointers (e.g., *sum*, $diff$). The root may start computations from a terminal symbol (as a top-down execution) or from start symbols (in a bottom-up processing). A branch (such as **if** $c_1 < 0$ **then** ...) is represented by an operation in a row entry which needs to return TRUE to fire an entire column of 1's the branch belongs to. Using the rough table of Fig. 2, the following is done:

$$\textbf{if}\ \ c_1 < 0\ \textbf{then}\ \ sum = c_0 + c_1$$

$$\textbf{if}\ \ c_1 \geq 0\ \textbf{then}\ \ diff = c_0 - c_1$$

where c_0 and c_1 are calculated in a distributed computation controlled by the rough table.

	b_0	b_1	b_2	b_3	c_0	c_1	sum	$diff$
a_0	1							
a_1	1							
a_2		1						
a_3		1						
a_4			1					
a_5			1					
a_6				1				
a_7				1				
b_0					1			
b_1					1			
b_2						1		
b_3						1		
c_0							1	1
c_1							1	1
$c_1 < 0$							1	
add	1	1	1	1	1	1	1	
$c_1 \geq 0$								1
sub								1

Fig. 2. A Rough Table to Control Distributed Computations.

Any right side of the production rule in the rough grammar graph of a lower-level (e.g., an *add* rule: $(b_2,\ add,\ b_3) \longrightarrow c_1)$ can be demanded by the left side of a higher-level rough-grammar rule (e.g., by the root *add* rule: $(c_0,\ add,\ c_1,\ c_1 < 0) \longrightarrow sum)$. Hypotheses can be spread in this way (e.g., as demands for software).

Values 1 in an entire column of the rough table indicate parallel predecessors of a node labeled by the right side of a rough grammar production rule and being a column pointer. The predecessors are treated as operands and operators providing computation for a **join** node. Any branch condition is also an operator. The node uses for its execution the operator and operands received from the predecessors and returns the approximation of the received operands. Each outcome (if it is not empty) is applied as a predecessor (a row pointer) to the next stage of the parallel processing. Synchronization is provided by the rough table (i.e., by the rough matrix extended by metrics of operators and operands): the computation is fired when a full set of the operands arrives for the operations of a production rule specified by 1's of a particular column. A few complete sets of 1's in different columns may fire a few different productions at a time in parallel, e.g., pointed to by column pointers b_1 or b_3 in Fig. 2. A sequence of values 1 in one row indicates parallel successors for a **fork** node, i.e., a set of destinations of a single operand or an operator. The rough table may be treated not only as a casual schedule of tasks, but also as a parallel program.

Any production rule (located in the rough grammar graph at a lower-level) can be demanded indirectly by a higher-level rough-grammar rule through its right side. Demands for recursive computations can be spread in this way. All the productions leading nowhere are disregarded by not demanding them. The rough production rule returns NIL, if demands cannot be satisfied (e.g., if a datum is missing). Simply, semantics for the right side of the rough grammar rule are checked (i.e., whether it reflects an expectation, or not). All the rough grammar graph branches continue until one (in the *AND* graph) or all (in the *OR* graph) values of the operand are NIL or until a terminal T is reached. All parents getting operands equal to NIL die thereby stopping any further unnecessary derivation.

3.2. Properties of the Rough Grammar. The details of rough grammar's properties, including novel dynamic task management approaches using the rough table and pipelining, and basic differences between the rough grammar and the classical (Chomsky) grammars, have been presented in [5]. Here, we mention them only briefly for completeness.

Typical formal context-free grammar terminates at terminal symbols only. Constraining all productions (e.g., checking some relations on data) permits an explicit planning of the productions in the run time. Explicit dynamic modification of the schedule of tasks cannot be achieved using the formal context-free grammars.

The rough grammar is active: its rough table is suitable to control parallel computations by demanding both operators and data and then their executions. The flow of the parallel execution may be affected by explicit conditions listed as operators in the production rules. A classical formal grammar production rule is passive: it waits until an external procedure makes all the possible replacements of symbols. The rough grammar is also capable of spreading in parallel the demands (to achieve goals) from the graph root or updated demands from the grammar graph leaves towards the root in the data-driven execution.

The rough grammar can spread distributed computations in a systematic fashion:

a) As a data driven execution (requests for software when some data become available);
b) As a demand-driven (top-down) transmission of codes for data; and
c) As a demand for both data and codes for a required production rule of the rough grammar.

This demand for data and codes in onc selected direction of a processor net yields the optimal pipeline-like global load balancing.

The rough grammar demanding data and codes is dynamic: its production rules (listing operators (e.g., procedures and functions) and their operands) can be created or deleted at the run time. Each production rule may be seen to correspond to a task and its operands in the task table. The main difference is, that production rules of the rough grammar are passed with acknowledged requests for service together with the predecessor's code to the servers in one prespecified direction of the net making the execution similar to a pipeline. The codes and data demanded at a current moment are swapped by servers or by predecessors for direct use making the distributed system relatively free from waits and from idle subspaces of net, and thus purposeful and entirely dynamic.

The receiver of a demand (token) will identify the readiness of the requested code and data (e.g., their names, types and addresses) and will schedule them for transfer to the destination address. Receiving or having the requested code, a target processor can poll the predecessor for the values of the operands matching formal specification of the required data types and the data meanings (optionally). Failing to get the expected code or data may lead to a new demand (as a top-down request), modified by recent responses (i.e., by a full metrics of the recently received code or data).

4. Experimental Results. In a previous paper [5], we discussed a significant improvement in the performance parameters of our dynamic task management over static task schedulers. The study indicated that underutilized resources existing on some nodes in static scheduling are wasted, while other nodes are overloaded and unable to meet the demand for processing. Other practical results of the implementation of the rough grammar in computer vision on a sequential machine are published in [4, 6].

In current study, the performance parameters: allocation time, node busyness and speedup, are computed for the entirely dynamic execution in which all tasks are rolled in one direction in the pipeline manner. The tasks are moved to the next stage when the quantum set per task expires. An overhead associated with the rough table is also considered. This is compared (Fig. 3) with three cases studied in [5]:

a) Classical static schedule;
b) Decentralized task scheduling in which static preallocation is not needed but the *wait_factor* number of nodes wait until their requests are serviced;
c) Entirely dynamic control of execution in which the shortest tasks must wait until the longest task complete execution at each stage.

Quantum	Static	Diffusive	Dynamic	Optimal
1.0	0.0008	0.52	0.52	0.60
0.7	0.0008	0.52	0.52	0.75
0.4	0.0009	0.51	0.51	0.89
0.1	0.0009	0.51	0.51	0.99

Fig. 3. Node Busyness for Various Lengths of Quantum (% of tasks completed).

The simulations show, that the busyness is almost one hundred percent at each node for an arbitrary algorithm and without knowing the task execution times in advance (Fig. 3). We also completely eliminate any unpredictable waits for CPUs. The method is almost ideally scalable: the speedup improvement is linear at any stage (Fig. 4). The linear improvement at subsequent stages is achieved because of keeping busyness all the time very close to 1. Higher linear improvement is achieved by allocating the next nodes for a smaller quantum (e.g., equal to the time when 10% of tasks complete their execution) and passing all the tasks forward when the quantum expires.

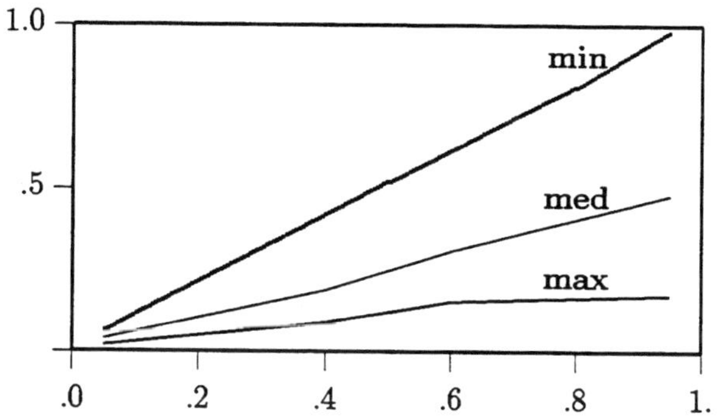

Fig. 4. Linearity of Relative Speedup Improvement vs. Task Cardinality (Depending on the Rough Table Overhead: min/med/max).

Linearity of the improvement makes the rough architecture highly predictable and scalable, and thus very suitable for real-time computations. For a given deadline, it becomes basically necessary to divide the sequential average run time T_s of all tasks at an average stage by the speedup and multiply the result by the number of parallel stages (assuming an unlimited amount of processors at each stage of parallel execution). The run time of the longest tasks moved to the last stage should be also accounted for. If the deadline is not met, the run times must be reduced by using faster processors, because it is not possible to shorten the tasks.

5. Conclusion. Using the rough grammar we sequence dynamically all the tasks in a processor net in a pipeline fashion. The duration of each pipeline stage is not normalized to the longest task, but to the duration of one of the shorter tasks, by which a reduction of the idle and wait times of nodes to a minimum is achieved. The organization of our dynamic distributed task control via the rough grammar is very time effective if process (task) execution time is longer in average than the average time of code transfer. In particular, high predictability and scalability is achieved.

Other advantages of rolling the entire code according to the rough grammar are as follows:

a) The resulting architecture is extremely fault-tolerant if direct predecessors are not set free immediately after their completion but are kept inactive with their codes for some time as checkpoints for quick fault recovery [5].

b) The rough table update can be done without delay, because it is kept together with each currently executing process and the update request does not need to be sent to the host.

c) The net is deadlock free, since the processors required for the entire job are only the dependent (immediate) nodes and are fully preallocated by a dynamic pipeline execution.

There are also disadvantages: firstly, entire jobs are transferred, including rough tables; secondly, for fastest execution uninterrupted by disk swaps, job size in the longest branch should basically be smaller than the size of the smallest private storage at each node.

Our rough architecture [5] obeys Amdahl's law limiting the speedup S on a parallel machine composed of p processors with an algorithm in which a fraction f of tasks is inherently sequential. The maximum speedup S on a two-stage parallel machine is:

$$S = 1/(f + (1 - f)/p) \tag{5.1}$$

The speedup in average on our rough architecture (a multiprocessor system involving two or more stages) is linear as a function of the number of tasks executed at any single stage for an arbitrary algorithm. This is because a full availability of processors for tasks is assumed at each stage of parallel execution and the pipelining assures this.

REFERENCES

[1] H. EL-REWINI, T.G. LEWIS, H.H. ALI, Task Scheduling in Parallel and Distributed Systems, Prentice Hall, Englewood Cliffs, NJ, 1994

[2] P. MEHRA, B.W. WAH, Load Balancing: An Automated Learning Approach, World Scientific, Singapore, 1995

[3] Z. PAWLAK, Rough Sets: Theoretical Aspects of Reasoning about Data, Kluwer Academic Publishers, Dordrecht, 1991

[4] Z.M. WÓJCIK, Rough Approximation of Shapes in Pattern Recognition, Computer Vision Graphics and Image Processing, Vol. 40, pp. 228-249, 1987

[5] Z.M. WÓJCIK, B.E. WÓJCIK, Rough Grammar for Efficient and Fault Tolerant Computing on a Distributed System, IEEE Trans. Software Engineering, Vol. 17, No. 7, pp. 652-668, July 1991

[6] Z.M. WÓJCIK, B.E. WÓJCIK, A Rough Grammar for a Linguistic Recognition of Image Patches, Signal Processing, Vol. 19, pp. 119-138, 1990

A HIERARCHICAL FAULT-TOLERANT RING PROTOCOL FOR DISTRIBUTED REAL-TIME SYSTEMS

TURHAN TUNALI* , KAYHAN ERCIYEŞ* , AND ZEHRA SOYSERT*

Abstract. A synchronous communication protocol is designed and implemented for a distributed real-time system. The protocol operates on hierarchical rings and forms the communication backbone of a cluster based distributed system model that is designed to provide various distributed system functions such as clock synchronization, total event ordering, process group management, multicasting and fault tolerance. The multilevel hierarchy of the cluster based system model allows intracluster communication to be carried out independent of other clusters and hence provides parallelism in communication of cluster nodes. The intercluster communication among cluster *representatives* allows the *leader* to uniquely dictate various decisions to the whole system. The semantics of fault management for the cluster based model is also given and the interrelation of this fault mode with various layers of the system architecture is given by state transition diagrams. Finally, a distributed clock synchronization algorithm is implemented using the protocol and its performance is discussed.

Key words. cluster computing, fault tolerance, synchronous protocol, real-time systems

1. Introduction. In distributed system applications, the implementation of fault tolerant techniques such as data replication increases the network traffic considerably, causing congestion and other complications. Various techniques have been developed to decrease the message complexity while providing high availability [1], [2]. The key concepts used in these techniques are the group communication protocols and multicasting. Among the important contributions to the field are Isis [3], Horus [4], Totem [5] and Transis [6] projects. These are all event-driven asynchronous distributed systems. Although these systems can be successfully used in applications such as transaction processing, banking and stock market trading and replicated database systems, their real-time capabilities are limited. Only Totem has features for real time, however, the extended virtual synchrony model used is still based on an asynchronous model. In [7], based on asynchronous model, checkpoints are used to develop a fault-tolerant algorithm for distributed real-time systems.

On the other hand, synchronous models may yield better performance for real-time applications. For example, Delta-4 project uses synchronized clocks for the applications and logical clocks for multicast message ordering [8]. AAS is developed for air traffic control and uses a clock-driven and event-triggered approach [9]. MARS is developed for process control and uses a clock-driven and time-triggered approach [10], [11]. However, for geographically distributed systems, the situation is further complicated in synchronous models due to the requirement of a globally synchronized clock. Moreover, it is well known that these models require high communication bandwidth to yield acceptable performance in real-time applications.

*International Computer Institute, Ege University, Bornova, İzmir 35100 Turkey ({tunali,erciyes,soysert}@ube.ege.edu.tr).

A distributed real-time system requires a real-time network which guarantees a bounded message delivery time, a distributed real-time operating system that manages resources of the whole system efficiently and timely as a single operating system and some "middleware" functionality to provide all this real-time platform to the distributed real-time applications. The aim of this study is to provide this "middleware" distributed real-time functionality with scalable and synchronous ring protocols embedded within each other. The reason for using such a protocol stems from the physical models of distributed real-time systems that are in fact clusters of processing nodes connected by some communication medium. As an example, a process control system can be considered where clusters may be mapped to processing cells. Providing fault-tolerant communication between a number of nodes running real-time applications is another aspect of our study.

In this work, a cluster based approach is applied to a synchronous system model with the expectation of reducing the network overheads while providing a suitable communication medium for real-time applications. This approach needs the development of a fault tolerance model that should be glued to the underlying communication protocol within the clusters and between the clusters. This fault tolerance model should not be confused with the fault tolerance concept at the application layer. The latter is entirely independent of fault tolerance at the communication layer and any popular scheme such as replication can be used at that layer. At the communication level, the difficulty arises due to the crash failure model accepted. To maintain the *intracluster* and *intercluster* communication, a model that contains *ordinary cluster node*, *cluster representative* and *leader* concepts is developed. The communication protocol is designed to run these three processes at appropriate levels. In case of failures, the protocol rebuilds the system and starts functioning again. Even though a two-level approach will be given here, the protocol can be implemented for more than two levels without loss of generality.

The paper is organized as follows. In Section 2, the distributed system model is given and its interrelation with communication is stressed. In Section 3, the ring based protocol is described together with state diagrams and algorithms. In Section 4, the implementation is explained and results on regular operation, fault scenarios and clock synchronization are discussed. Concluding remarks are given in Section 5.

2. The System Model. In a sense, our protocol provides a communication infrastructure on top of which various layers can be built as in [12]. However, our protocol assumes a synchronous model. Our distributed real-time system model is formed from clusters of computing nodes. Depending on the represented layer in the architecture, the word "node" will be used both for processors and processes. The nodes within a cluster are assumed to be physically located close to each other as workstations in a local area network. Each cluster has a *representative* that communicates with the *leader*. The leader requests information from cluster representatives via the ring protocol operating at a higher level that

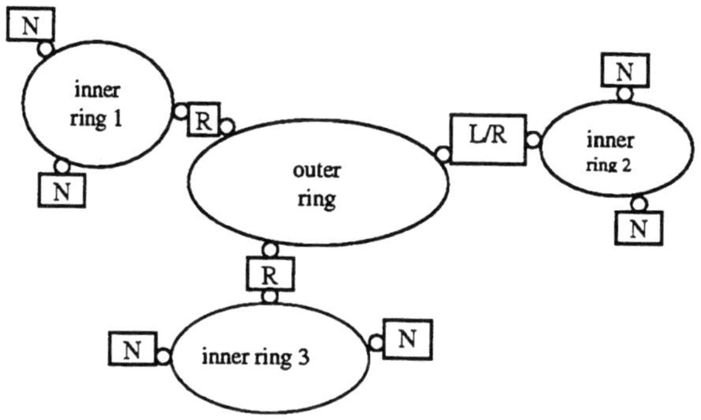

FIG. 2.1. *The two level communication hierarchy where L is the leader, R is a representative and N is an ordinary node*

only consists of the cluster representatives and the leader. Each representative, receiving this request, passes it to the nodes within their respective clusters. Within each cluster, the communication is also carried out by using the ring protocol, but this time, the protocol is used at a lower level consisting of the nodes of a cluster including the cluster representative. The main idea here is that, exactly the same protocol is used in these two different levels of communication. It should also be noted that clusters can easily join the system and this provides scalability. Figure 2.1 illustrates the communication hierarchy.

The application considered in this study that will use this model consists of various layers. The lowest level is the distributed clock synchronization. This is due to the assumption that the system model is synchronous. At this level, the cluster based model is implemented with nodes being the processors. In clock synchronization algorithm, the clock leader requests clock information from the nodes and upon receipt of the clock information, the clock leader decides on the new clock value and dictates this to the whole system via the cluster representatives. This operation is repeated at each period and the clocks are synchronized. The clock synchronization module is implemented and the results are given in Section 4.

Above the clock level, there is the distributed scheduler whose operation is similar to that of the clock level as far as the cluster model is concerned. The nodes are again the processors, the clusters are the same clusters, however, the representatives and leader of this level are not necessarily the same nodes as that of the clock level. In other words, the cluster topology is considered to be fixed for all layers of the architecture, however, the formation of the representatives and the leader of this level is entirely independent of that of the clock level.

Above the scheduler is the group membership layer. The cluster based model

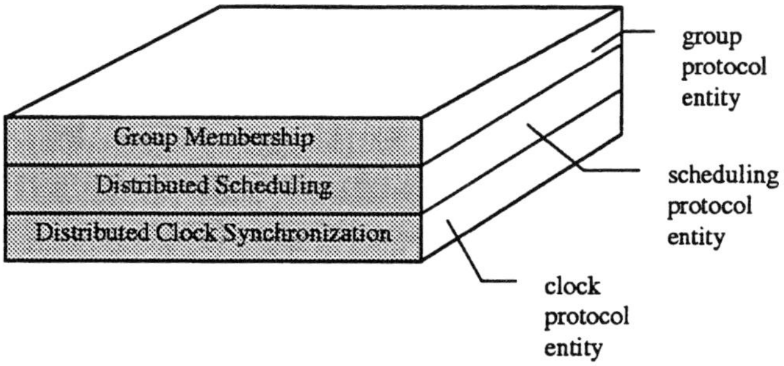

FIG. 2.2. *Two dimensions of the system model*

Control	Node R/O Info	Node Write Info

FIG. 3.1. *Structure of inframe*

is again applied to this layer. The clusters are again defined by the original topology, but this time the nodes are the processes running on the processors of the respective clusters. The processes may belong to a particular group that is defined independent of the cluster topology. That is, for each process group, the cluster based model is applied once to determine the group leader, cluster representatives of the group and the nodes in clusters belonging to the group.

The above outlined structure stresses that the cluster based model is repeatedly applied to the various levels of the distributed system architecture. In a sense, these architectural layers of clock synchronization, distributed scheduler and group management form one dimension of the overall model. The other dimension is the two level hierarchy of the cluster based model that is repeatedly applied to the architectural layers. It is important to see that the two dimensions are entirely independent of each other. Figure 2.2 illustrates the two dimensions of the system model.

3. Protocol for Cluster Based Model. The cluster based model needs special semantics to solve the fault tolerance problem at the communication layer. This section describes the protocol that contains fault tolerance semantics particularly developed for the cluster based model. It is an essential feature of the whole system.

The general operation of the protocol is as follows. Every representative controls the circulation of a message frame within its cluster. This message frame will be called *inframe* and the intracluster ring will be called *inner ring*. The inframe contains two main parts. The first part, called *global information*, contains the information that is sent by the leader such as the global clock value or ordered event list. This part is *read only* for the nodes and it dictates the leader's decision about the previous cycle. The second part is filled by the nodes.

Control	Rep R/O Info	Rep Write Info

FIG. 3.2. *Structure of outframe*

Message_Type	Message_Info_Slots (Optional)	Source	Destination

FIG. 3.3. *Structure of control messages*

It contains node information such as the local clock value or local event list with time stamps, to be sent to the leader. The structure of inframe is shown in Figure 3.1.

Every node in a cluster knows the addresses of its predecessor, successor and representative in the cluster ring. If the predecessor (successor) of a node is the representative, then, that node also knows the address of the predecessor (successor) of the representative. The reason for this requirement is that when the representative crashes the other nodes should be able to repair the ring. All the nodes in all of the clusters know the address of the leader.

The leader controls the circulation of the message frame in the outer ring. This frame will be called the *outframe*. As in inframe, the outframe also contains two main sections. The first section contains the information that is sent by the leader such as the global clock value or ordered event list. This section is *read only* for the representatives. The second section is filled by the representatives. It contains the forwarded node information such as the local clock value or local event list with time stamps. The structure of outframe is shown in Figure 3.2. As in inner ring, every representative knows the address of its predecessor and successor in the outer ring. If the predecessor (successor) of a representative is the leader, then the representative also knows the address of the predecessor (successor) of the leader.

The protocol can be examined in three different modes of operations: NODE, REPRESENTATIVE, and LEADER. Figure 3.3 shows the structure of the control messages used in the algorithms.

When a NODE process is activated, it is furnished with the address of the cluster representative that it intends to join and the identification number of the cluster. It submits a *join request* to the representative. Then it waits for *new neighbor info* that contains the addresses of a predecessor, successor and the leader together with some sequencing information. When it receives the new neighbor information, it updates its configuration and starts waiting for the *ring check inframe* which is a final check circulated by the cluster representative. Acknowledging the ring check inframe, the node starts waiting for the data inframe to fill up the local information. As the inframe arrives, it reads the first section that contains the globally finalized information. It then fills up the appropriate fields to report its local information and starts waiting for the next inframe. If the inframe is late, it sends point to point *are you alive* messages to its predecessor and successor. If its predecessor and/or successor is dead, it informs the representative and waits for a new information. The representative

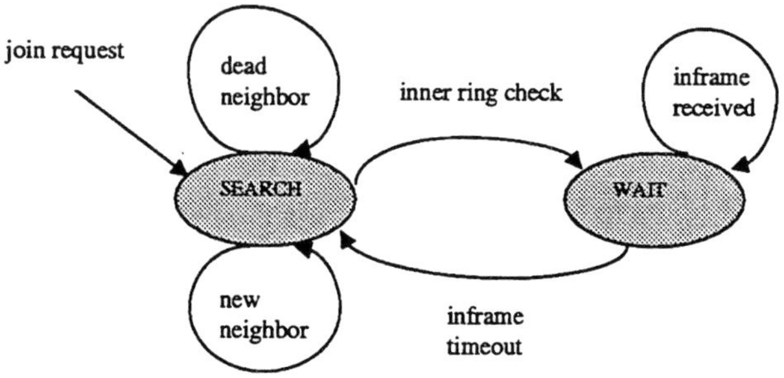

FIG. 3.4. *Node state diagram*

bypassing the dead node provides new predecessor or successor address to the node and the node acknowledging this, starts waiting for the inframe.

If the representative is dead, this is noticed by its neighbors, namely by its predecessor and successor. The successor of the dead representative becomes the new representative. Having the address of the dead representative's predecessor, the new representative repairs the ring and informs this predecessor. The node algorithm is given in Appendix A. Figure 3.4 shows the state diagram of the node algorithm.

When a REPRESENTATIVE process is activated, it is furnished with a predecessor and successor address on the cluster ring. It issues a *gather info inframe* to collect the cluster addresses and let the cluster nodes know that it is the new representative. The node algorithm assures that every node in the cluster has its predecessor and successor address before the new representative process is activated. The gather info inframe contains the address of the predecessor of the new representative that is to be collected by the successor of the new representative. This precaution is for a possible failure of the representative in future. By this way, the neighbor will have chance to bypass the dead representative in case of a failure. As the gather info circulates, the last node before the representative, that is the predecessor of the representative collects the address of the successor of the representative, again for ring repair purposes.

Upon receiving the gather info inframe, the nodes update their records, fill in their addresses and acknowledge. After making sure of the status of its nodes, the new representative sends a *join request message* to the leader. The new representative starts waiting for outer ring neighbor information from the leader. The leader, forming the new outer ring, furnishes the new representative with a predecessor address and successor address. The leader then circulates a *ring check outframe*. After acknowledging the ring check, the new representative is ready for routine operations.

The representative issues an inframe and waits. When it receives the inframe, it waits for the outframe. As the outframe is received, it reads the global

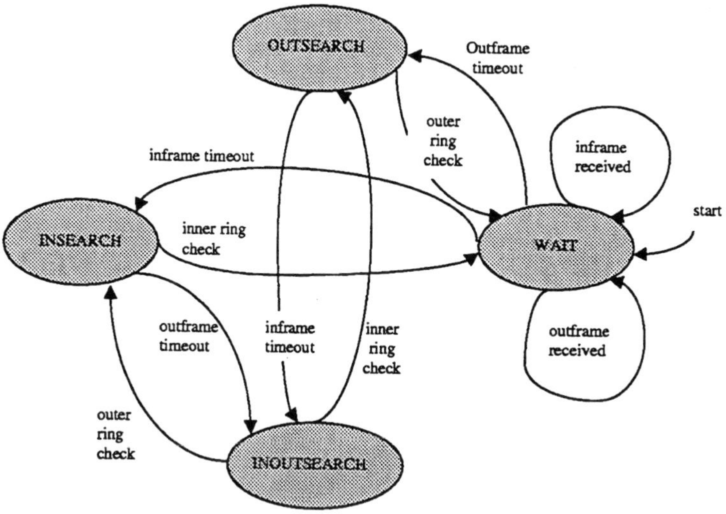

FIG. 3.5. *Representative state diagram*

information, writes the local information and forwards the ouframe to its successor. It then issues the next inframe with the most recent global information to be forwarded. If the outframe arrives before the inframe, the representative holds the outframe for a limited time. If inframe is still late, it releases the outframe with empty inner ring info information and *inner ring trouble* marked. If the inframe arrives before the outframe, the representative holds the new inframe to be issued for a limited time. If the outframe is still not in, the representative issues the new inframe with *outer ring trouble* marked.

If the inframe is late, it starts an *inner ring search* timer and sends *are you alive* to its inner ring neighboring nodes. If everyone is alive and the timer goes off, it issues a ring check inframe and upon the completion of the circulation of ring check, the representative issues inframe. If a node is dead, the representative discards the node from the ring and furnishes new addresses to the predecessor and successor of the dead node and then circulates a ring check inframe. Then it retransmits the last inframe. If there is a join request from a node, the representative honors this only in its wait state. It modifies the ring, informs the related nodes and retransmits the last inframe. The representative algorithm is given in Appendix B. The state diagram of the representative is given in Figure 3.5.

If the outframe is late, the representative sends point to point *are you alive* messages to its outer ring predecessor and successor. If either of its predecessor or successor is dead, it informs the leader and waits for a new outer ring neigh-

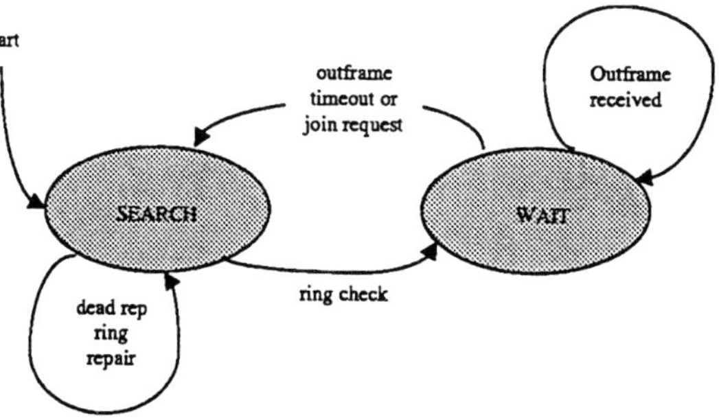

FIG. 3.6. *Leader state diagram*

bor information. The leader bypassing the dead representative provides new predecessor or successor address to the representative and the representative acknowledging this, starts waiting for the outframe.

If the leader is dead, its successor takes over. Having the address of the dead leader's predecessor, the new leader repairs the outer ring and informs this predecessor. It should be noted that the representative acts similar to a leader in the inner ring and similar to a node in the outer ring.

When the leader process is activated, it issues a *gather info outframe*. Upon receiving the gather info outframe, the representatives update their records, fill in their addresses and acknowledge. As in inner ring, necessary measures are taken to bypass the leader in case of failure. They also update the leader address field in their inframes. After making sure of the status of its representatives, the new leader is ready for routine operations. It sorts the collected local information and issues an outframe containing the global information.

If the outframe is late, the leader starts an *outer ring search* timer and sends *are you alive* to its predecessor and successor. If everyone is alive and the timer goes off, it issues a ring check. If a representative is dead, it discards the representative from the outer ring and furnishes new addresses to the predecessor and successor of the dead representative. Then it retransmits the last outframe. If there is a new representative message, the leader modifies the ring, informs the related representatives and retransmits the last outframe. The leader algorithm is given in Appendix C. Figure 3.6 shows the state diagram for the leader process.

The protocol assumes that, if a node crashes, the representative does not crash during the ring repair period which is measured to take less than 50 milliseconds in our implementation. Multiple node crashes are allowed. However, the protocol again assumes that, if a representative crashes, no other node crashes during the new representative startup process. This means that, if an

TABLE 4.1
Average ring cycle completion times of the first topology in msec.

Message size	Cluster1	Cluster2	Cluster3	Outer Ring
1K	5.254	13.696	3.003	19.456
2K	9.821	19.195	6.803	28.225
4K	14.179	25.132	10.872	43.421
8K	24.725	39.341	20.930	62.665

TABLE 4.2
Average ring cycle completion times of the second topology in msec.

Message size	Cluster1	Cluster2	Cluster3	Outer Ring
464 bytes	3.906	4.880	5.856	9.760

event violating the above assumptions happens within a cluster, then that cluster will be discarded from the whole system and the rest of the system will continue functioning.

The above assumptions are also valid for the operation of the outer ring. In case of leader and a neighbor representative failing at the same time, the whole system collapses and has to be restarted. However, the probability of such an event is quite low since different clusters usually reside in different LAN segments.

Note that the deterministic nature of the protocol is suitable for supporting real-time applications. The synchronous behavior can easily be exploited to provide necessary services for applications. In the following section, implementation of clock synchronization will be reported.

4. Implementation. The protocol is implemented on a network of workstations. In the first part of our experiments, the network consisted of three clusters, each having three nodes with one of the clusters having two of the nodes on the same machine. All nodes were DEC Alpha workstations that are located in Ege University campus and running OSF1/Mach operating system. The clusters were all on different 10 Mbps Ethernet segments. The outer ring was 100 Mbps FDDI. Initially, the implementation was limited to the routine operation of the synchronization of inframe and outframe. The frame synchronization rate achieved is an essential measure for the performance of the protocol when no crash occurs. Therefore, the maximal rate achieved at this level gives a good idea about the cycle period both for the inner ring and outer ring. Four different sizes are used for the messages: 1K, 2K, 4K and 8K. The outframe issue period was taken as 100 msec. Table 4.1 shows the average completion times of ring cycles in milliseconds based on 30 observations. As it can be seen from the table, outframe issue period is well above the cluster periods to guarantee that inframes are ready waiting for the outframe. Representatives issued their inframes as they received outframes.

In the second part, we have implemented the system on a similar topology

TABLE 4.3
Average crash recovery times in msec.

Crash scenario	Recovery	Average crash recovery time
Single node crash in a cluster	Recovery of cluster	22.590
Simultaneous two node crashes in a cluster	Recovery of cluster	25.725
Total collapse of a cluster	Recovery of the outer ring	31.784
Single representative crash	Recovery of the whole system	55.867

as above, but this time two of the clusters contained four nodes each and the third cluster contained three nodes. All the nodes were on different machines. With a fixed message payload of 464 bytes, the average ring cycle completion times are given in Table 4.2. The measurements are based on 20 observations. Even though the second topology contains more nodes, when compared with Table 4.1, Table 4.2 figures are much more improved. We have continued our experiments with the second topology in the following.

For the crash scenarios, *are you alive* timer is set to 5 msec. *Issue inframe* and *release outframe* timers are set to 5 msec. *Inframe* and *outframe* timers are set to 200 msec. Table 4.3 lists average recovery times of various scenarios in msec. The averaging is done on 20 observations. The crash figures show that, with 100 msec frame issue period, the system solves the problem within the issue period and the normal operation is not interrupted.

Using the second topology, a simple clock synchronization algorithm is implemented. The local clock values are collected from nodes and forwarded to the leader. During the forwarding process, a fixed correction term per hop is used to account for the time spent during the communication. The leader simply takes the average and dictates it as the global clock value. The representatives forward this global clock value to their nodes. Both the representatives and nodes normalize the value of clock for the time passed during communication. The frame issue period used in this implementation is 200 msec. The drifts in the local clock values are measured and the results are given in Table 4.4. The results are averaged on 20 observations. The minimum drift is measured as 0.048 msec. and the maximum drift is measured as 5.760 msec. Table 4.4 also contains clock drifts in 5, 10 and 20 sec. ranges when no correction is done. As can be seen from the table, the clock values drastically improve when the algorithm is implemented.

5. Conclusion. A cluster based distributed system model is considered for a ring-based hierarchical communication protocol developed together with its imbedded fault-tolerant cluster membership algorithm. The cluster concept

TABLE 4.4
Average clock drifts measured at nodes in msec.

Clock scenario	Cluster1	Cluster2	Cluster3
Uncorrected Clock Drifts (5 sec.)	5.963 7.940 7.219 6.832	6.242 5.672 8.450 8.324	5.231 5.734 6.675
Uncorrected Clock Drifts (10 sec.)	8.439 8.963 8.231 7.171	7.903 6.356 8.909 8.654	6.434 7.423 8.284
Uncorrected Clock Drifts (20 sec.)	10.524 9.520 10.359 9.036	10.939 9.632 9.158 9.236	7.564 10.345 9.453
Corrected Clock Drifts (frame issue period=200msec.	2.089 1.902 2.187 1.980	2.172 1.883 1.658 2.012	1.765 1.806 2.196

is considered on a hardware basis such as the computers on the same Ethernet segment. The fault-tolerance algorithm developed allows the protocol to maintain communication in case of crash failures. The synchronous nature of the communication algorithm can easily be exploited for real-time applications. As an application, a clock synchronization algorithm is implemented using our protocol. Crash scenarios are tested and performance is reported.

The current work is progressing in two steps: Firstly, managing processing power using the ring protocol is being implemented. In this case, each representative periodically monitors availability of the processors in its cluster. When a node receives an asynchronous real-time processing request, it checks whether this can be fulfilled locally. If not, the representative is informed which may or may not find a potential receiver in the cluster to process the request. If the request can not be met within the cluster, it is forwarded to the outer ring to find a possible receiver in another cluster. The shadow process concept is used in this case to eliminate the need for process migration. The second implementation involves using process groups and active replication to provide fault tolerance to the application. To provide such a feature, the order of messages sent to copies of a process must be preserved. The inner and outer ring protocols function similarly in this case where events are gathered locally in each cluster, delivered to the leader, which determines the order and dictates the result to the nodes which contain the replicated process.

REFERENCES

[1] D. Malki, *Multicast Communication for High Availability*, Ph. D. Dissertation, Hebrew University in Jerulsalem (1994).

[2] Y. Amir, *Replication Using Group Communication Over a Partitioned Network*, Ph. D. Dissertation, Hebrew University in Jerusalem (1995).

[3] K.P. Birman and R. Cooper, *The ISIS Project: Real Experience with Fault-Tolerant Programming System*, Technical Report, Department of Computer Science, Cornell University (1993).

[4] R. Van Renesse, K.P. Birman and S. Maffeis, *Horus: A Flexible Group Communication System*, Communications of the ACM, Special Section on Group Communication, 39-4, (1996).

[5] L.E. Moser et.al., *Totem: A Fault Tolerant Multicast Group Communication System*, Communications of the ACM, Special Section on Group Communication, 39-4 (1996).

[6] D. Malki and D. Dolev, *The Transis Approach to High Availability Cluster Communication*, Communications of the ACM, Special Section on Group Communication, 39-4 (1996).

[7] Z.M. Wojcik and B.E. Wojcik, *Optimal Algorithm for Real-Time Fault Tolerant Distributed Processing Using Checkpoints*, Informatica, Vol.19, (1995), pp. 111–122.

[8] S. Mishra and R. Schlichting, *Abstractions for Constructing Dependable Distributed Systems*, Technical Report, TR92-19, Department of Computer Science, University of Arizona (1992).

[9] F. Cristian, *Understanding Fault-Tolerant Distributed Systems*, Technical Report, Department of Computer Science, University of California, San Diego (1993).

[10] H. Kopetz et al., *Distributed Fault-Tolerant Real-Time System: The MARS Approach*, IEEE Micro, Vol.9, (1989), pp. 25–40.

[11] S. Mullender (Ed.), *Distributed Systems*, Second Edition, ACM Press, 1993.

[12] O. Babaoglu et al., *RELACS: A Communications Infrastructure for Constructing Reliable Applications in Large-Scale Distributed Systems*, Technical Report UBLCS-94-15, Laboratory for Computer Science, University of Bologna, Italy (1995).

Appendix A. Node algorithm.

```
Node_process
{
send_message(join_request, my_node, repr);
wait_for_neighbor_info;
curstate=SEARCH;
cycle
  wait_for_event;
  switch (event_type);
    RING_CHECK_INFRAME_RECEIVED:
      mark_ack_slot;
      release_ring_check_inframe;
      start_timer(inframe);
      if (curstate=SEARCH)
        curstate=WAIT;
    INFRAME_RECEIVED :
      if (curstate=WAIT)
        if (not_outer_ring_trouble)
          read_global_info;
          write_local_info;
        release_inframe;
        start_timer(inframe);
    INFRAME_TIMEOUT:
      curstate=SEARCH;
```

```
      send_message(are_you_alive,my_node,pred);
      send_message(are_you_alive,my_node,successor);
      start_timer(are_you_alive);
    AREYOUALIVE_TIMEOUT:
      if (my_pred=rep and my_pred=dead)
        send_message (I_am_your_new_successor,my_node,pred_of_dead_rep);
        wakeup(Representative_process);
      else
        send_message (dead_neighbor,dead_neighbor_addr,my_node,repr);
    GATHER_RING_INFO_INFRAME_RECEIVED:
      if (curstate=WAIT)
        curstate=SEARCH;
        stop_timer(inframe);
      update (rep_info);
      mark_address_slot;
      release_inframe;
    NEW_NEIGHBOR_MESSAGE_RECEIVED:
      if (curstate=WAIT)
        stop_timer (inframe);
        curstate=SEARCH;
      update (neighbor_info);
    ARE_YOU_ALIVE_MESSAGE_RECEIVED:
      if (curstate=WAIT)
        curstate=SEARCH;
      send_message (I_am_alive,my_node,asking_neighbor);
      send_message(are_you_alive,my_node,other_neighbor);
endcycle
}
```

Appendix B. Representative algorithm.

```
Representative_process
{
issue_inframe(gather_ring_info,my_addr,my_successor,ring_addr_slots);
wait_for_gather_ring_info;
issue_inframe(ring_check);
wait_for_ring_check_ack;
send_message(cluster_join_request,my_node,leader);
wait_for_new_outer_neighbor_info;
wait_for_ring_check_outframe;
start_timer(outframe);
issue_inframe(data,global_info_slots,local_info_slots);
start_timer(inframe);
curstate=WAIT;
cycle
  wait_for_event;
  switch (event_type);
    INFRAME_RECEIVED :
      stop_timer(inframe);
      read_local_info;
      if (outframe_waiting)
        update(cluster_info_slot);
        release_outframe;
        start_timer(outframe);
        issue_inframe (data,glob_info_slots,local_info_slots);
        start_timer(inframe);
      start_timer(issue_inframe);
```

```
ISSUE_INFRAME_TIMEOUT:
  issue_inframe (outer_ring_trouble);
OUTFRAME_RECEIVED :
  stop_timer(outframe);
  read_global _info;
  if(curstate=WAIT)
    if (inframe_in)
      update(cluster_info_slot);
      release_outframe;
      start_timer(outframe);
      issue_inframe (data,glob_info,local_info_slots);
      start_timer(inframe);
    else
      start_timer(release_outframe);
  if(curstate=INSEARCH)
    mark (inner_ring_trouble);
    release_ouframe;
    start_timer(outframe);
RELEASE_OUTFRAME_TIMEOUT:
  set (inner_ring_trouble);
  release_ouframe;
  start_timer(outframe);
 INFRAME_TIMEOUT:
  if(curstate=WAIT)
    curstate=INSEARCH;
  else if(curstate=OUTSEARCH)
    curstate=INOUTSEARCH;
  start_timer(insearch);
  send_message (are_you_alive,my_node,in_pred);
  send_message(are_you_alive,my_node,in_successor);
  start_timer(in_are_you_alive);
IN_ARE_YOU_ALIVE_TIMEOUT:
  stop_timer(in_search);
  if (pred=dead)
    send_message (new_succes,my_node_addr,my_succes_addr,my_node,dead_node's_pred);
  else
    send_message (new_pred,my_node_addr,my_pred_addr,my_node,dead_node's_succes);
  issue_inframe(ring_check);
INSEARCH_TIMEOUT:
  issue_inframe(ring_check);
INNER_RING_CHECK_RECEIVED:
  if(curstate=INSEARCH)
    curstate=WAIT;
    issue_inframe(data,glob_info,local_info_slots);
    start_timer(inframe);
  else
    curstate=OUTSEARCH;
    issue_inframe (outer_ring_trouble,glob_info_slots,local_info_slots);
    start_timer(inframe);
OUTER_RING_CHECK_RECEIVED:
  if(curstate=OUTSEARCH)
    curstate=WAIT;
    start_timer(outframe);
  else
    curstate=INSEARCH;
    start_timer(outframe);
OUTER_RING_CHECK_RECEIVED:
```

```
        if(curstate=OUTSEARCH)
            curstate=WAIT;
            start_timer(outframe);
        else if (curstate=INOUTSEARCH)
            curstate=INSEARCH;
            start_timer (outframe);
    DEAD_NEIGHBOR_MESSAGE_RECEIVED:
        stop_timer(in_search);
        if (dead_node=my_successor)
            send_message (rep's_new_successor,dead_node's_successor,my_node,my_in_pred);
        send_message (new_pred,dead_node_pred_addr,my_node,dead_node's_successor);
        send_message (new_success,dead_node_succ_addr,my_node,dead_node's_pred);
        issue_ inframe(ring_check);
    OUTFRAME_TIMEOUT:
        if(curstate=WAIT)
            curstate=OUTSEARCH;
        else if (curstate=INSEARCH)
            curstate=INOUTSEARCH;
        send_message(out_are_you_alive,my_node,out_pred);
        send_message(out_are_you_alive,my_node,out_successor);
        start_timer(out_are_you_alive);
    OUT_ARE_YOU_ALIVE_TIMEOUT:
        if (my_out_pred=leader and my_out_pred=dead)
            send_message (I_am_your_new_out_successor,my_node,pred_of_dead_leader);
            wakeup (Leader_process);
        else
            send_message (dead_neighbor,dead_neighbor's_addr,my_node,leader);
    GATHER_RING_INFO_OUTFRAME_RECEIVED:
        update (leader_info);
        if (curstate=WAIT)
            curstate=OUTSEARCH;
        else if (curstate=INSEARCH)
            curstate=INOUTSEARCH;
        stop_timer(outframe);
        mark_address_slot;
        release_outframe;
    NEW_NODE_JOIN_REQUEST_RECEIVED:
        curstate=INSEARCH;
        send_message (new_successor,new_node's_addr,my_node,in_pred);
        send_message (rep's_pred,new_node's_addr,my_node,in_successor);
        send_message (nghbor_info,pred_addr,succes_addr,rep's_succes,my_node,new_node);
        issue_inframe(ring_check);
endcycle
}
```

Appendix C. Leader algorithm.

```
Leader_process
{
issue_inframe(gather_ring_info,my_addr,my_successor,ring_addr_slots,);
wait_for_gather_ring_info;
issue_outframe(ring_check);
wait_for_ring_check_ack;
issue_outframe(data,last_glob_info,local_info_slots);
start_timer(outframe);
cycle
  wait_for_event;
  switch (event_type);
    OUTFRAME_RECEIVED :
      read_local_info_slots;
      form_global_info;
      issue_outframe(data,glob_info,local_info_slots);
      start_timer(outframe);
    OUTFRAME_TIMEOUT:
      curstate=SEARCH;
      start_timer (ring_search);
      send_message(are_you_alive,my_node,pred);
      send_message(are_you_alive,my_node,successor);
      start_timer(are_you_alive);
    ARE_YOU_ALIVE_TIMEOUT:
      stop_timer (ring_search);
      if (pred=dead)
        send_message (new_succesor,my_addr,my_successor's_addr,my_node,dead_rep's_pred);
      else
        send_message (new_pred,my_addr,my_pred's_addr,my_node,dead_rep's_successor);
      issue_ouframe(ring_check);
    DEAD_NEIGHBOR_MESSAGE_RECEIVED:
      stop_timer (ring_search);
      if (dead_neigh=my_successor)
        send_message (leader's_new_successor,dead_neighbor's_successor,my_node,my_pred);
      send_message (new_pred,dead_rep's_pred_addr,my_node,dead_rep's_successor);
      send_message (new_successor,dead_rep's_successor_addr,my_node,dead_rep's_pred);
      issue_ouframe(ring_check);
    RING_SEARCH_TIMEOUT:
      issue_ouframe(ring_check);
    RING_CHECK_RECEIVED:
      curstate=WAIT;
      issue_outframe(data);
      start_timer(outframe);
    NEW_REP_JOIN_REQUEST_RECEIVED:
      curstate=SEARCH;
      send_message (new_successor,new_rep's_addr,my_node,my_pred);
      send_message (leader's_pred,new_rep's_addr,my_node,my_successor);
      send_message (nghbor_info,pred's_addr,succes's_addr,leader's_succes,my_node,new_rep);
      issue_outframe(ring_check);
endcycle
}
```

REAL-TIME MULTICAST IN WIRELESS COMMUNICATION

BARBARA D. GANNOD AND SOURAV BHATTACHARYA *

Abstract. This paper presents methods for the reconfiguration of a multicast tree at the instance of node migration in cellular wireless networks. We consider a novel, and highly practical, formulation of the real-time multicast problem. Unlike the traditional notion of source to leaf node message transmission time being the measure for real-time, we consider the multicast tree re-construction time (in the event of a node migration) as the measure for real-time constraints. The overall goal is to minimize both the delays: *i)* delay of re-constructing the multicast tree and *ii)* source to destination transmission delay. In this paper, we introduce and provide solutions for the first objective, while the current research in real-time multicast tree considers the latter objective only. We propose two heuristics to solve the real-time multicast tree re-construction problem, one as a foreground and the other as a background algorithm, and present analysis and simulation results for several factors that contribute differently to the re-construction delay.

Key words. cellular structure, hypercube topology, media access control, real-time multicast, wireless network

1. Introduction. Wireless technology has become commonplace in our everyday lives. Beepers, cellular telephones, and laptop computers are among the many devices that allow us to stay connected and productive, even while we are "on the move." The demand for mobile communication has made wireless technology an important focus for today's computer and communication industries. A wireless network is a collection of autonomous computers in which no physical (or 'wired') connections exist between the computers. The nodes in a wireless network can be *stationary* or *mobile*. In a stationary wireless network, the location of the nodes and the network topology is fixed. The only difference from a typical wired LAN is that wireless technology is used to support communication among the nodes in the network. In a mobile, wireless network, nodes may change location often. Consequently, the network topology is dynamic. The creation of high performance, portable computers and the desire for mobility has driven wireless networks to support a "global network" that will allow the user to access the capabilities of the network at any time without regard to location or mobility. The advent of mobile wireless networks has created many new possibilities and many new challenges for parallel and distributed computing applications.

Most wireless (for the remainder of the paper we assume that a 'wireless' network is also mobile) networks are based on cellular technology that uses centralized control to manage the network. In particular, the service area of the network is divided into a number of cells, and the nodes in the network can communicate through a single access point called a *base station*. Although this centralized management scheme allows fairly simple management, it has obvious drawbacks (lack of fault tolerance, in particular). Consequently, current

*Department of Computer Science & Engineering Arizona State University Tempe, AZ 85287-5406, USA, {bgannod,sourav}@asu.edu

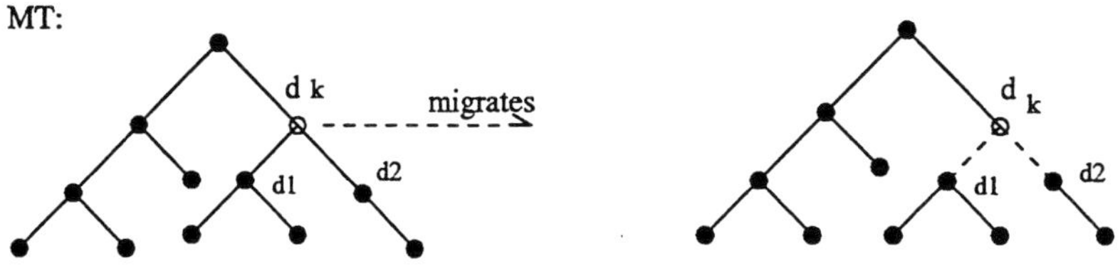

FIG. 1. *Multicast tree re-construction example. a) node d_k migrates in an existing multicast tree, b) nods d1 and d2 become orphan due to migration of node d_k.*

research is based on wireless networks that employ a distributed management scheme, such as *ad-hoc* wireless networks. In an ad-hoc wireless network, all nodes are equipped with routing capabilities. Thus, routing, as well as other network management issues, can be distributed.

Ad-hoc cellular networks are particularly appealing for parallel and distributed networking applications because the nodes in the network can be arranged in a logical topology [1]. Logical topologies have been used both for parallel architectures and computer networks. Popular logical topologies include the 2-D mesh, torus, hypercube, manhattan street network, hierarchical tree structures, etc. Using logical topologies allows mobile computing to benefit from network architecture concepts and associated advantages, e.g., systematic routing and simplified network management. Most logical topologies in which performance plays a large role have a diameter (*diameter* = length of the longest path between any two nodes in the network) greater than one. In such *multihop* topologies, a message may need to traverse several hops to reach its destination. This will require routing through intermediate nodes, each repeating the packet on a new wavelength, until the packet is finally transmitted on a wavelength that can be received by the intended destination.

1.1. Problem Statement and Contributions. In this paper, we address *multicast communication* in ad-hoc wireless networks. Multicast is a communication paradigm in which a single node in the network, called the *source*, sends a message to a subset of nodes, called *destinations*, in the network. We focus on real-time issues and constraints for multicast communication. In particular, we define a new performance metric for real-time multicast - delay of reconstruction of the multicast tree at the instance of *node migration*. In a cellular network, node migration occurs when a mobile node moves from one cell into a neighboring cell. When a node in the multicast tree migrates, the nodes connected to the former become orphans and the multicast tree becomes disconnected. Figure 1 illustrates the idea of node migration. When node d_k of the multicast tree MT moves away, its children d_1 and d_2 become orphans (i.e., d_1 and d_2 become disconnected from the rest of the tree).

Our goal is to rebuild the multicast tree dynamically. In particular, the tree is to be reconfigured with the least amount of time delay. To our knowledge, no previous research has been done in this area. We propose two approaches for reconfiguring the multicast tree, and we discuss performance issues for each. These two approaches are as follows, where the first one is a foreground computation based algorithm and the second one is based on background computation:

- Request-Reply-Rejection (RRR). When a node migrates, orphan nodes request other nodes to be their parent; the node receiving the request either accepts or rejects the request depending on timing constraints. Eventually a potential parent will accept the request, and the broken multicast tree is reconfigured. This algorithm is invoked, when a node migration (and, creation of the orphan nodes) takes place - thus, it is a foreground computation based approach.
- Look-ahead Alternate Parent (LAP). Each node holds a local parent table containing a number of alternate parent-ids; the node can be attached immediately to any of the alternate parents when it becomes orphan. This algorithm expects to have the table containing the alternate parent-ids available, using a background computation approach.

1.2. Performance Metrics for Real-Time Multicast. Existing research results in real-time multicast concentrate on the worst case source to destination node message transmission time as the measure of real-time performance. Optimization goals have been used in multicast algorithms to determine what constitute a 'good' tree. As stated, one such goal is providing minimum delay along the tree, which is important for such multimedia applications as real-time video conferencing. Another optimization goal is to use the resources of the network as efficiently as possible. Dijkstra's shortest path algorithm [2] has been used to generate the shortest paths from the source to destination nodes; this provides the solution for delay optimization. Multicast algorithms that perform cost optimization have been based on computing the minimum Steiner tree which is an NP-complete problem [3]. A large body of research has been conducted in the area of traffic optimized multicast tree construction for popular parallel architecture topologies, e.g., 2D mesh [4], or hypercube [5], and this research has also been extended to the area of fault-tolerant multicast trees [6].

In this paper we consider a dual formation of the real-time multicast problem - namely, the time required to reconfigure the multicast tree when a node changes its physical location. Node migration is very common and frequent in wireless networks. A node migration may temporarily disconnect the multicast tree. When node migration occurs, both the source to destination delay and the delay of reconstruction are critical issues. Thus, the metric used in this paper, namely the delay of tree re-construction, is a new and important practical metric for real-time multicast operations over ad-hoc cellular networks. The contribution of this paper is in this context, viz. providing solutions to this new metric or objective of real-time multicast for ad-hoc cellular networks.

1.3. Applications of Real-Time Multicast in AD-HOC Wireless Networks. Multicast communication in a real-time environment is an important issue. Following is a non-exhaustive list of applications for this work:

- A scientific, nomadic environment. For example, scientists stationed at several different cites may gather seismic data and employ a parallel algorithm that predicts future seismic activities.
- Embedded military supercomputing applications in which fault tolerance is a concern. For example, tanks, trucks, planes, etc., may be connected via a wireless network. They can gather data, send it to other nodes in the network, and use distributed algorithms to make decisions based on that data. Clearly centralized management of the network is undesirable since the enemy make bring down the entire network by destroying the centralized point of control. Besides, for rapid deployability reasons ad-hoc cellular networks (i.e., without base stations) with fully distributed control operations are preferred.
- Intelligent incast or multicast, where the primary job of the nodes is to gather data to be sent to a supercomputing center where the data is used.
- Intelligent incast or multicast in which strict time deadlines are used to steer immediate actions. For example, consider the study of weather phenomenon such as tornadoes. Several mobile nodes may gather data, send data to other nodes, and use the data to make predictions about the path of the tornado. Time critical decisions must be made.

The remainder of the paper is organized as follows. In Section 2, we illustrate various underlying ideas in wireless networks, logical interconnect topologies, cellular interconnection structure and media access control. We then define our problem domain and extend this definition in formulating the problem of node migration. We convey an overview of applicability of current research also. In Section 3, we define the basics of hypercube multicast followed by our proposed two solution approaches, along with their pseudocodes. Section 4 discusses the issues of network management and proposes a number of analytical results related to this research. We also give a probability analysis of the approaches in this section. Section 5 presents the simulation environment and simulation results. Finally, we conclude and present future research areas in Section 6.

2. Background Wireless AD-HOC Networks and Problem Formulation. This section introduces background ideas in wireless network, logical interconnect topologies, cellular interconnection structure and media access control. Then comparisons to current research of our contribution is presented.

2.1. Mobile Wireless Networking. The organization of wireless networks is constantly evolving. Most modern wireless networks are based on a cellular structure, in which the service area is physically partitioned into different *cells*. Cells can be considered to be the basic service areas. The main advantage of the cellular concept lies in the reusability of frequencies for spectrum efficiency. Frequencies assigned to a number of nodes in one cell can be reused by the nodes in a non-adjacent cell (using a map coloring concept).

Network management is a complex issue in wireless networks. The network protocols must be able to handle mobility issues in order to provide seamless services. At any given time, each node in the network is a member of a single cell (usually the cell in closest proximity). Because nodes are mobile, they may frequently change their cell-membership (as a new cell becomes 'closer'). When a node changes its membership from one cell to another, it is said to undergo *cell migration*. Cell migration is an important responsibility of the network manager. One implication of cell migration is that, unlike wired networks, connections between nodes in a wireless network are not static. Cell boundaries, on the other hand, can be static or dynamic. Static cell boundaries are created to serve a specific geographic area, while dynamic cell boundaries are created to achieve uniform load-balancing among cells, among other flexibilities and benefits. Dynamic cell boundaries require much more complex network management strategies. We focus on static cell boundaries.

Many cellular networks follow a centralized management scheme that uses a *base station* organization. In this approach, the service area of a wireless network is subdivided into different contiguous cells. Each cell has a single (fixed) base station that handles network management issues for the entire cell. When a node boots up in a given cell, it must register with the local base station. All communication between nodes is handled by the base station. If node u wants to send a message to node v within the same cell, node u first sends the message to the base station, and the base station then forwards the message to node v. Thus, we can view the network within a cell as having a logical star topology. When node migration occurs from cell i to cell j, the base station of cell i contacts the base station of cell j to make arrangements for cell j to take over management of the migrating node. Thus cell migration is often referred to as "cellular handover" in a cellular network managed by base stations. At first glance this scheme seems attractive; since the base station has complete information, it can make perfect decisions. It enlarges the coverage area of communication and relieves the nodes from network management responsibilities. Unfortunately, the base station structure has some serious drawbacks such as the vulnerability of the base station, the need for an extensive infrastructure and asymmetric node configurations.

Another option, more fault tolerance and more scalability, for cellular networks is to use a distributed network management scheme. In an *ad-hoc cellular network*, several mobile nodes come together in a small area and establish peer-to-peer communication among themselves without the use of a base station. This scheme uses a symmetric node configuration, and a distributed logical topology among the nodes can be enforced. In general, ad-hoc networks cannot presume a fully connected network topology since a fully connected topology requires the node degree to grow linearly with the size of the network. Our research is based on an embedded logical topology interconnecting the mobile nodes in an ad-hoc distributed cellular structure.

2.2. Logical Interconnect Topology and Its Advantages. For scalability reasons, a completely connected topology is not feasible. An arbitrary topology may have to follow a centralized approach, which involves complex

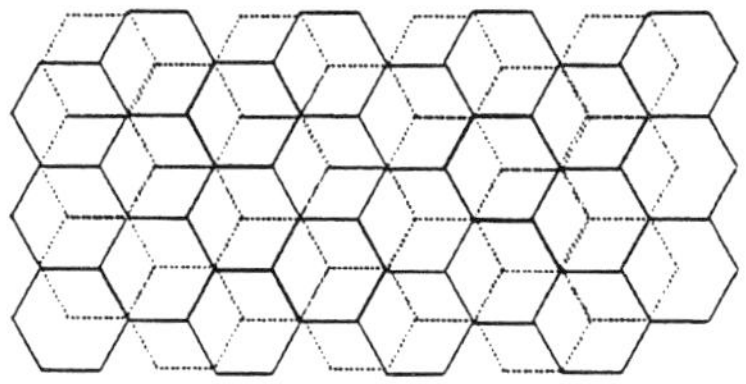

FIG. 2. *Cellular Interconnection Structure: a) solid hexagon = FBINTRA, b) dotted hexagon = FBINTER.*

network management. The nodes in an arbitrary topology need to know the connectivity among them for message transmission; so either a centralized approach or a distributed approach with each node having global status information is required. Following these arguments, a symmetric logical topology is a better choice; it drives performance and scalability because the connectivity pattern determines the length of message-passing pathways through intermediate nodes and links. In the context of logical topologies, the following metrics are among those that are important:

- The *communication diameter* metric is the maximum number of links that a message must traverse between any source and any destination node while taking the shortest available path.
- The *degree* of a node is the number of neighbors it has. A scalable topology should preferably incur minimal increases in node degree as the number of nodes in the topology increases.
- The *size* of the network topology is the total number of nodes in the network.

An ideal logical topology would have a small (compared to size) communication diameter and a small (if not, fixed) node degree that grows slowly (if at all) as the number of nodes increases. Various types of logical topologies have been proposed. In a *ring* topology, each processor has exactly two neighbors; thus, a ring topology has a fixed node degree of two. A *2D mesh* is a planar structure that has nodes arranged in a grid of rows and columns, such that a node is connected by the grid's horizontal and vertical links to its immediate neighbors in four directions. Adding wrap-around links for the border nodes in a mesh creates a *torus* and reduces the communication diameter. A *hypercube* topology arranges nodes in an *d*-dimensional cube. *Tree* topologies have a regular, hierarchical structure of node levels that creates a tree appearance by having each lower level contain more nodes than the previous level. An overview of different logical topologies and their cost-benefit tradeoffs can be found in [7].

2.3. Cellular Interconnection Structure. In our proposed cellular structure, we introduce the notion of "frequency-band used for intercell (FBINTER)" and "frequency-band used for intra-cell (FBINTRA)". Each cell is considered to be a hexagonal structure, and the cell boundary is static. Figure 2 depicts the concept of FBINTER and FBINTRA.

Solid hexagons represent FBINTRA; dotted hexagon represents FBINTER. Nodes are scattered across the cells; all nodes are symmetric. Nodes at the intra-cell boundary may hold more responsibilities for FBINTER communication, and they constitute FBINTER. One of the primary reasons to adopt a cellular structure is to increase the effective total bandwidth by reusing different frequencies in different cells. A number of frequency channels are allocated for the nodes within each cell for message transmission. Nodes belonging to two adjacent cells cannot use the same frequency range. Likewise, two adjacent FBINTRA nodes cannot be assigned the same frequencies. Note, however, that two non-adjacent FBINTRA or two non-adjacent FBINTER can share the same frequency bands. As a result of frequency reuse, the total available communication bandwidth for all nodes becomes much larger. Furthermore, frequency reuse not only saves the spectrum but also reduces transmission power by reducing cell size. When a node changes its cell membership by migrating from one cell to one of the adjacent cells, it is assigned to use any one of the unallocated frequencies of the latter. Media access control for the wireless medium, and dynamic algorithms to adapt to changing traffic load are presented in authors' current research [8, 9].

2.4. Problem Discussion and Applicability of Previous Research. We consider the multicast reconfiguration problem on an ad-hoc cellular network. For ease of multicast operation, rapid maintainability and other advantages of symmetric topologies, we embed the multicast tree on the top of a mesh of hypercubes topology. Our purpose is not to generate the 'best' multicast tree, but to reconstruct a disconnected one. Heuristics multicast algorithms for hypercubes are proposed in [5, 6, 10], any of which can be used to construct the initial multicast tree.

When a forwarding or destination node in the multicast tree moves to an adjacent cell, a number of other multicast tree nodes may become orphan. A rapid placement of the migrated node into the hypercube topology is first needed, and then a rapid reconfiguration of the multicast tree is required. The time delay of the multicast tree re-construction is our problem focus. Maintaining the height balance and node degree of the tree help us to achieve small re-construction delay.

A number of related, but orthogonal, research issues require clarification. Dijkstra's shortest path algorithm [2] and the Steiner tree generation problem [3, 11] employed for delay optimization and cost optimization constraints in real-time multicast can produce traffic and tree height minimized real-time multicast trees. However, they do not consider multicast re-construction.

Some heuristics for the Steiner tree problem have been developed that take polynomial time and produce near optimal results [12]. In [13] KMB algorithm, a network is abstracted to a complete graph consisting of edges that represent the shortest paths between the source node and the destination nodes. These research results do not provide any means for minimizing the re-construction delay. [3] examines the dynamic update of the tree if destination nodes join or leave the tree occasionally. The dynamic algorithms proposed for the *multipoint problem* satisfy bandwidth constraints based on minimum spanning tree algorithms for the Steiner tree problem. [14] discusses optimization on both traffic cost and delay; however, they assume that cost and delay functions are identical. [15] proposes two heuristics (which we call the KPP algorithm) that address delay-bounded Steiner trees; the KPP algorithm extends the KMB algorithm by taking into account an integer-valued delay bound in the construction of shortest paths. [16] proposes a source-based multicast algorithm that can set variable delay bounds on destinations and can handle variants of network cost optimization goals. [17] considers real-time multicast applications which are required to meet specified time and geographical (spatial) constraints. It improves steadiness and tightness metrics, defined as functions of maximum and minimum individual point-to-point delay. However, none of this research considers the re-construction of the multicast tree.

Most of these research results concentrate on the delay-bound restrictions of the real-time multicast problem. The nodes in the underlying network topology are either static or do not change their physical positions frequently. Since we study wireless networks, where nodes are constantly moving around the cells, the scenario is different. The deadline issue is more critical, and network updates are more common. Moreover, we are considering the minimum time required to rebuild the suddenly torn or disconnected multicast tree. These two metrics are our primary concern.

3. Proposed Solution Approaches. We consider *ad-hoc* cellular infrastructure, where the nodes are connected using a logical topology, namely the mesh of hypercube. The proposed multicast re-construction algorithms combine the design attributes of both source-based and distributed multicast. This unifies the advantages of both along with the benefits of adaptiveness. Our goal is to minimize the delay of re-construction of the multicast tree in the event of a node migration. Thus, the objective is to derive solutions within specified time bound and also compute alternate solutions during idle period which will eventually result in increased optimality and reliability. The two heuristic solutions are described in the following, along with their pseudocodes. Performance of these approaches is shown in Sections 4 and 5.

3.1. Basics of Hypercube Multicast. Hypercube structure has been the subject of extensive research [18, 19, 20]. Topological properties of the hypercube, e.g., regularity, symmetry, extensibility, small diameter, and the embeddability of many other topologies (such as ring, mesh, and tree) have been discovered. Heuristic multicast algorithms for hypercubes are proposed in [5, 6, 10].

Since our choice of logical topology includes the hypercube, some well-known properties of hypercube are repeated as background information. A r-dimensional hypercube, or r-cube consists of $R = 2^r$ nodes. In the r-cube graph, $Q_r(V,E)$, for a vertex $v \in V(Q_r)$, $a(v)$ will represent the r-bit binary address of v; $|a(v)|$ denote the number of 1's in binary number $a(v)$. Then, $e = (u,v) \in E(Q_r)$ if and only if $|a(v) \oplus a(u)| = 1$. This implies that $deg_{Q_r}(u) = r$ for every node $u \in V(Q_r)$. Furthermore, if $a(v) \oplus a(u) = 2^i$, edge e is said to

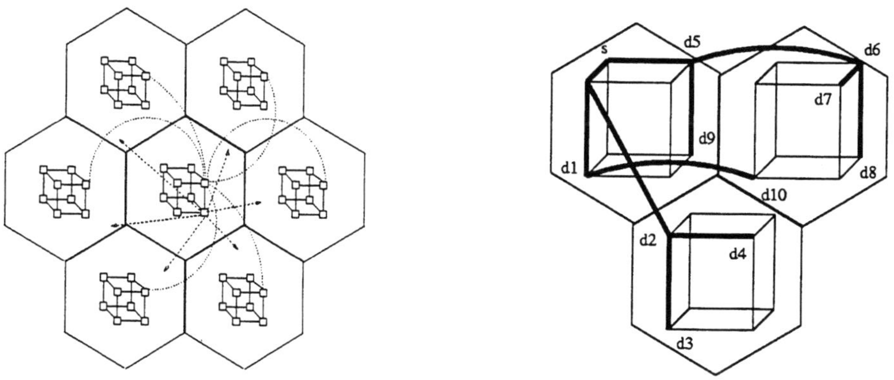

FIG. 3. *a) Hierarchical hypercube interconnection network - for simplicity only one set of inter-cell links are shown; b) Multicast embedded on hypercube, s = source,* $d_1 \cdots d_8$ *are des tination nodes.*

be at dimension i. Any particular node in the r-cube, with an r-bit address as $b_{r-1}b_{r-2}\cdots b_1b_0$, has r Gray-adjacent neighbors. The *distance* (the length of a shortest path, in number of links) between two nodes is equal to the *Hamming distance* of their binary addresses.

The cost model of multicast communication we assume is the one when a node with k outgoing edges can simultaneously transmit the multicast data along each one of the k edges, and not have to serialize among these links. This model is per the findings in [21].

3.2. Timely Re-Construction of Fragmented Multicast Tree. In a cellular network, the nodes are scattered across all the cells. Following the notion of *ad-hoc* cellular networks and logical topology, we propose a "mesh of hypercubes" topology for the intra- and intercell networks. Our choice of the "mesh of hypercube" topology is merely a design selection - any other topology can also be used. Figure 3 shows an example of the cellular infrastructure where nodes are connected using the underlying mesh of hypercube topology. Nodes within each cell are connected as a binary hypercube, while the nodes across the cells are connected as a hexagonal mesh. Solid lines indicate logical channel within the cells (intracell), dashed lines indicate logical channels across the cells (intercell). For simplicity, we have shown a 3-dimensional hypercube within each cell, however dimension four and higher are better for realistic scenarios. In addition, we have only shown the intercell connections for a single node. All other nodes will have similar intercell adjacencies.

We consider the multicast reconfiguration problem on this cellular network. For ease of multicast operation, rapid maintainability and other well known advantages of symmetric topologies, we embed the multicast tree on the top of the mesh of hypercubes. Our purpose is not to generate the 'best' multicast tree, but to reconstruct a disconnected one. Heuristics multicast algorithms for hypercubes are proposed in [5, 6, 10], any of which can be used to construct the initial multicast tree. Figure 3b shows a multicast tree constructed on top of the hypercube where S is the source node, and $d_1, d_2, \cdots d_n$ are n destination nodes. Destination nodes may be spread across different cells. Multicast includes internal or forwarding nodes.

3.3. Orphan Node Creation Circumstances. As depicted in Figure 1, an orphan node is created when its parent node migrates (in fact, two orphan nodes are created). A node can also become an orphan, if it migrates and it is a destination node in the multicast tree. We identify three possible situations for creation of the orphan nodes, as listed below:

- The migratory node is a leaf node. In this case, by definition, the leaf node is a destination node. Since, this node migrates to a new cell, it becomes an orphan and requires to find a new parent node (belonging to the multicast tree).
- The migratory node is an intermediate node, but not a multicast destination. In this case, the migratory node itself does not need to re-connect to the multicast tree. But, its children nodes (be they multicast destinations, or non-destination but intermediate nodes) become orphans and require to find new parents. Note that, the nodes that become orphans and need to find parent nodes in this case, may not have migrated.
- The migratory node is an intermediate node, and is also a multicast destination. In this case, the migratory node needs to find a new parent after moving into the new cell, and at the same time its children become orphans and each one of them require to find a new parent node.

Regardless of whether the node became an orphan due to its own migration, or its former parent node's migration - the net effect is identical, i.e., the fact that it requires to find a new parent. We proposed three algorithms in this section to make an orphan node find a new parent. Figure 4 depicts the problem. When the forwarding destination node d_{11} moves to an adjacent cell, d_6 and d_9 become orphans. A rapid placement of the migrated node into the hypercube topology is first needed, and then a rapid reconfiguration of the multicast tree is required. The time delay of the multicast tree re-construction is our problem focus. Maintaining the height balance and node degree of the tree help us to achieve small re-construction delay.

Let $G(V, E)$ be a graph, with the node set $V(G) = V$ and edge set $E(G) = E$ representing a multicast tree embedded on the hypercube. Let V_i denote the set of all nodes within cell i. Then, $V = V_1 \cup V_2 ... \cup V_n$, where $V_i \cap V_j = \phi$. Following the cell migration of d_k, the disconnected fragments of the multicast tree must be connected within deadline constraints, while at the same time trying to maintain a *height balanced* multicast tree (*i.e.*, a tree in which the distance between the root and the leaf nodes is kept small). Let $V_{i'}(V_{j'})$ denote the set of nodes within cell $i(j)$ after the migration of node d_k. Then, $V_{i'} = V_i - \{d_k\}$, and $V_{j'} = V_j + \{d_k\}$.

During multicast tree re-construction, a large number of design questions arise, e.g., the worst case delay from the source to leaf node (which is the focus of

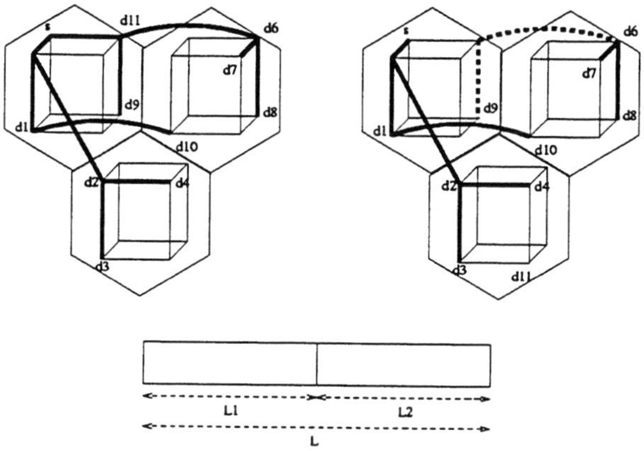

FIG. 4. *Node d_{11} migrates: a) before move, b) after move; c) Relative Bit Positions of Cell ID, and Node Id.*

previous research), minimization of the time for reconstruction of a disconnected multicast tree (which is the focus of our proposed research), the height balance property of the tree, the fan out of each node, etc.

3.4. Definitions and Design Approach. .

Proposition: *For a hexagonal repetitive cell structure, let the intra-cell topology be a (d-6)-cube and the inter-cell topology be a hexagonal mesh. Then, each node in this mesh-of-hypercube will have an outdegree of d.*

Each cell consists of a (d-6)-cube, i.e., each node has $(d-6)$ edges to $(d-6)$ neighbors within the same cell. For hexagonal cell structure, each cell is surrounded by 6 cells, since, each node has an edge/link that connects it to the corresponding node of each one of the six adjacent cells. Therefore, the total number of edges connected to each node is $(d-6)+6=d$.

Gray-coding of nodes: Figure 4c shows the bit-positions of the cell-id ($L1$) and the node-id ($L2$).

1. All nodes within any particular cell have identical value of $L1$, i.e., the Cell-Id.
2. $L2$ represents $(d-6)$-bit id of the node in $(d-6)$-cube contained within particular cell.

Cell-id is defined as follows. Each cell has a row id and a column id. Figure 5 illustrates row and column configuration for hexagonal cellular structure. Each cell in a row has the same row number; cells in the left diagonals have the same column number. Selection of left diagonal as column id is arbitrary; selection of right diagonals would have given a dual, but analogous effect.

$L1 = \lceil (log_2(\text{maxrow})) \rceil + \lceil (log_2(\text{maxcol})) \rceil$ and $L2 = d-6$, where maxrow = maximum number of rows, maxcol = maximum number of columns and $d-6$ = number of bits needed to represent the nodes within a cell for $d-6$ dimensional

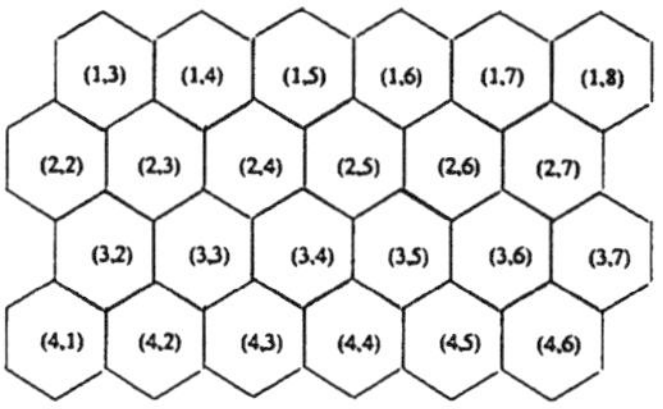

FIG. 5. *Row and Column Id Configuration of Hexagonal Cellular Structure.*

hypercube.

Theorem 1: *Two nodes are topologically adjacent iff any of the following properties hold* :

1. Two nodes have same cell-id (*i.e.*, nodes are in the same cell) and node id is gray-adjacent.
2. Two nodes have same node-id and any of the followings holds:
   (a) $row_i = row_j$, $col_i = col_j \pm 1$
   (b) $row_i = row_j \pm 1$, $col_i = col_j$
   (c) $row_i = row_j + 1$, $col_i = col_j - 1$
   (d) $row_i = row_j - 1$, $col_i = col_j + 1$. This condition, and the above one will change, if the right diagonal is the column-id.

Example: Figure 5 clarifies the idea of node adjacency for the second case *i.e.*, when two nodes have the same node-id. Cell {*1,3*} and {*2,3*} are adjacent (condition (b)); cell {*1,4*} and {*2,3*} are adjacent (condition (c)); cell {*1,3*} and {*2,4*} are not adjacent since none of the conditions hold.

Path Length Reduction Approach: To minimize the maximum hops distance from the root to anyone of the leaf nodes, a balanced tree creation is desirable, instead of a skewed one. Thus, if the multicast tree is uniformly spread and balanced to begin with, and during each tree re-construction phase, if the orphan node(s) can connect to a new parent belonging to a tree level same as that of the previous parent, then the balanced property of the tree remains unchanged. Otherwise, the tree may become progressively imbalanced, and some of the leaf nodes will get unduly further from the root, causing additional delay. Towards this objective, we propose the following *design objective*:

> An orphan node (u), whose former parent node was at tree level l, should connect to a new parent node at a tree level that is least different from l, if not $= l$. In other words, the new parent node should be selected from among those that are topologically adjacent to u, and have minimum level difference from l.

3.5. Request-Reply-Rejection (RRR). The first solution approach, named as "Request-Reply-Rejection" (RRR) is designed to operate at run-time, i.e., to be invoked at a time the multicast tree gets fragmented (due to node migration) and requires to be connected or re-constructed. It is a foreground approach, however, in principle it can also be used in background computation based approach, namely the "Lookahead Alternate Parent" (LAP), proposed next.

We assume that the initial multicast tree is height balanced since the current multicast tree generation algorithms or heuristics may achieve this. Note that the height balanced property ensures that no destination node in the multicast tree has unduly long path length delay compared to the other destination nodes. This assumption has been taken to economize the worst case message propagation delay from the source node to the destination node. The goal is to reconfigure a suddenly broken multicast tree in a way such that the newly constructed multicast tree remains height balanced. Figure 1 illustrates a scenario of orphan nodes. Figure 6 illustrates the pseudo-codes for RRR approach.

An orphan node at the l-th level will attempt to find a parent so that it can reconnect to the tree at a level as close to l as possible in order to keep the resultant tree height-balanced. Also, the node requested to be the new parent must be hypercube adjacent to the requesting one (*i.e.*, the orphan). For a $(d-6)$-cube with mesh topology on top, one node may have d adjacent nodes. So, the time complexity of the RRR algorithm is $O(d)$ times the complexity of a single parent node seek. Since, individual parent node ids are computed by Gray-adjacencies, each parent seek operation takes $O(1)$ time, resulting in a total of $O(d)$ time complexity of RRR. The RRR algorithm can also be used to improve the multicast tree. During idle time, any node connected to a parent may use the same approach to find a more optimal parent, and consequently update the multicast tree.

The approach of RRR can be extended to background computation also, as will be discussed with the LAP algorithm. A final comment applies to our proposed approach to maintaining a "good shape" multicast tree, and avoid creating a skewed shape one. If a skewed multicast tree is gradually formed, due to a series of re-construction steps, it may hurt the source-to-leaf delivery delay. To prevent such occurrence, ideally, each re-construction step should maintain a height-balanced tree, where the difference between the maximum and minimum height of the leaves is at most one.

However, including this check in each step of the RRR algorithm can make the algorithm computationally expensive. Besides, there is no guarantee that among the available set of topologically adjacent parents of the orphan node at least one would offer height-balance maintaining connection. In some cases, the only connection left could be a new parent node that is > 2 levels different from the previous parent of the orphan node, leading to a height imbalanced tree.

Our proposed solution approach is to first list all the available parent nods, per topological adjacency. Next, these available parent nodes are sorted in the tree level discrepancy from the previous parent of the orphan node. Clearly, the first element of the sorted list would offer a parent node that is closest in tree height level to the former parent of the orphan node, which is the design choice for tree re-construction.

Input: $G(V, E)$= multicast tree with underlying mesh-of-hypercube topology spanning over all the cells; s= source node, D= set of destination nodes, I= set of intermediate nodes.
v = the node which has become orphan and requires to find a new parent;
threshold = maximum allowable fan out of a prospective parent node;
Output: Parent(v), which will re-construct the tree.
Procedure RRR (v)
  if ($v \in D \cup I$)
    $l \leftarrow$ tree_level(n); $S = \phi$ /* S_i denote the i-th element of the set S. */
    $\forall u \in$ {mesh-of-hypercube adjacent to v} $\wedge u \in (D \cup I)$ do $S = S \cup u$
    $\forall u \in S$, height_diff(u) = $|(tree\_level(u) - l)|$
    Sort the elements of S in increasing order of height_diff() value of the set members
    $i = 1$; parent(v) = S_1
    while (deg(parent(v)) > threshold) $\wedge i < |S|$ Do   parent(v) = S_{i+1}; $i = i+1$;
    if deg(S_i > threshold) **then** parent(v) = S_1;
  else node v is not in multicast tree, no action required;
End Procedure RRR

FIG. 6. *Pseudo-code algorithm for RRR*

3.6. Look-ahead Alternate Parent - LAP. This approach is based upon precomputed alternate multicast tree reconstruction techniques. In the LAP algorithm, each node has a local parent table containing current the parent-id and a number of alternate parents-ids computed in the background. Due to one or more node migrations, when orphan node(s) are created, each orphan node readily selects one alternate parent from its alternate-parent table. Ideally, this approach would be able to re-construct the multicast tree in zero wait time; however, in practice a small table lookup delay would be involved. Also, if the alternate parent table is not ready and available, then associated delays for executing the RRR algorithm in the background would also account as a foreground delay.

Following is the sequence of events that will happen for the LAP:

- **time 0**. The multicast tree is in operation. Each node in the multicast tree, as a background computation, computes a set of alternate parent node ids ready, and available, to carry out re-construction, if needed.
- **time 0 + Δt**. A node, v, migrates from one cell to another breaking the multicast tree. A few of the other nodes in the multicast tree, including v itself, may become orphans. Each orphan node carries out a lookup at its alternate-parent table, and selects a suitable (based on path length reduction approach) alternate-parent to re-construct the multicast tree.
- **time 0 + $\Delta t + \delta$**. Now, since the tree is again connected, multicast traffic flows as expected. However, based on the new tree-connectivity and topological adjacency information, each node carries out a new set of alternate-parent table computations.

Input: $G(V, E)$= multicast tree with underlying mesh-of-hypercube topology spanning over all the cells; S= source node, D= set of destination nodes, I= set of intermediate nodes.
v = the node which has become orphan and requires to find a new parent;
threshold = maximum allowable fan out of a prospective parent node;
Output: Parent(v), which will re-construct the tree.

```
Procedure LAP (n)/* invoked at a node v becoming orphan */
  if (v ∈ D ∪ I)
      if table_empty
          if v has recently migrated then parent_table = Φ;
          if parent_table = Φ              then p = Request_Reply_Reject(v);
            else p = parent_table_1; i = 1;
                while (parent_table_i not active ∧i < |parent_table|)
                    p= parent_table_{i+1}; i = i + 1; endWhile
                if i = |parent_table| then print "topology fragmented, exception error";
                return(p);
  else node v is not in multicast tree;
End Procedure LAP
Procedure Background_LAP (v)
if (time mod κ) = 0 ∧ (v ∈ D ∪ I)
      l ← tree_level(v); S = φ /* S_i denote the i-th element of the set S.
      ∀x ∈ {mesh-of-hypercube adjacent to v} ∧x ∈ (D ∪ I) do          S = S ∪ x
      ∀x ∈ S, height_diff(x) = |(tree_level(x) − l)|
      Sort the elements of S in increasing order of height_diff() value of the set members
  else node v is not in multicast tree;
End Procedure Background_LAP
```

FIG. 7. *Pseudo-code algorithm for LAP*

3.7. Background vs. Foreground Computation. The LAP algorithm requires to execute the RRR algorithm, or an equivalent one in the background. Each node has a local parent table containing a number of alternate parent-ids; these parents are sought and computed during the idle time (when data transmission rate is low). Background computation requires some extra administrative overhead and initiate substantial amount of network management activity during slack period. It also enhances buffer cost. However, at the cost of all these, the advantage is that the fragmented multicast tree can be re-connected instantaneously; thus very fast or real-time multicast tree reconstruction can be achieved.

On the contrary, RRR method employs foreground computation only; it keeps on building the broken tree heuristically and seeks a better balanced tree (refer to the discussion on "Path Reduction Approach") to reduce transmission time from the source to the destination node. Foreground computation does not carry extra network management overhead and storage cost of the alternate parent nodes or links. But, consequently, it can not restore the multicast tree instantaneously like in the cases of LAP approach. Therefore, depending on the reuse of response time required, the RRR method may not suite real-time applications. The RRR method is essentially what the background computation of LAP does.

Load factor plays a significant role in each case. Load factor is the data transmission rate. When load factor is low, background computation can be facilitated; when load factor rises high, foreground computation is required.

4. Analysis of Solution Approaches. This section discusses the issues of network management and derives a number of analytical results related to the proposed heuristics. Probability analysis of the LAP approach and the optimization objectives are given in this section. Finally, we present a geometric analysis of the possible (entry, exit) points of a mobile node within a cell and based on the relative speed of the mobile node and cell sizes we arrive at the probability that a mobile node will miss its deadline for immediate reconstruction of the multicast tree upon migration.

4.1. Network Management with Empty Slot Assignment. We assume that each cell consists of a hypercube of dimension $d-6$; so the maximum number of nodes in each cell is 2^{d-6}. Each node is logically represented to fill up a *slot*, where a slot is a placeholder for a physical node in the event of a node arrival. There can be a maximum of 2^{d-6} slots in a cell. At a given time, all the slots may not be occupied, since the cell may not be fully populated by mobile nodes. Slots become empty (or free) when a node migration occurs. When a node migrates from one cell to another, an empty slot is created in the former cell, while a previously empty slot in the new cell is marked as occupied. Assignment and re-assignment of the free slots is governed by the network manager. Migration of one or more nodes from a complete logical topology may create a fragmented logical topology, *e.g.*, an incomplete mesh or incomplete hypercube. The analysis of such incomplete topologies, particularly the issue of routing in fragmented topologies, is an attractive research area, but beyond the scope of this paper.

4.2. Probability Analysis of LAP . Assume that a node's migratory behavior is independent of all other nodes. Let p be the probability that one node changes its cell membership. If a node has one current parent and $\alpha - 1$ alternate parents then

$$Prob\{\text{all } \alpha \text{ parents move simultaneously}\} = p^\alpha << p.$$

After constructing the lookahead parent table,

$$Prob\{\text{instantaneous connection required}\} = Prob\{\text{current parent moves}\} = p.$$

Therefore, $Prob\{\text{instantaneous connection impossible}\} = 1-p^\alpha$. For a node, if each alternate parent entry requires σ space, then the total space required by each node is:

$$\text{Average space requirement }, S_{LAP} = \alpha \times \sigma$$

Probability of maintaining a reliable connection , $R_{LAP} = 1 - p^{\alpha}$

Let the maximum time to connect a node instantaneously with alternate parent be Δt. If the maximum data rate is K_{LAP} bps, then temporary buffer space required, $TS_{LAP} = K_{LAP} \times \Delta t$ bits. In other words, if a node has TS_{LAP} bits buffer space for data then for K_{LAP} bps maximum data transmission rate the maximum duration a node can be orphan is Δt. Beyond that, there will be a loss of data. Therefore:

1. Each node should contain adequate buffer space, to account for the distributed multicast stream.
2. A disconnected node should be able to synchronize with the multicast bit-stream upon tree re-construction.

4.3. Deadline Miss Probability. We analyze the different geometrically feasible trajectories of a mobile node through a particular cell and estimate the average time lag between entry into and exit from the cell. From this average time, and assuming a computational capacity of the processors in the mobile node (viz. the background computation time needed for the LAP algorithm, or foreground computation for the RRR algorithm) we derive the probability of missing the deadline to instantaneously reconfigure the multicast tree.

4.3.1. Time Delay for LAP or RRR Construction. The shortest path algorithm [2] can be modified to seek the alternate parent in the LAP algorithm. The LAP algorithm is executed in the background, while RRR is executed in foreground - in either case, the time complexity of the algorithm is $O(|MT_V|^2)$, where $|MT_V|$ is the number of nodes in the multicast tree. The height-balance constraint, *i.e.*, the fact that alternate parents can only be chosen from a small subset of possibilities, may further accelerate the algorithm. However, we take the worst case $O(|MT_V|^2)$, as the time to derive a re-construction pattern of the multicast tree.

For realistic applications, the range of values for $|MT_V|$ is limited to a few thousand at most. This makes the computational overhead for the (background) LAP or (foreground) RRR algorithms in the range of a few million (since 1 million $= 1000^2$) CPU cycles. With a Pentium 300 MHz CPU, such a computation will require less than a second. The fastest moving vehicle traveling at, say, a speed of 120 miles per hour, will pass $\frac{1}{30}$ miles, or approximately 60 yards in a second. If the mobile node passes less than 60 yards in a cell before causing a second handover, then immediately after the second handover, the fragmented multicast tree may not be ready for re-construction. For distances traversed more than 60 yards in a cell, the LAP or RRR algorithms will be fast enough to have the fragmented multicast tree ready for immediate re-construction.

The basis of our deadline miss ratio computation is based on this approach of comparing the time taken by a standard processor to compute the LAP and RRR algorithms, and the time-equivalent of the distance traversed cutting through the cell by the mobile node.

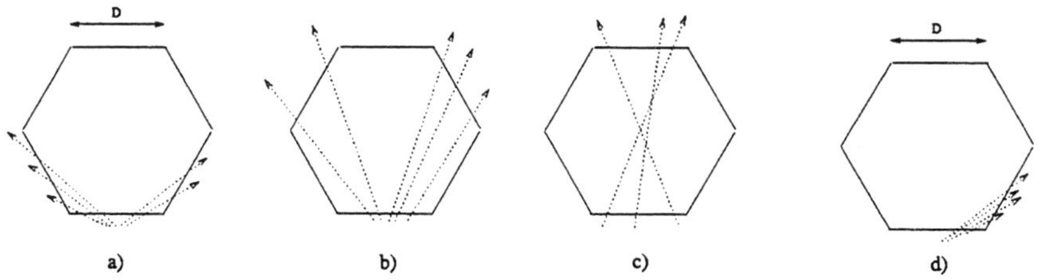

FIG. 8. *a-c) Hexagonal cell structure, and three types of (entry, exit) directions; d) Short distance trajectories through a cell.*

4.3.2. Average Distance Analysis. Figure 8 shows a hexagonal cell structure, where without loss of generality, the mobile node enters through the bottom horizontal edge. Suppose that each side of the hexagon is divided into D equal segments, and that a mobile node may enter or exit only at these discrete points. Depending on the direction of the trajectory, assuming a linear segment, the mobile node will exit along anyone of the five other sides. Among these five sides, pairwise immediate left and right, and pairwise immediate second left and second right sides are symmetric. This causes three distinct cases for analysis, as shown in cases (A), (B) and (C) respectively.

Let D be the length of each side of the hexagonal cell. Let a particular mobile node enter at the i-th grid point, and exit at the j-th grid point along the immediate right side, as shown in Figure 8a. The linear distance, which the mobile traverses within the cell can be shown to be:

$$x_1(i,j) = \sqrt{(j sin 60^o)^2 + (i + j cos 60^o)^2}$$

Likewise, if the mobile node exits at the j-th grid point along the second right side, as shown in Figure 8b, then the linear distance traversed by the mobile node can be shown to be:

$$x_2(i,j) = \sqrt{(2DCos30^o - jCos30^o)^2 + (i + jSin30^o)^2}$$

At the third combination, if the mobile node exits at the j-th grid point along the diagonally opposite side, as shown in Figure 8c, then the linear distance traversed by the mobile node is:

$$x_3(i,j) = \sqrt{4D^2Cos^2 30^o + (i-j)^2}$$

We use the above distances to calculate the average distance that a node travels through the cell. For simplicity we use the square of the distances. We define the following,

$$X_1 = \sum_{i=1}^{D}\sum_{j=1}^{D} x_1(i,j)^2; \quad X_2 = \sum_{i=1}^{D}\sum_{j=1}^{D+1} x_2(i,j)^2; \quad X_3 = \sum_{i=1}^{D+1}\sum_{j=1}^{D+1} x_3(i,j)^2$$

Then we calculate the total of the square of the distances as,

$$\text{Total Square Distance} = 2 \times X_1 + 2 \times X_2 + X_3 = O(D^4)$$

Since there are D^2 grid-pair points along each axis, and there are five possible exit sides, a total of $5D^2$ grid-pair points are summed above. Thus, the average square distance equals

$$\frac{O(D^4)}{5D^2} = O(D^2)$$

For even the smallest size hexagonal grids, the range of values for D is large enough to make the average distance ($\sqrt{O(D^2)} = O(D)$) larger than the time it takes for a fast CPU to execute the $O(|MT_V|^2)$ algorithm. Therefore, on average the multicast re-construction algorithm is unlikely to miss its deadline.

4.3.3. Deadline Miss Ratio. However, in a case where the mobile node enters at an angle nearing an edge corner, and immediately exits around the corner along the nearby side (Figure 8d), the distance traversed by the mobile node within the cell may be smaller than the $O(|MT_V|^2)$ delay of the multicast tree re-construction algorithm. In such a case, the deadline may be missed, as the mobile node, after entering the new cell (i.e., after second handoff) does not find a re-constructed multicast tree to switch to instantaneously. In such cases, a small but noticeable delay may be observed until the $O(|MT_V|^2)$ algorithm for LAP or RRR completes execution. We estimate the possibility of such occurrence in the following.

The Deadline Miss Ratio (DMR) is defined as the fraction of mobile node trajectories (viz. entry-exit grid-pair points) that traverse a rectilinear distance that is less than a given threshold – a distance small enough to be traversed faster than the execution of the $O(|MT_V|^2)$ LAP or RRR algorithms.

Let S denote the speed of the mobile node in unit time. The time taken by the LAP or RRR algorithms to execute, *i.e.*, $O(|MT_V|^2)$, is equivalent to $\Delta = S \times O(|MT_V|^2)$ distance traversal by the mobile node. Since, this distance is small, it is only feasible that trajectories of type (A) (refer Figure 8a,b,c) can be shorter than this distance.

The question is: what pairwise combination of (i, j) values lead to $x_1(i, j) \leq \Delta$? The geometric median for the (i, j) values is achieved when $i = j$, leading to the following computation:

$$\Delta \geq x_1(i,j) = \sqrt{(j sin60^o)^2 + (i + j cos60^o)^2}, \text{ with, } i = j$$

$$\Delta \geq \sqrt{3}i, \text{ Or, } i \leq \frac{\Delta}{\sqrt{3}}$$

This implies that one of the co-ordinates of the (i, j)-pair will require to be $\leq \frac{\Delta}{\sqrt{3}}$. Since, i and j are symmetric, without loss of generality, we can vary one variable i. For each one of the $\frac{\Delta}{\sqrt{3}}$ values of i, the value of j could vary between 1 to $\frac{\Delta}{\sqrt{3}}$. This makes a total of $\frac{\Delta}{\sqrt{3}}^2$ combination of trajectories that can have a linear distance less than Δ. Since, there are a total of $5D^2$ (entry, exit) grid-pair possibilities, the deadline miss ratio value is computed as:

$$\text{DMR} = \frac{\frac{\Delta^2}{3}}{5D^2}$$

As can be observed, for realistic values of D (cell size) and Δ (*i.e.*, S, the speed of the mobile, and $|MT_V|$ as the multicast tree size), the deadline miss probability is small.

4.3.4. Overhead of Background Computation. Another important parameter that must be considered is the total amount of background computation required to allow the LAP algorithm to provide a parent that will allow instantaneous reconfiguration of the multicast tree upon node migration. The lookahead parent table is recomputed every k time units. Suppose that a mobile node is traveling through a cell at speed S along an average length trajectory of length d. Then the number of times that the background computation will be executed is: $(\lfloor \frac{d}{Sk} \rfloor)$.

Furthermore, the time needed to traverse the trajectory of length d is $(\frac{d}{S})$. Since each background computation requires $O(|MT_V|^2)$ time, the average overhead due to background computation is

$$\frac{(\frac{d}{Sk})O(|MT_V|^2)}{\frac{d}{S}} = \frac{O(|MT_V|^2)}{k}.$$

We can adjust the frequency (k) of doing background computation so that the background computation does not interfere with the application's performance. Smaller values of k will result in more reliable alternate parent information at the cost of a larger percentage of overhead from background computation. Larger values of k will reduce the background computation, but will give less reliable alternate parent information. For ad-hoc cellular networks with frequent migrations and very dynamic topologies, smaller values are suitable. For networks with fairly stable topologies, larger values of k are appropriate.

5. Performance Measures.

5.1. Simulation Environment. Simulation results are shown for the look-ahead alternate parent (LAP) approach. A 64-cell cellular network is considered with each cell having a 3-cube. Each node has 3 hypercube-neighbors, and 6 other neighbors from 6 adjacent cell hypercubes. We start each simulation with an initial multicast tree structure. Subsequently, during node migration different parts of the multicast tree are broken, and the re-construction process is done employing our proposed algorithm for LAP.

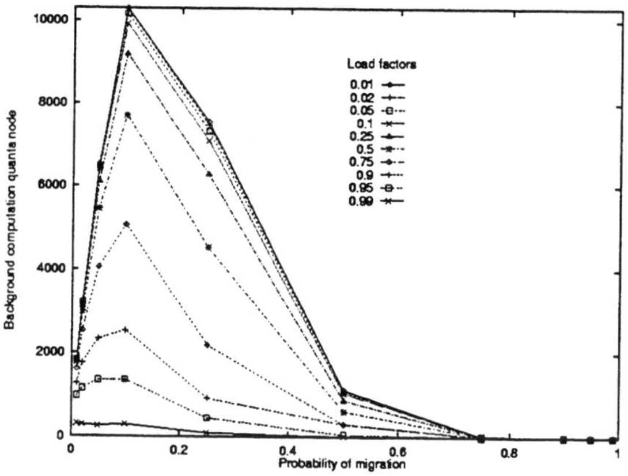

FIG. 9. *Probability of migration vs. Background computation quanta node*

5.2. Input/Output Parameters. We have considered four input parameters: probability of migration, load factor, child limit and parent limit. Ten output metrics are used for performance measure (only few are shown in the plots due to lack of space): occurrence of data interruption due to node migration, occurrence of 'no-data' interruption due to node migration, number of successful 'seek to connect' (i.e., number of times an orphan is successfully connected), number of failures in 'seek to connect', number of data transmission during instantaneous connection, number of successful data transmission, number of quanta in background computation, number of idle quanta, worst-case reconstruction delay and average reconstruction delay.

5.3. Simulation Plots and Discussion. Simulation is continued until steady state is reached. During a steady state, the multicast tree consists of some orphan nodes; alternate parent table of some other nodes are also partially filled up. The program is run for 500 time units and parameters are measured in "node-time quanta".

Figure 9 shows *probability of migration* vs. *number of quanta in background computation.* A constant amount of background computation is done at zero *probability of migration.* At the instant when each node has already filled up its alternate parent table or there are no nodes that can be chosen as an alternate parent, nodes will not spend time in background computation. As *probability of migration* increases, updation of alternate parent table will be increased. But again, beyond a certain point all quanta will be spent in migration. As load factor increases, background computation decreases. This implies the tradeoff between background and foreground approach.

Figures 10a and 10b show the plots of *probability of migration* vs. *average and worst-case reconfiguration delay.* For the simplicity in simulation, we have considered a 3-dimensional hypercube, where number of empty slots is low. However, dimension 4 and higher are better for realistic scenarios. Aver-

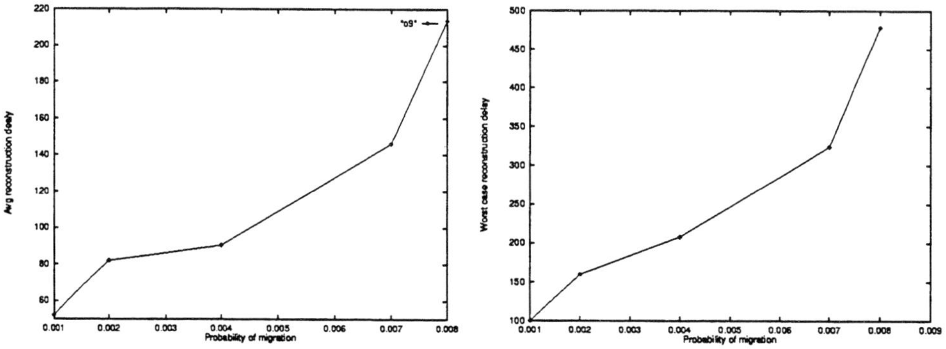

FIG. 10. *a) Probability of migration vs. Average reconstruction delay, b) Probability of migration vs. Worst-case reconstruction delay.*

age reconfiguration delay and worst-case reconfiguration delay rise rapidly with probability of node migration. In both cases, the delay exceeds the limit after certain point of probability of migration. If we increase dimension of the hypercube, this point will shift rightward.

6. Conclusions and Future Work. We have considered the real-time multicast tree problem for wireless network with frequent node migration. The dual formulation of real-time multicast problem has been proposed. We have given emphasis on the practical importance of the issue of multicast reconstruction time (in the event of a node migration) and proposed two solution heuristics. We have discussed their performance issues and derived the optimization objectives. Our simulator measures different performance metrics as a function of different system configurations when a node migration occurs. The simulation results provide us with performance results which very closely resemble our analytical findings. Our ongoing research is currently being extended into an implementation phase on a testbed which includes wireless PCs, ATM-interconnected workstations and high-speed Myrinet switches.

REFERENCES

[1] C. KWANG-CHENG, "Medium Access Control of Wireless LANs for Mobile Computing," *IEEE Networks*, pp. 50–63, September/October 1994.

[2] E. DIJKSTRA, "A Note on Two Problems in Connection with Graphs," *Numerische Mathematik*, Vol. 1, pp. 269–271, 1959.

[3] B. WAXMAN, "Delay-Bounded Steiner Tree Algorithm for Performance-Driven Layout," *Journal on Selected Areas in Communication*, Vol. 6, pp. 1617–1622, December 1988.

[4] P.K. MCKINLEY, H. XU, A-H. ESFAHANIAN, AND L. M. NI, "Unicast-Based Multicast Communication in Wormhole-Routed Networks," *IEEE Transactions on Parallel and Distributed Systems*, Vol. 5, pp. 1252–1265, December 1994.

[5] X. LIN AND L. M. NI, "Multicast Communication in Multicomputer Networks," *Proceedings of 1990 Intl Conf. on Parallel Processing*, pp. III 114–118, August 1990.

[6] S. BHATTACHARYA, C. L. ALBERT, AND W. TSAI, "Fault-Tolerant Multicasting on Hypercubes," *Journal of Parallel and Distributed Computing*, Vol. 23, pp. 418–428, 1994.

[7] A. Y. ZOMAYA, ED., *Parallel and Distributed Computing Handbook*, McGraw-Hill, New York, 1996.

[8] L. K. NAHAR AND S. BHATTACHARYA, "Dynamic Network Management for Firmware Controlled Network Topology," *Proceedings of the COMPSAC '96*, Seoul, Korea, pp. 398–399, August 1996.

[9] C.-C. YU AND S. BHATTACHARYA, "Real-Time Traffic Management on Optical Networks Using Dynamic Control of Cycle Duration," *Lecture Notes in Computer Science*, D. K. PANDA and C. B. STUNKEL, eds., Vol. 1362, pp. 174–188, Springer-Verlag, Berlin, 1998.

[10] Y. LAN, A. ESFAHANIAN, AND L. M.NI, "Multicast in Hypercube Multiprocessors," *Journal of Parallel and Distributed Computing*, Vol. 8, pp. 30–41, 1990.

[11] S. HAKIMI, "Steiner's Problem in Graphs and Its Implication," *Networks*, Vol. 1, pp. 113–133, 1971.

[12] H. TAKAHASHI AND A. MATSUYAMA, "An Approximate Solution for the Steiner Problem in Graphs," *Mathematica Japonica*, Vol. 6, pp. 573–577, 1990.

[13] L. KOU, G. MARKOWSKY, AND L. BERMAN, "A Fast Algorithm for Steiner Trees," *Acta Informatica*, Vol. 15, pp. 141–145, 1981.

[14] K. BHARAT-KUMAR AND J. JAFFE, "Routing to Multiple Destination in Computer Networks," *IEEE Trans. on Communications*, Vol. COM-31, pp. 343–351, 1983.

[15] V. P. KOMPELLA, J. C. PASQUALE, AND G. C. POLYZOS, "Multicast Routing for Multimedia Communication," *IEEE/ACM Transactions on Networking*, Vol. 1, No. 3, pp. 286–292, 1993.

[16] Z. QING, M. PARSA, AND J. J. GARCIA-LUNA-ACEVES, "A Source-Based Algorithm for Delay-Constrained Minimum-Cost Multicasting," *INFOCOM*, 1995.

[17] M. R.POKAM AND G. MICHEL, "Guaranteeing Spatial Coherence in Real-Time Multicasting," *International Symposium on Information Theory*, p. 41, May 1995.

[18] T. LEE AND J. P. HAYES, "Fault Tolerant Communication Scheme for Hypercube Computers," *IEEE Trans. Comput.*, Vol. 41, pp. 1242–1256, October 1992.

[19] Y. SAAD AND M. SCHULTZ, "Data Communication in Hypercubes," Technical Report YALEU/DCS/RR-428, Dept.of Computer Science, Yale University, 1985.

[20] H. SULLIVAN AND T. BASHKOW, "A Large Scale, Homogeneous, Fully Distributed Parallel Machine," *Proc. 4th Symp. on Computer Architecture*, pp. 105–117, 1977.

[21] Y.-J. TSAI AND P. K. MCKINLEY "An Extended Dominating Node Approach to Collective Communication in All-Port Wormhole-Routed 2D Meshes," *Proceedings of the Scalable High-Performance Computing Conference, May 23–25, 1994, Knoxville, Tennessee*, pp. 199–206, IEEE Computer Society Press, Los Alamitos, Calif., 1994.

REAL-TIME NETWORK APPLICATIONS PROGRAMMING

ABDELMALEK BENZEKRI AND PHILIPPE SARAFOGLOU *

Abstract. Real-time network applications need a special attention. Mechanisms allowing them to face delay variation on the flow delivery must be available as much as resource reservation and admission control for QOS guarantee of all the flows being accepted within the network. This paper presents an integrated stack of protocols enabling real-time network programming. The programming issues held by IP multicast, RTP, RTCP and RSVP protocols are discussed in details and tackled in both Sun Solaris and MS Windows NT environments.

Key words. IP multicast, RTP, RTCP, RSVP, socket programming

1. Introduction. Many works propose extensions to networks architectures in order to provide integrated services supporting real-time to meet the growing need for a variety of new applications, including teleconferencing, distance learning, telescience and distributed simulation. These applications built thanks to the client/server model are also coming up with new concepts in the way they are settled. Traditional network applications enforce the client party to pull information, i.e. the client program asks the server for the information needed. The new generation of applications introduces the push principle based on the information delivery by the server party, the client program just showing its interest. Multimedia applications such as video conferencing obey the push mechanism: the server program is responsible for the information flow while the client programs listen. To manage efficiently network resources, group management protocols allowing multicast transport over a network have been designed. This new way of resource access has other implications especially when dealing with quality of service (QOS).

Traditional networks were conceived offering point-to-point best-effort data delivery. But real-time applications require some control of end-to-end packet delays. Real-time QOS is not the only issue for the next generation traffic management. Network operators in their wish of optimising network resources are requesting the ability to control the sharing of bandwidth on a particular link among different classes of traffic. By assigning the required amount of bandwidth to real-time applications, the "unused" bandwidth remains available at other times. Such a management facilility is commonly called controlled link-sharing. The integrated service model stands for best-effort service, real-time service, and controlled link sharing [10, 16].

The new Internet generation model proposes a set of extensions built upon some key assumptions. "Resource reservation" and "admission control" are the key building blocks of the service. The RSVP protocol is designed to set up a flow-specific state in the endsystems and in the routers along the path of a flow. Packet scheduling (rather than simply forwarding on a FIFO policy), flows

*IRIT/SIERA, Université Paul Sabatier, 118 Route de Narbonne, F31062 Toulouse Cedex 04, France (benzekri@irit.fr, sarafogl@irit.fr)

classification (for traffic control and accounting) and admission control (granting the requested QOS without impacting earlier guarantees) must accompany the reservation protocol. Other arguments that do not defend the key assumptions above, such as "infinite bandwidth", "prioritizing", "applications adaptivity" have led to the design of protocols supporting real-time applications without managing delays variation accross networks. Multicast protocols and new real-time transport protocols such as RTP/RTCP provide means for the applications to adapt their QOS requirements to any characteristic of a network. These protocols are not incompatible with RSVP. On the contrary, if combined they all together offer the possibility to satisfy real-time requirements while managing the resource sharing within a network.

RTP/RTCP and RSVP can be used within a TCP/IP network but are not specific to the Internet. Their use within a native ATM network is also possible [2]. In this paper, we present a protocol stack for real-time applications, in Section 2. This stack involves RTP/RTCP, RSVP, and IP multicast. Section 3 deals with the programming interfaces that are offered around such protocols. Section 4 shows how to build real-time client/server applications focusing on the Solaris and Windows NT environments.

2. The Protocol Stack for Real-Time Network Applications. Multimedia network applications are increasingly being developed. Audio and video flows enforce soft real-time constraints. New network technologies are coming up with facilities taking into account such requirements where QOS management is of central importance.

The "push" based applications rely on point-to-multipoint packet forwarding. The IP multicast, connectionless oriented mode, optimizes the information transport among the network. The addressing scheme defines a group address and group management facilities for dynamic join/leave operations treated by the Internet routers. In a connection oriented network, multicast signaling present in the ATM technology for instance allows such resource optimisation. Moreover, in new internetworking architectures like Multi Protocol over ATM, the MARS services adapting the IP multicast over ATM are specified (Multicast Address Resolution Server) [4, 12].

RTP/RTCP protocols augment the knowledge of an application party with regard to time delivery within a session. The application may then adapt its behaviour in order to meet the real-time requirements. That is to say that no mechanism is offered by RTP/RTCP to guarantee QOS requirements. To achieve these goals, we need a specific protocol to reserve the bandwidth and to manage the packet forwarding within the network. A given guaranteed flow must not have an impact on another, the remaining bandwidth of a link being shared among best-effort traffic.

The protocol stack we are dealing with involves the protocols mentioned above. This stack supports a wide variety of real-time applications and not only multimedia ones. On the other hand it is open to the Internet domain even if the network is native ATM. Normally, the RTP/RTCP protocols provide a transport interface to applications. But in order to facilitate the socket progamming, RTP/RTCP is used over UDP.

2.1. IP Multicast [10]. IP individual addresses are generally used for end-to-end communication. When an information concerns all hosts within a subnet, broadcasting can be used. When an information concerns a logical group of stations within a network, broadcasting will dramatically decrease the performance of the network as far as the message will flood the whole network, even the non-concerned subnets. Another solution consists in setting as many communications as pairs of endsystems within the group, but it increases the number of messages to process within the network with the fact that the replicate packets will arrive at the different destinations with a great variability in time. The alternative was introduced thanks to the Internet Group Management Protocol (IGMP) allowing a performant multicast over the network.

IP multicast makes use of the specific class D of addresses where packets are forwarded within the network only to the subnets that notified their interest in receiving packets related to declared group addresses. A member of a group must register with an IGMP router, joining the group. When a packet arrives at a router including a multicast address, either it is forwarded to the subnets where related members are, or it is discarded. If many subnets are concerned then the router replicates the packet accordingly. This has the advantage to substancially save the bandwidth while optimizing the end-to-end delivery.

The other advantage of IP multicast is that the notion of a group is dynamic. Any member can join/leave the group at the moment it likes. Furthermore, group membership is not exclusive: one host can join several groups at the same time.

Routers implementing IGMP are very few within the Internet but their number increases day after day. To face this lack, a virtual network on the Internet called Mbone providing the multicast service has been set up [11]. Mbone consists in tunnels between IGMP routers, the latter encapsulate multicast packets they forward to the next IGMP router in a unicast manner over a traditional IP section. A multicast router that wants to send a multicast packet across a tunnel will prepend another IP header, set the destination address in the new header to be the unicast address of the multicast router at the other end of the tunnel, and set the IP protocol field in the new header to be 4 (which means the next protocol is IP). The multicast router at the other end of the tunnel receives the packet, strips off the encapsulating IP header, and forwards the packet as appropriate.

Many cooperative applications can be built in this environment [5, 6, 14]. Thanks to its bandwidth saving and its performant delivery, real-time cooperative network applications in the Internet will require such services. In order to augment and manage the quality of network access for these applications, we recommend the use of a stack offering admission control and resource reservation while allowing the application to adapt to the network quality, variability and knowledge. RSVP and RTP/RTCP protocols serve this purpose and are presented in the following sub-sections.

2.2. Real-Time Protocol, Real-Time Control Protocol [17].

2.2.1. RTP Overview [1, 7, 21]. The RTP protocol has been adopted by IETF to provide real-time end-to-end data transport within the Internet and is generally used over UDP. Multiplexing and checksum control is available thanks to UDP. RTP can be employed with unicast or multicast flows, and its flexibility (its ability to adapt to a specific class of application) allows an open design of real-time applications, in contrast to the proprietary solutions. RTP can be used by multimedia applications but not only, continuous data archive, real-time monitoring, distributed simulation and virtual reality may benefit from its service.

RTP doesn't guarantee the real-time delivery or any other QOS guarantee. But it provides facilities for synchronisation, loss detection, content security and identification allowing the application to deal with the QOS management.

Data flows are carried in the "payload" field of a segment whose identifier gives information on the flow format. Profiles may be specified defining extensions or modifications to RTP that are specific to a particular class of applications. This incompleteness allows the protocol to carry different flow types defined by a profile specification which is a real advantage in many proprietary and flow specific nonreusable solutions. Sequencing and timestamping are the other mechanisms offered to applications in order to manage the end-to-end flow transport. Each recipient part is intended to process a sliding window buffer, discarding segments that do not arrive in time.

RTP can be directly implemented over IP, ICMP and IGMP thanks to the raw sockets. But the major available actual releases are based on UDP, allowing ports multiplexing and checksum control. The programming using RTP (cf. Section 3) consists in fact in the header creation whose format contains a 12-byte fixed part specifying the synchronisation source and the above mandatory mechanisms held by the protocol. Another important feature concerns the contributing sources inserted by a mixer. Mixers are RTP-level relays to be placed near low-bandwidth areas to adapt a high quality flow to low-bandwidth parts of the network. Mixers reconstruct, translate, and forward flow encodings to the lower-bandwidth context.

2.2.2. RTCP [17]. Data transport is augmented by a control protocol RTCP to allow monitoring of the data delivery in a manner scalable to large multicast networks. Based on a periodic transmission of control packets to all participants in an RTP session, RTCP provides feedback on the quality of data distribution (related to the flow and congestion control functions of underlying protocols). Multiple data streams in a set of RTP sessions that may concern a participant and means to associate them, especially when resuming after any kind of network failure, are provided by RTCP. All participants should send RTCP control packets required by the two functions above. The rate must therefore be controlled to scale up to a large number of participants. One direct impact on applications is that each participant in an RTP session is aware of the others and can independently observe the number of participants. Group management for cooperative applications can hence be provided thanks to RTCP.

2.3. Introduction to RSVP [8, 16, 18].

2.3.1. What is RSVP. RSVP is a bandwidth reservation protocol, designed for a multicast environment and accomodating heterogeneous recipient oriented service needs. A session is defined by the common IP multicast destination address of the receivers. The latter should reserve the required bandwidth related to the QOS they like as they know what they want and what they can pay for. Receiver initiation handles heterogeneous receivers easily, each receiver simply asking for an appropriate reservation. Moreover, the receiver initiation has no impact either on the source part or on the other receiver parts.

To achieve resource reservation, the protocol must be implemented in both endsystems and routers. Another major characteristic is that resources are reserved according to the flow sense. Duplex communications need two independent simplex reservations. Routers involving RSVP have to distribute the control requests along the flow path. A soft state is employed in order to manage the reservation status among the routers and endsystems. Periodic messages are therefore required to maintain the soft state, and if not exchanged the reserved resources become immediately available for the rest of the traffic.

As RSVP can not be deployed at one go within the Internet, RSVP should "remain available" over a network portion where routers do not implement it. The best-effort policy related to these routers may be a source of quality of service degradation. Nevertheless, the routing policies already available in some modern routing protocols such as OSPF provide a "type of service" routing facility that should avoid this degradation if possible, depending on the traffic load. RFC 2236 presents a new routing model considering QOS both inside and outside autonomous systems (QOS intra/extra domain routing).

2.3.2. Protocol Overview. RSVP is part of the network layer and needs the IP protocol to forward its messages. Routing protocols are not part of RSVP but they have a great impact on it. RSVP messages, identified by the protocol number 46, are exchanged along the path between RSVP routers. Raw IP datagrams can be used to this end, but as a lot of systems do not provide them, RSVP messages can be encapsulated in UDP segments for communications between an endsystem and the first (resp. last) RSVP router whose reserved ports are 1698 (resp. 1699). For more details see Annex C of RFC2205.

An RSVP session is viewed as a flow with a destination address, a transport protocol and a port number. Sessions are independent from ech other. Receivers are then identified and the resources they require have to be specified. In order to state the resource requirements, an application must specify the desired QOS using the flow descriptors. A flowspec parameter describes the required QOS "rspec" and the traffic flow "tspec". Another parameter, the filterspec, identifies the IP source and the UDP/TCP port in option, defining the flow packets receiving the resources. Assuming the admission control succeeds, the flowspec is used to parameterize a resource class in the packet scheduler, while the filterspec will be instantiated in the packet classifier to map the appropriate packets into this class.

To aggregate the resource requirements of multiple receivers, RSVP offers several different reservation "styles". The first reservation option concerns the reservation processing for different senders within the same session either shared or distinct. Another option controls the senders selection by addressing explicitly the filterspec or in case of a wildcard, implicitly determining the whole set of senders. The table below lists the reservation styles (column) and sender selection (rows).

	Distinct Reservation	Shared Reservation
Explicit Selection (senders specified in RESV message)	FixedFilter Style	SharedExplicit Style
Wildcard Selection (dynamic filter where session participants are not previously known or specified)	None Defined	WildcardFilter Style

TABLE 2.1
Reservation Styles

The Wildcard-Filter style is a combination of shared reservation and a wildcard sender selection. This creates a single reservation which is shared by all flows from upstream senders to a particular session (for example an open audio conference).

The Fixed-Filter style, a combination of a distinct reservation and an explicit sender selection, creates a reservation for a flow from a particular sender to a particular session. Other senders participating in the same session do not share the reservation (for example dowloading or multicast file transfer).

The Shared-Explicit style, a combination of a shared reservation and an explicit sender selection, creates a single reservation that is shared by explicitly selected (as specified by the filterspec(s)) senders (for example audio conferencing).

2.3.3. The RSVP Architecture. The RSVP architecture can be summarized in the figure below. The application asks the RSVP process for a particuliar QOS and the network simply grants or refuses it. The routing process must find a route supporting the resource reservation facing issues such as sufficient unreserved capacity for a new flow, adapting to a route failure or change. The admission control concerns resource availability. It requires that a router understand the demands that are currently being made on its assets and use some efficient algorithm to provide better link utilization (worst case bounds of each already commited flow, measuring actual usage by existing packet flows for admission purpose). The policy control consists in the verification of the access rights to the allocated resources. Authentication procedures of endsystems and routers are part of this module in order to ensure both the reservation and packet flow integrity. The use of Policy Data and Integrity objects [19] may be able to alleviate some of the impacts of denial-of-service attempts. The packet classifier serves the purpose of traffic control and accounting, each incoming packet must be mapped into some class corresponding to a broad category of flows or might hold a single flow. This classification is router-dependent according to its role in a certain configuration (a backbone router or near the periphery). The packet scheduler performs the reordering of the output queue, based on a priority mechanism, a round-robin scheduling scheme or any other scheme allowing an efficient access to a share of the link.

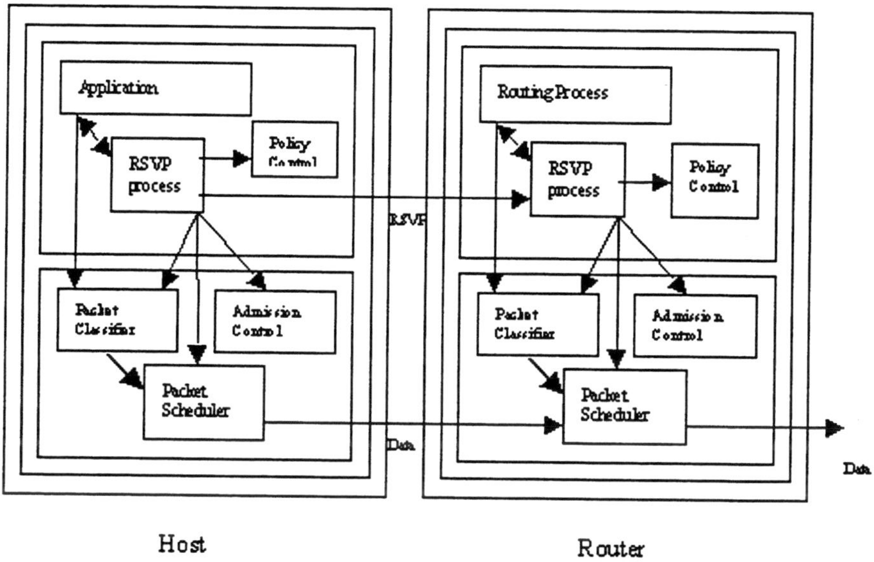

FIG. 2.1. *The RSVP Architecture*

2.3.4. The Reservation Establishment. The reservation establishment follows the general model below:

1. An RSVP sender transmits the PATH message along the path to the receiver of the flow, which message defines the RSVP session. The destination address may be a host address or a multicast group address.
2. Along the path, each RSVP router stores the state of the path, e.g., the IP address of the previous RSVP router, to proceed with RESV messages that will go back to the sender.
3. The RSVP receiver initiates a unicast reservation thanks to a RESV message upstream to the previous RSVP router. The flow descriptor characterizes the reservation.
4. As far as the reservation is satisfied, the RESV message follows the reverse path, RSVP router by RSVP router, until either it reaches the sender or the reservation is merged into an existing reservation if compatible.
5. Optionally, a receiver may request a confirmation message of the probably granted resources.

3. The Programming Interface Supporting Real-Time Applications. All the programming interfaces are built upon the socket API [13, 15, 22, 23]. We first present the RTP/RTCP primitives we have developed for the Windows NT and Solaris environments. We have used the Intel WS2RSVP structures to be employed with the Winsock2 API and the IETF RAPI library implemented with the Sun Solstice solution for the Solaris environment.

3.1. The RTP/RTCP Programming Interface. The library we developed consists in the data structures defining RTP and RTCP segments and the primitives creating, sending and receiving them. The data structures are defined in an "rtp.h" file which contains among others the `rtp_pkt_t` segment definition:

```
typedef struct {
  rtp_hdr_t * header;
  int header_size;
  rtp_payload_t * payload;
  int payload_size;
} rtp_pkt_t;
```

An RTP packet is represented by the `rtp_pkt_t` structure referencing a pointer to the fixed header structure specified in the RTP RFC, instantiated for the MPEG1 standard, the header length, a pointer to the payload structure and finally the payload length. The functions using this data structure have been grouped in the "rtp_base.c" file: `rtp_create`, `rtp_send` and `rtp_receive`:

```
rtp_pkt_t * rtp_create(int taille_payload, int marqueur,
                       u_int16 seq, u_int32 ssrc,
                       void * data);
void rtp_send (int sockfd, struct sockaddr_in client_ext,
               int taille_payload, int marqueur,
               u_int16 seq, u_int32 ssrc,
                void * data);
rtp_pkt_t * rtp_receive(int sockfd, struct sockaddr_in
               serveur_ext);
```

`rtp_create` creates a new RTP segment, initialises the header, using a marker to identify the flow, and data to fill the payload field. Information related to a 12-byte fixed header (e.g. no CSRC field) and the payload length are directly stored in the `rtp_pkt _t` structure.

`rtp_send` sends an RTP segment obtained by `rtp_create`. The `sendto()` socket primitive is used to send the RTP segment as a UDP datagram over an existing socket. The receiver is specified by the `client_ext` structure and the UDP segment length is obtained from the `rtp_pkt_t` structure.

`rtp_receive` receives an RTP packet in the `sockfd` socket. It initialises the `rtp_pkt_t` structure which is returned to the application.

RTCP data structures are also defined in the "rtp.h" file.

```
// one RTCP packet
typedef struct
   {rtcp_common_t common;    // common header
```

```
    union
   { // sender report (SR)
     struct {
       u_int32 ssrc;          // source this RTCP packet refers to
       u_int32 ntp_sec;       // NTP timestamp
       u_int32 ntp_frac;
       u_int32 rtp_ts;        // RTP timestamp
       u_int32 psent;         // packets sent
       u_int32 osent;         // octets sent
       rtcp_rr_t rr[1];       // variable-length list
     } sr;
     // reception report (RR)
     struct
     { u_int32 ssrc; // source generating this report
       rtcp_rr_t rr[1];       // variable-length list
     } rr;
     // BYE
     struct
     { u_int32 src[1];            // list of sources
       // can't express trailing text
     } bye;
     // source description (SDES)
     struct rtcp_sdes_t
     { u_int32 src;                  // first SSRC/CSRC
       rtcp_sdes_item_t item[1]; // list of SDES items
     } sdes;
   } r; } rtcp_t;
```

An RTCP segment contains a common `rtcp_common` and a structure union to be used according to the packet type. Several application specific packets can be defined:

- `app_lsdes` consisting in the `rtcp_common` and the `app_lsdes` (a light version of `sdes` allowing a simpler identification mechanism of the clients, where only the client's name is exchanged)
- "compound" `bye` consisting in `rtcp_common`, `app_lsdes`, and `bye` structures; it identifies the client leaving the session; `app_lsdes` packet must always preceed a "bye" packet (or simplicity, the two structures have been grouped in a compound packet to be transmitted)
- "compound" `rr` consisting in `rtcp_common`, `app_lsdes`, and `rr` structures; the server part must be able to identify the client transmitting a statistics packet RR.

We have grouped together the relevant structures. Data structure referring the statistics on the reception average quality looks as follows.

```
typedef struct
 {int nb_clients ;                //number of actual clients
  unsigned int fraction : 8 ;     //percentage of packets loss
```

```
        int lost :24 ;                  //number of packets loss
        u_int32 jitter ;                //jitter
  } stat_clients ;
```

Data structure related to the statistics specific to an identified client reception is shown below.

```
   struct cell_clt
     {char * nom ;
     unsigned int fraction :8 ;       // percentage of paquets loss
     int lost :24 ;                   // number of lost packets
     u_int32 jitter ;                 // jitter
     struct cell_clt * suivant ;      // chain list of clients
     };
      typedef struct cel_clt fiche_client ;
```

These two structures are updated each time an RTCP packet is received by the server. The functions using these structures can be found in the "rtcp_base.c" file, briefly described below. The names of the functions are selfexplanatory, so that no description is given. With `rtcp_rr_create` an RTCP "compound packet" of type RR is created and it returns a string to be sent. `rtcp_receive` allows the receipt of the RTCP packets sent by the clients using the `sockfd` socket. It updates `info` and `liste_clt` variables (statistics, QOS, group membership).

```
        char * rtcp_app_lsdes_create (char * nom);
        char * rtcp_bye_create(char * nom);
        char * rtcp_bye_create(char * nom);
        char * rtcp_rr_create(int nb_ssrc, u_int32 ssrc,
                              unsigned int fraction,
                              int lost, u_int32 last_seq,
                              u_int32 jitter, u_int32 lsr,
                              u_int32 dlsr, char * nom);
        void rtcp_send(int sockfd, struct sockaddr_in
                              client_ext, char *buffer);
        void rtcp_receive(int sockfd, struct sockaddr_in
                          serveur_ext, stat_clients *
                          info_cl, fiche_client *
                          liste_clt, int taille_lsdes) ;
```

3.2. The RSVP Programming Interface. For the Windows NT environment, the Winsock2 API specifies a generic interface, protocol independent, dealing with QOS requirements (RSVP, ATM, SP2) [23]. In this section, we are interested in the RSVP API. An application should use two separate interfaces, one for the QOS management, the other for the data transfer. An AF_INET socket is set normally for the data transfer, considering the group address if the multicast is needed. All QOS requests, addressed by RSVP should use a nonblocking SOCK_DGRAM socket instantiated with the IPPROTO_RSVP protocol identifier. Then, one should invoke the WSAIoctl() primitive for any

RSVP call. This socket may serve the purpose of many RSVP sessions but it is not mandatory. No explicite link does exist between the data transfer socket and the RSVP one. Recall that the packet flow is identified by the "flowspec" and "filterspec" parameters.

The data structures employed by the WSAIoctl() function are defined in the "WS2RSVP.h" file and we use the programming guideline provided by the Intel PCRSVP for the primitives chain [9]. In the Solaris environment, client/server programs make use of the `rapi_lib` library. Also, the Sun Solstice Bandwidth Reservation Protocol is a good support when designing them [3, 22].

We present below the programming means for managing an RSVP session (using the C++ programming language). For the Winsock2 environment, it looks as follows:

```
// an example of Creating an RSVP socket
hSock = socket (AF_INET, SOCK_DGRAM, IPPROTO_RSVP);
// an example of registering
iRetVal = WSAIoctl(hSock, SIO_RSVP_REGISTER, &Session,
                   sizeof(Session), &ErrStruct,
                   sizeof(ErrStruct),
                   &dwBytesRet, NULL, NULL);
if (iRetVal != 0)
{// RSVP REGISTER failed
printf("RSVP Register failed. Winsock Error Code = %d
       RSVP Error Code = %d\n", WSAGetLastError(),
       ErrStruct.errCode);}
```

For the Solaris environment, the `rapi_session()` call creates and initialises an API session and returns a session handle for further use. After a successful `rapi_session()` call, the application may receive up-calls indicating events and errors.

```
rapi_sid_t rapi_session(struct sockaddr *
                        addr_destination, int protid,
                        0, rapi_event_rtn_t
                        rsvp_callback, void *event_arg,
                        int * errno) ;
```

After setting an RSVP session, the server program starts sending a PATH message. For the server programs only, in the Winsock2 environment, it looks as follows:

```
// an  example of Sender call
SENDER_DATA   Sender;
// Fill sender info
// Fill sender tspec
Sender.dataTTL = 0;    // sender IP TTL value,
use the default value
Sender.lpPolicy = NULL; // Policy information,
may be set to NULL
// RSVP_SENDER call
```

```
iRetVal = WSAIoctl (hSock, SIO_RSVP_SENDER,
                    &Sender, sizeof(Sender),
                    &ErrStruct, sizeof(ErrStruct),
                    &dwBytesRet, NULL, NULL);
if (iRetVal != 0)
{// RSVP SENDER failed
printf ("RSVP Sender failed. Winsock Error Code = %d RSVP
        Error Code = %d\n", WSAGetLastError(),
        ErrStruct.errCode);
}
```

In the Solaris environment, it looks like this:

```
int rapi_IS_tspec_init (rapi_tspec_t * new_sender_tspec,
                        u_char version, float32_t rate,
                        float32_t depth, float32_t peak,
                        uint32_t min_unit, uint32_t
                        max_unit);
```

This function initializes an Integrated Services Tspec object before calling the `rapi_sender()` function to request PATH message generation. It can be used by the data sender application requesting the generation of RSVP PATH messages.

```
int rapi_sender (rapi_si_t sid, int flags,
                 struct sockaddr * host,
                 rapi_filter_t * sender_template,
                 rapi_tspec_t * sender_tspec,
                 rapi_adspec_t * sender_adspec,
                 rapi_policy_t * sender_policy, int TTL) ;
```

An application that intends to send a flow of data must issue a `rapi_sender()` call. Thereby, it specifies the parameters of its data flow. The RSVP daemon uses this flowspec to create PATH messages for this flow. Repeated calls of the `rapi_sender()` function with different parameters simply change the flowspec.

To handle an RSVP session both clients and servers have to notify themselves of their interest. This can be done as follows, for both client and server programs. In the Winsock2 environment, to receive RSVP status notification an application must register its interest in asynchronous notifications by using WSAAsyncSelect or WSAEventSelect (consult the WinSock 2 documentation for more details). RSVP requires that an application register for `FD_QOS` event. Once an RSVP notification is received by the application it can be retrieved by an `RSVP_Retrieve call`.

```
iRetVal = WSAIoctl (hSock, SIO_RSVP_RETRIEVE, NULL,
                    0, &RsvpReturn, RSVP_RETURN_SIZE,
                    &dwBytesRet, NULL, NULL);
```

The `RsvpReturn.infoType` contains the event type as follows:

- INFO_PATH : PATH message arrived at the receiver, we can make a Reserve call now.
- INFO_PATH_TEAR : PATH_TEAR message arrived at the receiver.

RSVP SP removes any installed reservation and a RESV_CHANGE message may follow.

- INFO_PATH_ERR : PATH_ERR message received by the sender. We may have to make the sender call again with the modified parameters to rectify the problem.
- INFO_PATH_TIMEOUT : Receiver gets a PATH_TIMEOUT message when RSVP SP stops receiving PATH refreshes. RSVP SP removes any installed reservation and a RESV_CHANGE message may follow.
- INFO_RESV : RESV message arrived at sender indicating a new/changed reservation.
- INFO_RESV_CONFIRM : Receiver gets this message if the confmFlag was set when reserve call was made.
- INFO_RESV_CHANGE : Receiver may get a RESV_CHANGE message if a previously installed reservation was changed or removed as a result of PATH_TEAR message.
- INFO_RESV_TIMEOUT: Sender gets a RESV_TIMEOUT message when RSVP SP stops receiving RESV refreshes.
- INFO_RESV_ERR : Receiver gets a RESV_ERR message if a reservation request fails.
- default: Unknown message

In the Solaris environment, the `rsvp_svattente_msg()` function has been written to manage the RSVP messages that arrive. It makes use of the `rapi_getfd()`, `FD_SET()` and `FD_ISSET()` functions available in the `rapi_lib` library.

```
void rsvp_svattente_msg(rapi_sid_t sid,rapi_event
info_t rsvp_arg);
```

Each time an RSVP session is set, a Unix socket is created to allow the communication within an endsystem with the RSVP daemon. The `FD_SET` allows to add the file descritpor to the list of file descriptors upon which the select primitive performs. When an event occurs, the `FD_ISSET()` function determines the file descriptor related to the event. Then, RSVP messages can be processed as for the Winsock2 environment. When a client receives a PATH message, it can start the reservation.

For the client only, in the Winsock2 environment, the respective code is shown below.

```
// Examples of receiver call  (Reserve)
RESERVE_DATA Reserve;
RSVP_FLOWDESC flowdesc;
RSVP_FILTERSPEC rsvp_filtspec;
//Fill Reserve structure
// fill in rsvp_filtspec
// fill in flowdesc
iRetVal = WSAIoctl (hSock, SIO_RSVP_RESERVE, &Reserve,
                    sizeof(Reserve), &ErrStruct,
                    sizeof(ErrStruct),
                    &dwBytesRet, NULL, NULL);
```

```
if (iRetVal != 0)
{ // RSVP RESERVE failed
printf ("RSVP Reserve failed. Winsock Error Code = %d RSVP
        Error Code = %d\n", WSAGetLastError(),
        ErrStruct.errCode);
}
```

In the Solaris environment, the following function converts a single Tspec object received from a PATH message into an Integrated Services Guaranteed Quality of Service flowspec object before calling the `rapi_reserve()` function to request RESV message generation. It can be used by the data receiver application requesting RSVP reservation, also shown below.

```
int rapi_IS_fspec_G_init(rapi_tspec_t * old_Tspec,
                         rapi_adspec_t * old_Adspec,
                         rapi_flowspec_t * new_Flowspec,
                         float32_t g_rate, uint32_t slack);
int rapi_reserve(rapi_sid_t Sid, int flags,
                 struct sockaddr_in *Rhost,
                 rapi_styleid_t StyleId,
                 rapi_stylex_t *Style_ext,
                 rapi_policy_t *Rcvr_policy,
                 int FilterSpecNo,
                 rapi_filter_t *FilterSpec_list,
                 int FlowSpecNo,
                 rapi_flowspec_t *FlowSpec_list);
```

If FlowSpecNo is zero, the `rapi_reserve()` call will remove any current reservation for the specified session. Otherwise, the parameters depend upon the following styles: WildcardFilter, FixedFilter, SharedExplicit.

4. Real-Time Network Application Programming. The application is structured according to the Client/Server model. The two programs must interact with the protocol stack within their respective endsystems. In fact, RTP and RTCP protocols are not implemented in the system kernel. They are related to the application and must then be part of it.

On the contrary, RSVP must be present and configured at both endsystems and routers. The daemon network interface uses the Internet Protocol which requires a protocol number to dispatch transport level traffic to the right protocol. Raw sockets can be used to communicate with the IP kernel module. If the hosts do not support raw IP, the RSVP daemon uses a UDP (or TCP) encapsulated mode (ports number 1698 and 1699 for RSVP).

The functional description of the client/server programs can be independent of the application semantics, regarding only the real-time networking requirements.

4.1. The Server Program. The server program must at least involve four functions independently of the subject of the application, which are:

- RSVP handling and flow specification notification

- Inform the RTP module to start emitting
- RTP handling, preparing the data flow and transmitting
- RTCP handling, maintaining statistics and managing a client table of presence.

In general, the above functionalities must execute concurrently, using shared data and needing synchronisation mechanisms. To program them, we make use of the multithreading tools available in both Windows NT and Solaris environments. Shared variables and mutual exclusion are used to achieve the threads cooperation. In our framework, we implemented both the client and the server programs with three threads each.

The server program involves a main thread dealing with the human/machine interface and the RSVP handling. The two others concern RTP and RTCP handling.

The RTP handling thread first creates a socket, initialises the multicast joining the group, enables the socket reuse for clients and/or servers on the same host, deactivates the loopback avoiding the receipt of what is being sent, makes known the communication socket and finally loops on the effective communication. The steps before entering the communication can be viewed as a fetch part of the program.

The RTCP handling thread starts the fetch part (the only change is that the socket binding must use the RTP port+1 for the RTCP port). Then the RTCP processing waits for a client to register (`app_lsdes` packet receipt), to leave the session (`bye` packet) or treating statistics on the quality of the session (`rr` packet).

The RSVP thread communicates with the RSVP daemon within a machine. First, it starts an RSVP session with the RSVP daemon, presenting the interest as a sender by describing the data flow. The RSVP thread then waits for RSVP events. In the case of a reservation request, the RSVP thread informs the RTP thread of the highest bandwidth allocated to the application in order to adapt to the network. Otherwise, an error message allows the RTP thread to know that the PATH message did not reach the receivers.

4.2. The Client Program. The client program performs at least the three functions below:

- RSVP handling especially the bandwidth reservation
- RTP reception
- RTCP handling; the client informs the server when joining the group and when leaving it. It also sends periodically statistics packets upon the quality of the session.

For the same reasons as for the server program, three threads can be used.

The main thread involves the human/machine interface and the RSVP handling. It also creates the RTP and RTCP threads. RSVP handling establishes a session with the RSVP daemon, and waits for the RSVP PATH event. The reservation request can therefore be issued. If confirmation of the requested bandwidth is needed, the thread waits for it and informs the RTP module about the allocation status. Recall that a soft state of the reserved resources must be maintained and that periodic reservation messages are sent by the RSVP daemon while the RSVP session is open. The RSVP thread informs the RTP module of the success or failure of the periodic reservation requests, and finally closes the RSVP session when the application wishes to terminate.

The RTP handling thread is the same as the server's one. The RTCP handling thread starts the fetch part (the only change is that the socket binding must use the RTP port+1 for the RTCP port). Next the RTCP processing notifies about its interest in joining the group (emission of the `app_lsdes` packet). Then, it initialises the structures that will store the application flow statistics. Hence, it loops calculating the actual statistics it sends periodically, occupying less than 5% of the bandwidth or every 2.5 second.

When, the client program wishes to exit, the RTCP thread sends an RTCP `bye` packet before leaving.

5. Conclusion and Future Work. In this paper, we dealt with real-time network applications programming. We presented a protocol stack providing a real support to real-time applications. This stack involves protocols for:

- optimizing the network packet load generated by the applications,
- facing the network quality of access modifications,
- reserving the receivers required bandwidth and controlling the network packet admission.

We implemented a video server application in a TCP/IP campus environment. Of course, in order to fully guarantee the resource reservation mapping real-time constraints within an internetwork, all the routers must involve the IGMP and RSVP protocols. The RTP/RTCP protocols, for their part, provide time delivery concerns allowing the application to adapt its behaviour in order to meet the real-time requirements.

We discussed the application programming interface we defined and/or used in both the Sun Solaris and Microsoft Windows NT environments. We also gave guidelines on the structuring of the client/server programs with regard to communication considerations, independently of the application semantics.

The push based applications allow the receiver parts to specify their requirements as they know what they want and what they can "pay" for it. The RSVP protocol has been defined accordingly, as the receiver reservation initiation has no impact either on the source part or on the other receiver parts. Nevertheless, the experiments we dealt with pointed out some issues one should consider if one receiver reserves less bandwidth than the sender really uses. Traffic admission within the RSVP router managing the link sharing related to the low bandwidth reservation will have to discard packets according to a certain policy. The RTP received flow will be different from the emitted flow and then RTCP will have to notify packets loss. Two issues must be faced:

- Is the received flow still "playable"? That is to say that the admission control must be aware of all the flow types.
- How the sender should interpret the packet loss as it is not aware of the

reservation made by the receiver party?

The second issue obligates the RTCP part of a receiver to act according to the reserved resources and not to claim quality that is not paid for. The first issue, which is very important, will take advantage of the mixers/translators services RTP should provide [RFC1889]. Translators are RTP relays between high and low bandwidth links. As such, we think they must be present in all the RSVP routers in order to adapt the input flow (high bandwidth) to the resources granted on the low bandwidth, making the output flow understandable and comprehensible by the receiver. A translator forwards RTP packets with their synchronization source (SSRC) identifier intact. It may change the encoding of the data and thus the RTP payload type and timestamp, probably assigning new sequence numbers to the outgoing packets.

Future work concerns the enhancement of the presented protocol stack, integrating services more efficiently for the support of real-time network applications.

REFERENCES

[1] B. Boute *Multicast over RTP: En quête d'applications*, ENST, France, 1997.

[2] E. Crawley (Ed.), L. Berger, S. Berson, F. Baker, M. Borden, J. Krawczyk, *A Framework for Integrated Services and RSVP over ATM*, May 1998.

[3] B. Braden, D. Hoffman *An RSVP Application Programming Interface Version 5*, June 1997.

[4] *IP Multicast over ATM Point-to-Multipoint Virtual Circuits*, CISCO Systems Inc., `http://hq.svzserv.kemerovo.su`

[5] P. Dax, *L'internet et le groupware: Le multicast*, ENST, France, 1997, `http://www-inf.enst.fr/~ dax/confs/multicast/`

[6] C. Elsen, D. Mercier, *Multimedia sur internet. RFC 1889, 1890 le couple de protocoles RTP/RTCP*, `http://www.enic.fr/enic/exposesrio96/rtp`

[7] J.P. Gautier *Multimedia sur IP: protocoles RTP ET RSVP*, Journee UREC/CCR du 26 novembre 1996, `http://www.urec.cnrs.fr/xcast/index.html`

[8] J. Jason, *Developping RSVP-Enabled Firewalls*, Intel Corporation, 1997.

[9] *Intel PC RSVP version 1.0 beta (Expiration: December 31, 1998)* `http://www.developer.intel.com/ial/rsvp/`

[10] *Writing IP Multicast-enabled Applications*, The IP Multicast Initiative (IPMI), `http://www.ipmulticast.com/`

[11] *MBONE & Multicast*, `http://www.research.microsoft.com/barc/mbone/`

[12] *Multi Protocol over ATM*, ATM Forum, `http://www.itsi.disa.mil/atmf/`

[13] *Socket Programming (with explanations)*, Vijay Mukhi's Computer Institute, `http://www.neca.com/~ vmis`

[14] B. Quinn, *Internet Multicasting*, Dr Dobb's Journal, October 1997.

[15] B. Quinn, D. Shute, *Windows Sockets Network Programming*, Addison-Wesley, Reading, Mass, 1995.

[16] R. Braden, D. Clark, S. Shenker, *Integrated Services in the Internet Architecture: An Overview*, RFC 1633, IETF Audio-Video Transport Working Group, June 1994.

[17] H. Schulzrinne, S. Casner, R. Frederick, V. Jacobson, *RTP: A Transport Protocol for Real-Time Applications*, RFC 1889, IETF Network Working Group, January 1996.

[18] R. Braden, L. Zhang, S. Berson, S. Herzog, S. Jamin, *Resource ReSerVation Protocol (RSVP)*, RFC 2205, IETF Network Working Group, September 1997.

[19] L. Berger, T. O'Malley, em RSVP Extensions for IPSEC Data Flows, RFC 2207, IETF Network Working Group, September 1997.

[20] W.R. Stevens, *Unix Network Programming (2nd Edition)*, Prentice Hall, Upper Saddle River, NJ, 1998.

[21] *FAQ RTP*, http://www.cs.columbia.edu/~ hgs/rtp

[22] *SolsticeTM Bandwiddth Reservation Protocol v1.0*, Sun Microsystems, Inc., Palo Alto, Calif, 1998, http://www.sun.com/solstice/telecom/bandwidth

[23] *Winsock 2 Overview and Pointers*, http://www.sockets.com/winsock2.htm

SOFTWARE DEVELOPMENT AND VERIFICATION OF DYNAMIC REAL-TIME DISTRIBUTED SYSTEMS BASED ON THE RADIO BROADCAST PARADIGM

JAN VAN KATWIJK, RUUD DE ROOIJ, SYLVIA STUURMAN AND HANS TOETENEL*

Abstract. The combination of an increased power of computer systems and a marriage between computing and communication causes an enormous increase in the complexity of applications in almost all domains. This also applies to the real-time and the embedded domains, where onstruction of distributed applications is a major research area. In our research, we develop a framework for the systematic development of distributed real-time control applications. We emphasize the use of pragmatic sound approaches in the design steps of the development process, preferrably based on some common architectural style. For analyzing and validating critical elements of design and implementation, we emphasize the use of formalisms, however. Complexity of applications is such that for real verification and validation, proof or model-checking techniques are required. We use formalized abstraction as a technique for obtaining the appropriate templates from design and implementation. These abstractions are then dealt with in a model-checking and analysis tool set. In this paper we show some elements of our approach, in particular we describe the architectural style that we are using, the Radio Broadcast Paradigm, and we demonstrate the viability of our approach by showing a case study.

Key words. distributed computations, real-time computing, software verification, radio broadcast paradigm

1. Introduction. The continuously increasing power of cheap computers and the integration between computer systems and communication mechanisms both have an enormous impact on applications. Applications become more and more distributed, obviously in the areas of business computing, but also in technical and control domains.

From our perspective, measurement and control applications are interesting since they depend, perhaps stronger than other kinds of applications, on the notion of time and on the reliability of the underlying networked systems. In distributed environments, these notions are hard to control, which influences design and implementation of distributed control applications considerably.

Part of the additional care to be given to the design of distributed control applications is based on the uncertainty in the stability of the environment: message passing in a network may not take a constant amount of time, networks may break down or be altered dynamically. Development of an application therefore should take into account an accurate characterization of the execution attributes of the underlying infrastructure. Characterization of the underlying infrastructure, and indicating requirements on the infrastructure is therefore an integrated element in the development cycle of this kind of applications.

* Department of Mathematics and Informatics, Delft University of Technology, P.O.Box 356, 2600 AJ Delft, The Netherlands. E-mail: {J.vanKatwijk|R.DeRooij|S.Stuurman|W.J.Toetenel}@twi.tudelft.nl

The objective of our research is to establish a framework for the systematic development of distributed real-time control applications. In our approach, practical development starts with the selection of an architectural style and an architecture that will fit the needs of the application. The selected architecture is supported by technology implementing the functionality of the architectural components. Such designs are gradually transformed into program code through the coding phase of system development.

The design process is supported by design analysis and simulation feedback. Analysis provides data that enables a more precise verification effort to be done. A classical example in this respect is the validation of timing properties of a system. Standard schedulability analysis provides a technique for analyzing whether or not real-time requirements are met, under the assumption that accurate execution characteristics are available. Here testing and simulation can provide accurate timing data that together with an abstract representation of the process structure of the implementation form the basis for formal analysis and simulation.

In our approach, we use abstraction as a technique for deriving the appropriate templates from design and implementation as an input to formal verification (see Figure 1.1).

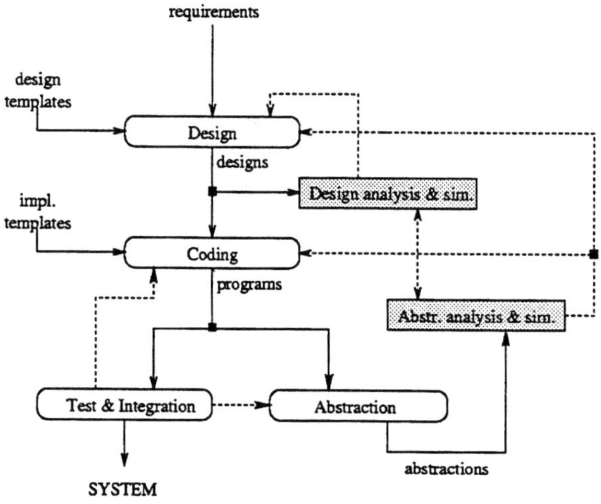

FIG. 1.1. *A Software Development Process*

In order for our approach to be successful, we need to be able to build models of the technology supporting the architectural models, to be used in validation of the architectural instances.

Analysis and verification can be addressed two ways. The classical way is that testing and analysis of implementations provide data on execution characteristics, after which the application is analyzed using this data. For many distributed applications this approach is not appropriate, simply because the application runs on different underlying systems with different characteristics.

However, an approach in which constraints on the architectural support mechanisms are derived, would be desirable. In such an approach, analysis of the application leads to a characterization of essential constraints in the underlying system that, when met, guarantee the application to operate correctly.

One of the key issues in our research is therefore to build models for both applications and underlying frameworks with which a qualitative and quantitative analysis of execution parameters and attributes in distributed real-time control systems is possible. In order to limit the scope of our research we use Java as our language of choice, and we use a radio broadcast model as basis for interprocess communication. For the latter, we developed a standardized implementation and a number of specification and analysis tools. Part of the research then focuses on the characterization of the radio broadcast model implementation with respect to applications running on it.

In this paper, we describe some elements of our development approach and discuss a (simplified) example of the analysis we pursue. The architecture we have chosen is the Radio Broadcast Paradigm (RBP), while the analysis technique used is parametric model-checking. In Section 2 we describe the RBP and briefly discuss its implementation in Java. In Section 3 we describe a case study, a distributed control application. In Section 4 we describe our analysis approach and the results of the application to a simplified model of the distributed control application. Finally, in Section 5, we summarize our results and describe our current work.

2. RBP and Its Implementation.

2.1. Subscription-based Communication. A subscription-based communication model abstracts from the physical communications structure by introducing communications "channels". A process interested in specific information "subscribes" to a channel. The real-world analogy to this action is tuning a radio to a certain frequency. After having subscribed to the channel, the process will receive all messages sent to the channel. Similarly, if a process wants to make information available to other processes, it can "publish" it on a channel, either an already existing one or a newly created one. In principle, the number of available channels is unlimited.

The properties described above make the subscription-based model appropriate for (data-dominated) embedded systems, which deal with a continuous information stream from the environment [3].

In most cases, the subscribers will be able to deal completely locally with the (temporary or permanent) absence of incoming messages. The fact that there are no hard-coded dependencies between processes opens the possibility for on-line change. Processes can be added, removed, and/or replaced without disturbing the information flow. The subscription paradigm thus provides a mechanism for very late binding.

2.2. Existing Models and Implementations. The subscription paradigm is a form of multi-cast communication, for which there are many implementations [5]. In this section, we briefly mention a number of existing implementations.

2.2.1. Splice. SPLICE (Subscription Paradigm for the Logical Interconnection of Concurrent Engines) is an implementation of the paradigm developed by Boasson [3] of Hollandse Signaal Apparaten. The main application area is embedded systems for command and control systems.

SPLICE extends the basic subscription-based communication model as described above, by providing a conceptual global data space. This data space is partitioned into data sorts (channels). Data sorts are typed; the structure of data elements (their fields and field types) must be specified before the data sort is used. In addition, it is possible to mark fields of the data sort as key fields. The global data space is a virtual one, it does not physically exist.

SPLICE provides a rich query mechanism so that applications can retrieve exactly the data they are interested in. In addition to queries, processes can put a filter on a local database. Whereas queries operate on the information already present in the local database, a filter is used to decide whether a newly received data item is stored in the database. Using filters enables a process to specify a more fine-grained selection of the information it wishes to process, and reduces the size of the local database.

SPLICE does not provide an operation to remove a data item from the global data space. Processes are allowed to remove items from their own local databases if they decide the specific data item is no longer needed, but a global remove-operation is not available.

2.2.2. JavaSpaces. JavaSpaces is a package of Java classes and interfaces, very recently developed by Sun Microsystems [11]. The package is meant to support the design of distributed applications using Java. At the moment of writing this article, only a beta version is available.

The two main concepts of JavaSpaces are "space" and "entry". The term "space" is used for the implementation of a JavaSpaces server. A space holds entries: typed groups of objects, expressed in a Java class. Three (atomic) operations are possible on entries:

- An entry may be *written* into a space. The result of this operation is a copy of the entry object, created in the space.
- An entry may be *read*, after which the space still holds the entry.
- An entry may be *taken*, after which the space no longer holds the entry.

With respect to the *read* and the *take* operations, JavaSpaces offers the possibility of matching against a template: entries in the space may be matched against an object that has some or all of its fields set to specific values (the template). The remaining fields act as wild-cards.

JavaSpaces offers still another kind of connection between clients of a space (or JavaSpaces server) and the space: clients may request a server to *notify* them, when an entry, matching a specific template, is written. Notification is done using a distributed event mechanism. This notify operation makes it possible to use the JavaSpaces package as an implementation of the subscription-based communication model.

Notifications may arrive in different orders on different clients, or may not arrive at all. The JavaSpaces server will make a "best effort" attempt to deliver the notification. The server will retry at least until the notifications request "lease" is expired. This "lease" is an amount of time, negotiated between the server and the client, during the request for notification. This concept of a lease is added to the JavaSpaces package to obtain more robustness, in case of failure of parts of a distributed application.

2.2.3. Other Implementations. A real-time publisher/subscriber model [12] was developed at Carnegie-Mellon as a basis for building replaceable software units. The emphasis is on real-time fault-tolerant systems. Next to the basic publish/subscribe model, a facility is provided to detect whether nodes in the network have failed, and when new nodes in the network have joined. The channels are therefore consistent to all publishers, i.e., all publishers on one channel will see the same subscribers at every time.

The Tibco Rendezvous Information Bus [14] is a commercial implementation of the subscription-based communication model. It is mainly intended for financial applications, such as for example the distribution of stock price information to dealer rooms. One of the interesting features is that when a process subscribes, it can leave part of the channel name unspecified. It will effectively be subscribed to all channels matching the given channel name.

The Java Shared Data Toolkit, a product of Sun Microsystems, is intended for collaborative interactive applications. It provides the concept of sessions which processes can join and leave dynamically. Within a session, processes can send messages to the other processes, as well as have the ability to create shared data structures. The JSDT can be used on top of a number of different communication mechanisms, such as sockets or Remote Method Invocation. Sun Microsystems offers JSDT and JavaSpaces as separate products intended for use in different application areas.

2.3. A Java Implementation of the Radio Broadcast Paradigm. In order to have a facility for doing experiments with the RBP and its implementation, we developed a library implementing the Radio Broadcast Paradigm [6]. Having a private implementation allows us to experiment with different implementation techniques and to instrument the library in order to obtain performance figures.

The library provides a Programming Interface (API), containing two Java classes and one Java interface (Figure 2.1).

An application that wishes to open a channel for publishing data, simply instantiates an object of class *Transmitter*, passing the name of the channel to the constructor.

To open a channel for receiving objects from a channel, the process instantiates an object of the class *Receiver*. The constructor of the *Receiver* class takes the channel name and an object which implements the *Listener* interface as its parameters. This *Listener* object is responsible for dealing with objects

```
public class Transmitter {
    public Transmitter(String channel);
    public void transmit(Object object);
    public void close();
}

public class Receiver {
    public Receiver(String channel, Listener listener);
    public void close();
}

public interface Listener {
    public void accept(Object object);
}
```

FIG. 2.1. *Public classes and methods in Radio Broadcast Paradigm library*

received from the channel (the concept of a *Listener* object is similar to the GUI call-back mechanism introduced in JDK 1.1). The only method which must be implemented by an object which implements the *Listener* interface, is the *accept*() method which is called whenever an object is received. It is up to the *Listener* object to handle the object.

The classes *Transmitter* and *Receiver*, and the interface *Listener*, are sufficient to build complete applications. The fact that *Transmitter* and *Receiver* objects may be on completely different machines is completely hidden from the programmer.

The need to define one's own classes implementing the *Listener* interface for even the most basic ways of handling incoming data is rather impractical. Therefore, the library contains a few *Listener* classes for simple processing tasks. They are summarized in Table 2.1.

StateListener	keeps last received object
QueueListener	places received objects in a queue
IndexListener	places incoming objects in a table indexed by a key value; new objects overwrite older objects with the same key
Filter	forwards received object to another Listener only if a specified predicate is valid
ClassListener	if incoming object is a class description in Java byte code format, this class is defined and t is linked dynamically with the Java virtual machine

TABLE 2.1
Listener classes

The behavior of *StateListeners*, *QueueListeners*, *IndexListeners* *Filters* is fairly intuitive. The *ClassListener* class is more complex, it opens up the possibility of dynamically updating the code in a running system. New parts of the software can be distributed in the architecture-neutral Java byte code format to all processes that have a *ClassListener* defined for a certain channel. The class will be defined and linked dynamically with the Java Virtual Machine in the receiving process. If the class contains any static initializers, these will be evaluated, thereby allowing a class to initialize itself, e.g., by starting a new thread. The *ClassListener* mechanism is similar to the on-demand loading of classes in Java-based web browsers. However, in our case, loading of classes is *push-based*. It is the transmitting side that decides if and when classes are to be sent. Since the usual Java dynamic class loading mechanisms are *pull-based*, missing class dependencies can be solved by loading the required class. In our case, missing class dependencies will cause the class defining and linking process to be suspended until the required class is received.

In the example given in Figure 2.2, we show how a *ClassListener* object is used to transfer actual byte code to another object after which the transferred code is executed. In this example, program *HelloProducer* constructs a *ClassDefinition* object containing the byte code for class *HelloPrinter*. *HelloPrinter* is a class that contains a static initializer which will cause the string "Hello, World" to be printed on the screen. *HelloConsumer* is a simple program which only defines a *ClassListener* and then waits indefinitely.

On execution, the code for the class *HelloPrinter* is sent to the *ClassListener* that is contained in objects of the class *HelloConsumer*, and the text "Hello, World" will be printed on the screen.

Even though the *transmit*() method takes an *Object* as parameter, only objects which directly or indirectly implement the interface *Serializable* can be transmitted. Objects not implementing this interface are silently discarded. The *Serializable* interface was introduced in Java 1.1 as part of the Object Serialization API. Our implementation of the Radio Broadcast Paradigm library uses these features internally to convert objects to byte arrays before passing them on to receivers. Even when sending objects within a single Java Virtual Machine, they are serialized and de-serialized.

Consistent serialization has the interesting consequence that any data structure that is transmitted, will become a "deep copy" when received. Consider for example a vector of objects. Applying the *clone*() method to such a vector will yield a copy of the vector, however, any reference in the vector refers to the same objects as the references in the original vector. However, sending and receiving the vector through the Radio Broadcast Paradigm library will yield a vector with references to *copies* of the elements of the original vector. This is important when considering the fact that one of the purposes of the Radio Broadcast Paradigm is to decouple processes as much as possible from each other.

2.4. Design Considerations. It is important to realize that the channels provided by the library are *unreliable*. Even though the library makes effort to

```
public class HelloPrinter {
  static { System.out.println("Hello, world"); }
}

class HelloProducer {
  public static void main(String[] args) {
    try {
       Object o =
        new ClassDefinition(Class.forName("HelloPrinter"));
       new Transmitter("hello").transmit(o);
    } catch (java.io.IOException e) { }
  }
}

class HelloConsumer {
  public static void main(String[] args) {
    new Receiver("hello", new ClassListener());
    pause(); // Wait indefinitely
  }
}
```

FIG. 2.2. *A simple example in which Java byte code is transferred*

get objects from transmitters to receivers, delivery of objects is not guaranteed. Similarly, the order in which objects are received is not guaranteed. Even though two objects sent sequentially by the same transmitter will be received in the same order by all receivers, two objects sent by different transmitters may be received in different orders by different receivers. An application cannot make any assumption about such issues.

Besides platform-dependent native-code solutions, the only form of communication between different Java virtual machines is the use of TCP/IP-based socket communication. Other high-level protocols, such as Java's Remote Method Invocation are built on top of this. Our implementation also uses TCP/IP sockets for communication between *Transmitters* and *Receivers* located in different Java virtual machines.

The implementation uses one "server" process for each machine in the network on which processes that use the subscription communications are run. Even on a single non-networked host, this server process is still necessary to provide the communications between several processes running concurrently on this machine. Figure 2.3 illustrates the possible communication paths; the "clients" in this figure are Java virtual machines which execute programs that use the subscription facilities.

Servers periodically send broadcast messages on the network, allowing other servers to locate each other without using (static) configuration files. It furthermore allows servers to detect when other servers have crashed (i.e., the absence of messages for a longer period of time).

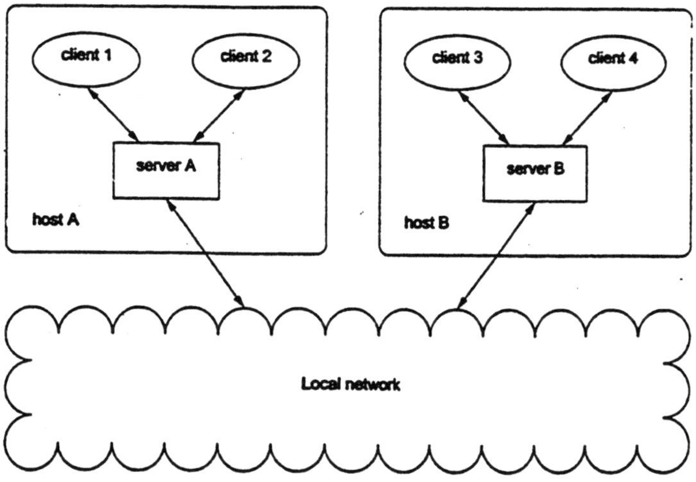

FIG. 2.3. *Communication between clients and servers*

For exchanging actual data over channels, server-to-server UDP messages are sent. The use of UDP, a datagram-oriented protocol, rather than the reliable TCP protocol is based on the assumption [3] that most embedded systems deal with a continuous stream of data from the environment, and that the environment serves as a back-up for occasionally missing a data item. Since TCP is a reliable stream-oriented protocol, the operating system will guarantee that all messages are delivered in the right order. If TCP was used, a packet dropped by the network would cause the data stream to stall until the dropped packet has been re-sent.

Clients communicate with servers using TCP rather than UDP, since using UDP, would have no advantage here. Communication between processes on a single host is always reliable, so the previous scenario in which a missed message causes a stall will not occur.

Periodically, the servers will communicate among each other, and to the clients attached to them, the set of channel names for which their clients have defined *Receiver* objects. Availability of this information minimizes the amount of data exchanged between servers and clients, and among servers.

A class diagram of the client-side library of the Radio Broadcast Paradigm implementation is shown in Figure 2.4. In this figure we show the *Transmitter*, *Receiver* and *Listener* classes. The *Transmitter* and *Receiver* objects contain a reference to the *Channel* object corresponding to the channel they are attached to.

For each channel name, a *channel* object exists. The mapping between channel names and *Channel* objects is maintained by a (single) *Registry* object. Finally, the *Forwarder* class, which is also a singleton, is responsible for communication with the server. It multiplexes and de-multiplexes incoming and outgoing data and control messages to a single TCP/IP connection.

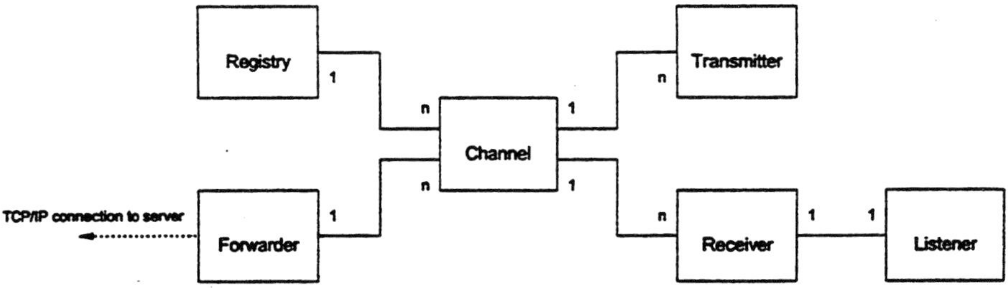

FIG. 2.4. *Class diagram of client-side library*

The server program contains a single "manager" object, and two objects for each connection to the server. These objects handle the incoming and outgoing data stream, respectively. The manager object keeps a table which contains the information on which channels are to be forwarded to which connections. In addition, there is a separate thread which periodically broadcasts to the network to discover the presence of other servers on the network. If a new server is found, a new connection is set up.

The use of Java provides a high degree of portability, the same Java code is used on MS Windows 95, MS Windows 98, MS Windows NT, several Linux versions, and Sun Solaris.

3. Controlling through Subscription: A Case Study.

3.1. Problem Description. Rotterdam is the world largest harbor. One of the largest container terminals in Rotterdam's harbor is fully automated. Cranes are used to carry the containers from a ship onto a lorry or from a lorry to a ship, from lorry onto stacks or onto a train or from trains or stacks onto a lorry.

The terminal employs a system of unmanned, automated vehicles transporting containers. The current system is running for several years now, and it is near its limitations. In a next-generation system, the number of lorries that can be handled has to increase dramatically, while the system should furthermore be able to handle lorries with different characteristics. Finally, traffic will be extended to include drives between terminals. There is no doubt that the complexity of the system will increase dramatically.

In order to get a good understanding of the problems involved in controlling the handling of these large amounts of containers, a prototype simulator/controller is being developed that is being used as a test-bed for a variety of implementation issues. The test-bed is based on control being distributed where each vehicle has its own controller dictating its behavior. The main reason for this design choice is that a distribution model conceptually fits perfectly to the situation of unmanned vehicles moving around. In practice, we will have to evaluate performance before deciding whether central or distributed control is more effective. Our implementation of the test-bed is using the earlier mentioned implementation of the RBP. The approach taken in our study was motivated by our cooperation with another group that is building a similar prototype using a centralized control approach, using called hierarchical semaphores [9] as controlling devices.

3.2. Requirements and Design Decisions. The current lorry handling system is able to handle a few dozen cranes and lorries. The system modeled through our test-bed should be usable for larger systems, systems with e.g. 1000 lorries rather than the 50, being served currently.

It is obvious that the new system will have to be able to handle changes in the number of lorries that are being dealt with during operation, however, the system also has to take into account the addition of lorries with different kinds of behavior. Main requirements for a solution are therefore:

scalability with respect to the number of lorries and the number of movements,

flexibility with respect to changes in the number of lorries and the behavioral patterns of the various vehicles operating on the terrain.

For this paper, it is assumed that a separate planner system exists that provides each vehicle with a plan: a function mapping the time to the position the vehicle should be (or should have been) at that moment. A complete plan provides information on where to collect the container, how to drive over the area and where to deliver the container.

In the design of a system based on an RBP, one must keep in mind that there is no guarantee that data will arrive, other then sending some precious data twice or more times. However, in a case like this, the loss of a single message is no disaster: the receiving processes temporarily use information slightly older than it should be.

3.3. Outline of the Control System. The control system we designed for our case study is discussed in detail in [13]. In this paper we briefly outline the ideas and the structure of the implementation.

The overall guiding principle in addressing the issue is separation of concerns. Separation of concerns on control is obtained by modeling a controlling process for each vehicle in the area, and by letting each controlling process be responsible for the control decisions for the movements of the associated vehicle. In order to do so, each vehicle controlling process needs a consistent view on the area it is in.

The system is built such that a vehicle control process can deduce a sequence of places that it will pass from its given plan. Essential in the model is that the process knows the planned position for the vehicle at any time. Furthermore, it knows the execution attributes of the vehicle it controls, such as the actual position, the velocity and the driving characteristics.

Vehicle control processes send their short-term plans (the part of the detail plan that should be followed in the immediate future) periodically through a channel. Such processes furthermore listen to the short-term plans of other vehicles and evaluate possible collisions. In order to obtain a reasonable behavior of the vehicles, each vehicle obeys a set of traffic rules, and knows the traffic rules of all other vehicles. Traffic rules can be as easy as:

- *the lorry with the lowest order number has precedence* or
- *the lorry that is in the greatest hurry has precedence*

or as complex as *a vehicle coming from right has precedence, unless the vehicle from left is delayed more than the vehicle from coming right.*

Under the assumption that any vehicle has a consistent view on the area, application of valid traffic rules allows a control process to take a decision on whether to continue, to stop or to alter the velocity in the presence of other vehicles.

We realize that in order for a lorry to take a decision, having a consistent view on the *whole* area is an overshoot. What is required is a consistent view of the direct environment of the lorry. Therefore, the area in which the vehicles move is partitioned in regions: a grid of for instance 10 by 10 coordinated points. To each region one particular channel is associated. A vehicle sends its short-term plan through the channel, associated with the region it is positioned in; it listens to the same region channel, and to the channels of the eight regions surrounding this region as well. Scalability is handled through this approach.

In Figure 3.1 we show two vehicles in different regions. Each sends (solid line) to the channel associated to the region it is positioned in. All vehicles in a given region listen to the same channel, and to the channels associated to the eight regions around it. Note that it is possible that more than just one vehicle drives around in one region.

Furthermore, to each region a region process is associated, that collects data of the vehicles driving in the region. It creates a summary which is sent through the "image channel", available for our visualization system. The visualizer can also be used to zoom in to one region, by telling it to listen to the associated channel. The short-term plans of the vehicles in that region may be inspected.

The traffic rules are a part of each vehicle process. Every vehicle process listens to a "rules" channel, which may be used to send a new version of these traffic rules. To avoid version conflicts, vehicles send the version number of the rules they use, together with their short-term plan. In case of a version conflict, a default rule is used by both parties.

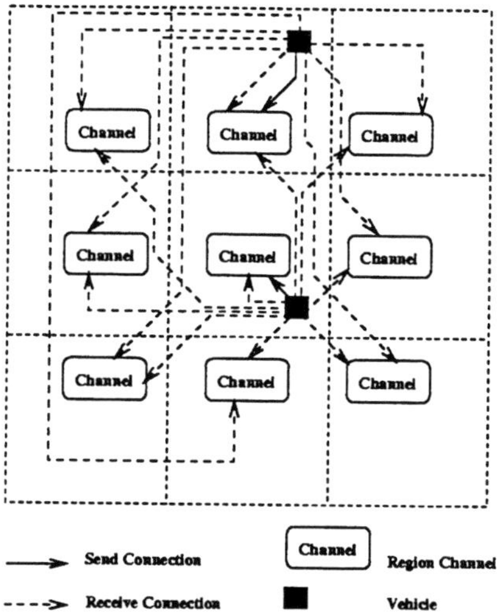

FIG. 3.1. *Vehicles in regions*

3.4. Implementation. The controller is built using the RBP library, that was discussed in Section 2.3. In Figure 3.2 we show the internal view of a vehicle process. In this figure, active (threaded) objects are represented by a rounded box, while sharp-edged boxes denote threadless objects.

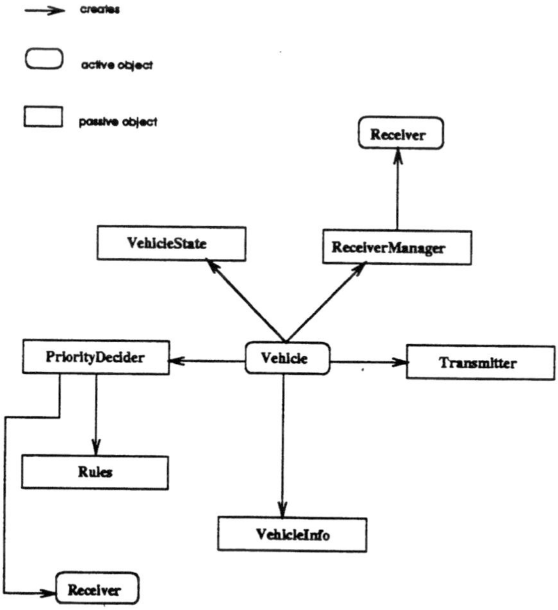

FIG. 3.2. *Objects in the Vehicle Process*

The vehicle process performs a loop:

- The *VehicleState* object is asked to construct an updated *VehicleInfo* object. This object contains relevant position information such as the vehicle identity, the speed and the current position of the vehicle, and the short-term plan of the vehicle. Furthermore, it contains the current version of the traffic rules.
- The *Transmitter* object is asked to transmit the newly created *VehicleInfo* object.
- In the meantime, the *Receiver* objects, that are connected to the *ReceiverManager* object listen for information from other vehicles. The *ReceiverManager* object is responsible for the choice of the channels to listen to. It selects these channels based on the position of the vehicle.
- Once every few time units, the *PriorityDecider* is asked to compute the next position the vehicle will drive to. This is based on the information gathered from the local environment and - obviously - on the traffic rules. The *VehicleState* object is updated.
- The traffic rules themselves may be updated when a new class definition is sent through the *Rules* channel.

4. Analysis of the Case Study.

4.1. Our Approach to Abstraction and Verification. As stated in the introduction of the paper, analysis and verification should provide feedback on the design and implementation of real-time distributed control systems. Our focus is on analyzing applications and deriving bounds for the execution parameters of the underlying system, i.e., the RBP implementation in our case. The technique we use for this kind of analysis is model-checking.

Model checking is becoming more and more part of the development process for hardware and software products. Companies like Intel and Lucent are using model-checking in their development processes and are even developing their own model-checkers. Model-checkers customized for hardware design are becoming commercially available [10]. Integration of model-checking in software development processes is not yet that far developed. There is, however, an increasing number of successful applications within the software industry, but it will take some time before it matches with the applications in the hardware sector.

The computational model that is generally used in the software case is (a variant of) the finite state automaton. The basic model of a finite state automaton provides only a basis for control abstraction. As the model was more widely used, constructions were added that enable the specification of data values and data transformation. To be of any use in the field of real-time systems, time and synchronization were added.

We designed a notation, eXtended Timed Graphs [2], an automaton-based formalism [1] with extensions in the area of data specification and a general form of control semantics. The primary use of the notation is as input notation for our model-checker [15].

The XTG notation is *not* meant to be a modeling language in itself. Other, better suited, modeling languages exist that focus more strongly on the various aspects of system and software design such as composition and decomposition, reuse, object-orientation, etc.

XTG is designed particularly for use as a verification language, it is supported by a more human-oriented specification language ATL, the Abstract Thread Language [16]. An ATL specification can be translated into XTG's. Such XTG's can be fed into the model-checker. In our approach, designs and implementations are abstracted into ATL specifications, that are fed into the model-checker.

Syntax and semantics of the behavioral constructions in ATL are based on C and Java. Furthermore, ATL supports a simple communications model which is loosely based on the subscription paradigm [3, 6]. Communication takes place along "channels". To send information on a channel, the send-operation is used, with the syntax "channelname.send(value)". To receive information from a channel, one defines a receiver thread. A receiver thread declaration consists of the receiver name, the variable which is used to store the value received from the channel, and a statement sequence to be executed every time the send-operation is invoked by some thread. A send-operation will not block until the receiver thread is ready to accept the communicated value. If a receiver thread is not idling, the value to be sent by the send-statement will be lost.

XTG and ATL share a single property specification language, a temporal logic based on CTL (Computation Tree Logic) [4] and TCTL (Timed CTL) [8]. The usage of these logics is strongly connected with the application of model-checking verification. TCTL variants are real-time extensions of CTL. These extensions either augment temporal operators with time bounds, or use reset quantifiers.

The core syntax of CTL defines two temporal operators, AU and EU. The formula $(\phi_1 AU \phi_2)$ is satisfied in a state if for all computation paths starting from that state, a state which satisfies ϕ_2 is encountered, and until that time ϕ_1 is satisfied. $(\phi_1 EU \phi_2)$ is satisfied if there is at least one such computation path. Derived operators are: $EF\phi$ (there is path on which there is state satisfying ϕ), $EG\phi$ (there is a path of which every state satisfies ϕ), $AF\phi$ (on all paths there is some state satisfying ϕ), and $AG\phi$ (on all paths every state satisfies ϕ).

Our CTL variant supports two types of atomic properties: boolean expressions over values of variables and clocks of both the system and the property, and location expressions. The latter take the form $g@l$, which expresses the fact that the graph g of the system is currently at location l.

To address resetting quantifiers, we use a technique found in other TCLT's, which consists of modeling the reset quantifier by assignments to specification clocks and variables. As an example, in our CTL variant (referred to as $\mathrm{CTL}_{\mathrm{XTG}}$ or simply CTL),

$$z := 0.AF(p \wedge z \leq 10)$$

expresses that p will always become true some time within ten time-units. A secondary benefit from this approach is that we can use symbolic constants in our property formulae (as suggested in [7]). Consider for example, the CTL formula

$$AG(t := count.AF(count = t + 1))$$

in which *count* is a system variable and t is property specification variable.

4.2. A Model of the Controller. The correctness of operation of the controller we discussed in Section 3.3 does also depend on the behavior of the underlying RBP implementation. As discussed in Section 1, we therefore should model the behavior of the controller implementation, identify the dependencies on the underlying implementation and derive bounds for the various parameter values. In this section, we demonstrate the usefulness of such analysis using a highly simplified version of the autonomous vehicle system as described in Section 3. In the simplified scenario discussed here, we take only two vehicles into account. These vehicles drive in a straight line towards each other as shown schematically in Figure 4.1.

Each vehicle maintains two positions, its own and the other one's, both represented by a simple integer value. It is assumed that the vehicle's own position is accurate, the position it believes the other vehicle has, is based on the information it received.

FIG. 4.1. *Scenario of the simplified model*

Even though this model is an oversimplification of the original system, it contains the essential elements: vehicles publishing their own position, and making decisions based on received information. The communications model is unreliable, in the sense that a message will be lost when a receiver is not listening, e.g. since it is busy processing a previous message.

In the ATL specification each of the two vehicles is modeled by means of a controlling process and a receiver process. The controlling process periodically sends the vehicle's position to the receiver process of the other vehicle. The controlling process of a vehicle retrieves the (assumed) position of the other vehicle from a variable shared with the receiver process. Figure 4.2 shows the code of the controlling process and the receiver of one of the vehicles. The code for the other vehicle (defining the position variable $p2$) is similar and is omitted here.

```
// Vehicle1's position
int p1 = Vehicle1Initial;
// Vehicle1's idea of Vehicle2's position
int q1 = Vehicle2Initial;
// Controlling process for Vehicle1
process Vehicle1 {
   forever {
      if (p1 >= RegionLeft && p1 <= RegionRight)
         plan1.send(p1+1);
         sleep(VehicleDelay);
      if ((q1-p1) > Distance || (p1-q1) > Distance)
         p1++;
   }
}
// Receiver process in vehicle 1
// receives position from Vehicle2
receiver plan2(int buffer) {
   sleep(ReceiverDelay);
   q1 = buffer;
}
```

FIG. 4.2. *ATL code of the vehicle*

Vehicle1Initial	0
RegionLeft	3
RegionRight	12
Vehicle2Initial	15
Distance	2
VehicleDelay	4
ReceiverDelay	7

FIG. 4.3. *Constants used in experiments*

4.3. Analysis of the Model. In our experiments we are interested in the the safety property "the two vehicles will never collide" and under which parameter values, i.e. indicating execution attributes of the underlying RBP implementation, the property holds. The non-collision property is expressed as `AG p1 != p2`. A vehicle might collide with the other one if the perceived position of the other vehicle differs sufficiently from the actual position of that vehicle. Such an inconsistent view might be obtained when processing of the received positions is too slow. Several verification experiments were performed based on the above model.

Verification of the non-collision property In a first experiment, we verified the safety property for a given set of constant values. The chosen values for the constants are shown in Table 4.3. As can be derived from the ATL description of the vehicle, *Vehicle1Initial* and *Vehicle2Initial* indicate the initial positions of the vehicles. *RegionLeft* and *RegionRight* indicate the region, *Distance* indicates the required minimum distance between the two vehicles, *VehicleDelay* indicates the time between two iterations of the *Vehicle* processes and *ReceiverDelay* indicates the receiver delay. The safety property turns out to hold.

Deriving the communications region In a second experiment we derived the smallest communications region possible for which no collision will occur. When the region is too small, the vehicles will not communicate their position fast enough to each other to allow a reaction. If

RegionLeft is made a parameter, the safety property is shown to be satisfied when RegionLeft ≤ 6. In the same way, the bound RegionRight $\geq$ 9 was derived.

Deriving upper-bounds for parameter values A third experiment was aimed to derive bounds on the various delays in the vehicle program. First, we determined an upper bound on the ReceiverDelay. Too high a value for the ReceiverDelay will cause the vehicles to collide, as they will not have a correct idea of the position of the other vehicle. Except for the value of ReceiverDelay, we used the same constant values as in Table 4.3. The safety property is satisfied for ReceiverDelay ≤ 7.

A similar (fourth) experiment was performed for the value of VehicleDelay. To ensure that the verification process ended, we needed to impose an upper-bound on the value of VehicleDelay, by replacing the statement

```
delay(VehicleDelay);
```

by

```
if (VehicleDelay < VehicleDelayMax)
    delay(VehicleDelay);
else
    delay(VehicleDelayMax);
```

where VehicleDelayMax is an appropriately chosen constant. After this modification, the property is satisfied for VehicleDelay ≥ 4.

Deriving dependencies between parameters In the fifth experiment, we took two parameters, VehicleDelay and ReceiverDelay. The values, derived by our model-checker PMC, for which the safety property is satisfied, are shown as the shaded area in Figure 4.4. In this experiment, we limited the values of VehicleDelay to the range from 0 to the value of VehicleDelayMax equal 10. The relationship between VehicleDelay and ReceiverDelay approximates a linear relation described by: ReceiverDelay $< 2 \times$ VehicleDelay. As the delay value in the vehicle controlling process gets longer, the communications layer is allowed to have a longer latency. The coefficient of 2 can be explained by the value of Distance (the minimal distance vehicles will try to keep between them). Changing the value of Distance, changes the coefficient as well.

Finally, (sixth experiment) we considered independent delays of both receivers. In Figure 4.5, we show the values of ReceiverDelay1 and ReceiverDelay2 for which the vehicles will not collide. From this figure, it can be seen that a longer communications latency in one direction can be compensated by a shorter delay in the other direction. This result shows a relationship which can not be described by an approximation of a linear relation. This can be explained by realizing that the vehicle controller process "samples" the position of the other vehicle at regular intervals of VehicleDelay. Changing the value of VehicleDelay will change the size of the "blocks" in the figure, although the shape will be similar.

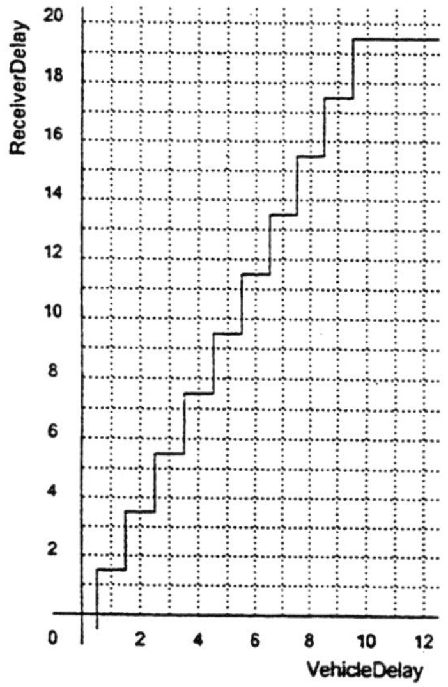

FIG. 4.4. *Verification result using* `VehicleDelay` *and* `ReceiverDelay` *as parameter; shaded area shows were property is satisfied*

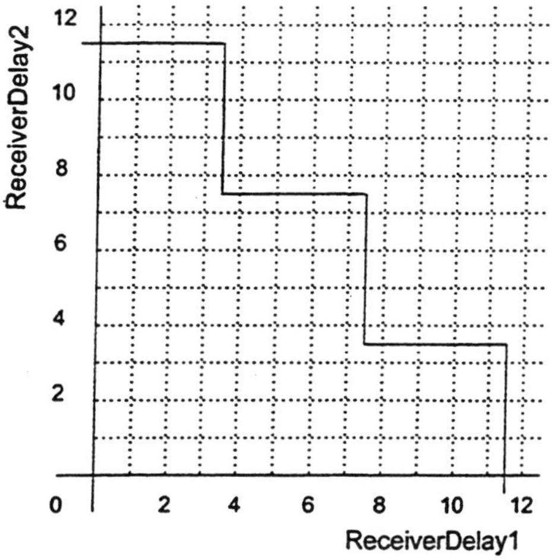

FIG. 4.5. *Verification result using* `ReceiverDelay1` *and* `ReceiverDelay2` *as parameter; shaded area shows were property is satisfied.*

Results. In Figure 4.6 the results of the verification experiments described above are presented. The objective of these experiments is to demonstrate the use of our tool-set for the (formal) derivation of values for which the required property holds. The parameter values themselves denote execution attributes of the underlying system. The result indicates the ranges for the values of the various attributes such that the property is guaranteed to hold.

#	Property	Parameters	Result
1	AG p1 != p2	—	positive
2	AG p1 != p2	RegionLeft	RegionLeft ≤ 6
	AG p1 != p2	RegionRight	RegionRight ≥ 9
3	AG p1 != p2	ReceiverDelay	ReceiverDelay ≤ 7
4	AG p1 != p2	VehicleDelay	VehicleDelay ≥ 4
5	AG p1 != p2	ReceiverDelay, VehicleDelay	Figure 4.4
6	AG p1 != p2	ReceiverDelay1, ReceiverDelay 2	Figure 4.5

FIG. 4.6. *Verification results*

4.4. Running the Model. The next step, obviously is to investigate under which conditions the underlying system has as its execution attributes values within the ranges specified above. In order to get some feeling of the results obtained analytically, we performed a series of experiments with the same system that was used a basis for analysis. The system simulated (and controlled) the behavior of two vehicles.

One vehicle had as its mission to drive from a point (0, 0) to the point (30, 0), the other had to drive the opposite way, both with a step-size 1. The experiments were done three times:

- once with both vehicles running on a Linux system,
- once with both vehicles running on a Windows NT system,
- once with one vehicle running on the Linux system, and the other on the NT system.

In all cases the simulation was checked for collision between the vehicles.

Varied parameter The parameter that was varied in the experiment, was the cycle-time of the vehicles. This cycle-time determines the *vehicledelay*, which amounts to the cycle-time plus 5 milliseconds.

Measured parameter The parameter that was measured was *ReceiverDelay* (the time between the moment a message is sent, and the moment it is received), in relation to the occurrence of collisions.

Default cycle-time of the vehicles was set to one second, meaning that each second, a vehicle checks the data it did receive giving information on the position of the other vehicle, and it computes its next step based on those data. Measurement shows that the time needed for the computation is approximately 5 milliseconds (on both systems). The actual cycle-time is therefore 1005 milliseconds, the measured *ReceiverDelay* showed to vary between 0 and 12 milliseconds, with consistent results in all three experiments. With these values for *cycletime* and *ReceiverDelay*, simulation showed that the vehicles always detect each other in time, and no collision occurs.

Varying the cycle-time gives consistent results. The measured *ReceiverDelay* varies between the same values, whether both vehicles are run on the Linux system, on the NT system, or both on a different machine. The results are presented in Figure 4.7.

Cycle-Time	ReceiverDelay	Detect on Time
1000	0-12	yes
5	5400-6600	no
100	2900-3800	no
300	500-600	sometimes
350	250-360	yes
500	170-370	yes

FIG. 4.7. *Results of the experiment*

It shows that a shorter *cycletime* results in a longer *ReceiverDelay*. For our network (where the *ReceiverDelay* does not depend on whether the vehicles run on different systems or on the same system), the critical value of the *cycletime* appears to be about 300 milliseconds: as long as the value of *cycletime* is larger, collisions are avoided. When shorter *cycletime*'s are chosen, collisions almost certainly will take place.

These results are consistent with what was derived from the results of the verification experiment, summarized in Figure 4.4. When *ReceiverDelay* becomes larger than 8 (twice 4), collisions cannot be avoided.

5. Conclusions and Further Work. In this study we introduced our approach to software development of dynamic real-time distributed systems based on complementary use of experimentation, abstraction and verification. The focus of our study was on a particular approach to model the middleware between distributed control applications and the underlying network structure, the Radio Broadcast Paradigm (RBP).

We created a test-bed for analyzing applications using our RBP through a Java implementation and experimented the RBP on an industrial case study. Abstraction of the Java implementation into a formal abstract language and the translation of the resulting representation into a modeling language for parametric verification enabled the derivation of constraints on the underlying execution environment. Our combined approach thus provides a sophisticated framework for the development of evolving distributed real-time systems.

Our experiments show that the approach is viable, the results of our experiments were very encouraging, although scaling is an issue. When more vehicles are involved, experiments based on model-checker predictions are more complex and the model-checking itself requires far more resources. One practical issue to be addressed is visualization of results, as more variables depend on each other, visual representations of the dependencies become complex.

Current validation runs were done on a large Linux machine, but could have been done on any PC. Our current experiments involve larger control configurations (over a dozen vehicles involved) than given here, and verification runs require somewhat more memory than available on an ordinary PC. However, due to the symmetry in the ATL specification, the amount of memory for model-checking in the complete verification remains within limits. The models provide useful insight in further optimizations in the model-checker.

Our current work consists of optimizing the model-checker, and developing robust translators for design notations like UML, Java and C languages into ATL specifications.

REFERENCES

[1] R. Alur and D. Dill, The Theory of Timed Automata, LNCS, Vol. 600, pp. 45–73, Springer-Verlag, Berlin, 1991.

[2] M. Ammerlaan, R. Lutje-Spelberg, and W. Toetenel, XTG – An Engineering Approach to Modelling and Analysis of Real-Time Systems, *Proceedings of the 10th Euromicro Workshop on Real-Time Systems*, pp. 88–97. IEEE Computer Society Press, 1998.

[3] M. BOASSON, Subscription as a Model for the Architecture of Embedded Systems, *Proceedings of the 2nd International Conference on Engineering of Complex Computer Systems*, pp. 130–133, IEEE Computer Society Press, 1996.

[4] E. CLARKE, E. EMERSON, AND A. SISTLA, Automatic Verification of Finite-State Concurrent Systems Using Temporal Logic Specifications, *ACM TOPLAS*, 8(2):244–263, 1986.

[5] G. COULOURIS, J. DOLLIMORE, AND T. KINDBERG, *Distributed Systems: Concepts and Design*. Second Edition, Addison-Wesley, Reading, Mass., 1994.

[6] R. C. M. DE ROOIJ, Subscription-Based Communication for Distributed Embedded Java Applications, *Proceedings of the Fourth Annual Conf. of the Advanced School for Computing and Imaging*, Lommel, Belgium, June 1998.

[7] T. HENZINGER, The Theory of Hybrid Automata, *LICS'96*, pp. 278–292, IEEE Computer Society Press, 1996.

[8] T. HENZINGER, X. NICOLLIN, J. SIFAKIS, AND S. YOVINE, Symbolic Model Checking for Real-Time Systems, *Information and Computation*, 111:193–244, 1994.

[9] J.J.M.EVERS, Ditrans, toekomst gericht gautomatiseerd containertransport. Technical Report TRAIL Studies nr 94/4, Delft University of Technology, 1994, ISBN 90-5584-004-1.

[10] R. KURSHAN, Formal Verification in a Commercial Setting, *Proceedings of the Design Automation Conference*, 1997.

[11] SUN MICROSYSTEMS, The JavaSpaces Specification, 1998, `http://www.javasoft.com/products/javaspaces/specs/js.pdf`

[12] R. RAJKUMAR AND M. GAGLIARDI, High Availability in the Real-Time Publisher/Subscriber Interprocess Cmmunication Model, *Proceedings 17th IEEE Real-Time Systems Symposium*, pp. 136–141, Washington, DC, Dec. 1996, IEEE Computer Society Press.

[13] S. STUURMAN AND J. VAN KATWIJK, On-line Change Mechanisms: the Software Architectural Level, *Proc. Sixth International Symposium on the Foundations of Software Engineering*, Orlando, Florida, November 1998, pp. 80–86, ACM.

[14] TIBCO, TIB/Rendezvous - White Paper, 1997, `http://www.rv.tibco.com/rvwhitepaper.html`.

[15] `http://tvs.twi.tudelft.nl`

[16] J. VAN KATWIJK, R. DE ROOIJ, AND W. TOETENEL, ATL Language Definition. Technical Report (to appear), Delft University of Technology, Faculty of Information Technology and Systems, 1999.

ON THE DISTRIBUTION OF CONTROL FUNCTIONS IN NEW-GENERATION ON-BOARD EMBEDDED REAL-TIME SYSTEMS

TULLIO VARDANEGA*

Abstract. The opening of the space business to the commercial market causes the cost and criticality of the on-board system to shift towards the payload component that delivers the value-added of the mission. As the cost of the payload increases, every effort is made to reduce the cost of the other elements of the spacecraft. The integration of the traditional on-board real-time control functions into a single platform component, denominated 'spacecraft bus', is one of the main effects of this cost-reduction effort. The new scenario is likely to require the allocation of additional real-time control functions to payload components. The immediate consequence of this phenomenon is the distribution of on-board services across the spacecraft. In earlier work we have presented an engineering approach to the construction of the real-time software embedded on-board integrated platform components. In this paper, we extend that approach to address the future scenario in which real-time control functions may be distributed across multiple processing nodes in the system.

Key words. fixed-priority preemptive scheduling, scheduling analysis, worst-case response time, end-to-end delivery time, holistic dependence, telecommand packets, telemetry packets, on-board data handling bus

1. Introduction. In earlier work [30], we have presented a novel process for the production of the mission-critical real-time software embedded on-board the control platforms of new-generation satellite systems. The motivation to our work originated from the rise of the "cheaper, faster, better" mission paradigm. One characteristic of this paradigm is to call for the integration of all the control functions allocated to the platform of the space segment (the so-called *spacecraft bus*) to a single processing node. In view of this requirement, our process had to accomplish three key objectives:

1. to facilitate the increase in the software productivity of the industrial process, expressed in terms of source lines delivered per hour, from the current range of 0.75—1.25 to the region of at least 4.0 (i.e. an aspect of the "faster" dimension of the new paradigm);

2. to facilitate the increase in the autonomous operation capability of the software product with a view of the reduction of service outage (i.e. an aspect of the "better" dimension of the new paradigm);

3. to master the increase in the functional complexity and real-time criticality of the system arising from 2. and the ever-growing application demands.

In [29] we have proven that our engineering approach serves well the application needs, meets the process requirements and is, therefore, ready for industrial utilisation.

*European Space Agency, Research and Technology Centre (TOS-ESD), Keplerlaan 1, PO Box 299, 2200 AG Noordwijk, The Netherlands (tullio@ws.estec.esa.nl).

In this paper we turn our attention to the impact that the increasingly crucial role of the *payload*, as the value-added provider of the spacecraft, will have on the architecture of the on-board system.

The trend towards an ever bigger payload component embedded in the on-board system stems from the commercial objective to use clusters of satellites for the implementation of a wide range of global-coverage multimedia services [19]. For satellite systems in this configuration (typically denominated *constellations*), virtually all of the customer-oriented services are allocated to the payload elements. In this scenario the platform is to operate as a dependable carrier of the value-added embedded in the payload, and an autonomous one, for the "cheaper" dimension of the mission paradigm calls for the drastic reduction of the ground control centres, with the consequent transfer of most control functions to the spacecraft bus.

As a reflection of this trend, the payload component is destined to acquire greater importance in terms of the cost and the product of the mission. This will inevitably imply the call for dedicated control capabilities that operate in co-ordination with the platform functions.

In that situation, the control functions allocated to the spacecraft will be *de facto* distributed across several processing nodes, so that the spacecraft bus will have to be regarded as a distributed system. In our vision, one processing node in the platform integrates all the traditional on-board control functions (typically denominated Attitude and Orbit Control and Data Handling Control) and co-ordinates with other nodes that control the activity of the payload elements embedded in the spacecraft. In this scenario, the platform retains the role of traffic manager for all the control communication between the spacecraft and the ground centre. This traffic consists of ground-issued telecommands and return telemetry (respectively denoted TC and TM) produced by the appropriate on-board service.

The issue we want to address in this paper is whether the process we have introduced in [30] will equally well serve the new application scenario. We are convinced that this is the case and prove so by building upon the research results discussed in the work of Tindell et al. at the University of York (UK), in particular, [26] and [27].

In the remainder of this paper we develop the essential component of our line of argument. In Section 2 we outline the process model we advocate for the construction of software systems in the domain. In Section 3 we recall the constructive elements of the engineering solution we adopt for the integration of all traditional on-board control functions on a single platform computer. In Section 4 we extend the capability of our solution to the distribution of selected on-board control functions to multiple processing nodes. In Section 5 we use one simple example to constructively demonstrate the feasibility of our approach. In Section 6, finally, we anticipate areas of future work for the furthering and consolidation of our proposal.

2. Process Model. Our process model calls for an *iterative* and *incremental* development philosophy as the means to master the feedback effect caused by the compression of the development schedule and the increasing complexity of new-generation systems. The process we envision bases on two conceptual pillars: the *design framework* and the *computational model.* The design framework is the development space that captures the iterations incurred in the establishment of the logical model of the system and in the verification of the feasibility of the corresponding physical model.

The computational model is the essential ingredient that steers this iterative process and leads it to convergence. In our vision, the notion of computational model defines: (a) the type of components for use in the construction of the real-time architecture of the system, the means availed for the communication and synchronisation between them, and the concurrency paradigm assumed for their run-time execution; (b) the execution properties and real-time attributes that characterise those components as well as the *constraints* placed on their use and interaction at run time; and (c) an underpinning analytical model that enables the static analysis of the real-time behaviour of systems constructed in terms of those components. The collection of these definitions constitute the abstract view of the architectural support for predictability availed to the software system design phase.

In the following, we outline our solution to the centralised and distributed version of new-generation systems by illustrating the relevant computational models and the principles of the associated analysis models.

3. The Centralised Solution.

3.1. Application Model. Satellite systems typically perform their operation under the supervision of a control centre based on ground. The ground centre exercises its authority on the on-board system by the issue of telecommands (TC) and the reception of status and verification information contained in the response telemetries (TM) sent back by the satellite.

The servicing of the TC/TM flow between on-board applications and the ground centre constitutes one of the two fundamental functions of the real-time software embedded in the satellite platform. This set of communication-related services is collectively termed *D*ata *H*andling *C*ontrol (DHC) subsystem.

The nature of most DHC services is eminently non-periodic. DHC services are typically executed in response to requests disjointly arriving either from the ground centre, for the issue of TC, or off on-board subsystems, for the issue of TM or the activation of other functions. DHC services have a sporadic nature (as opposed to generally aperiodic) in force of the fact that the typical on-board operation scenario is expressed in terms of definite mission-specific requirements that generally dismiss any residual indeterminacy. In addition to this core of sporadic activities, the DHC subsystem also includes a small number of naturally periodic activities such as health monitoring of status parameters and housekeeping. The DHC services must in general execute the required function and report to ground on the result within definite deadlines. Hence, most of the DHC services can be regarded as *mission-critical*. Failure to meet any of the associated real-time requirements may decrease the mission product or even compromise the mission.

Complementary to and equally important as the DHC services are the on-board functions aimed at the management of *A*ttitude determination and *O*rbit *C*ontrol (AOC) of the spacecraft. An orbiting satellite system acquires and maintains its assigned orbital position and trajectory by combined utilisation of a number of sensors (e.g.: Sun, star, Earth sensors, gyroscopes) and actuators (e.g.: torques, wheels, thrusters). The typical AOC functions are based around periodic acquisition of data from sensors, complex mathematical processing of such data based on specific control laws and determination of corrective actions required of actuators. Because of the nature of the applied control laws, AOC activities are mostly *periodic* with fixed known rates that are set to the highest possible frequency to achieve higher standards of control performance. The need to complete an entire control loop prior to the invocation of the next one imposes obvious, mission-critical requirements on the individual activities participating in the control loop.

Traditionally, the AOC and DHC components were allocated to physically disjoint subsystems that coexisted, as a federation of computing black-boxes, within one and the same platform. This architectural choice reflected the scarcity of resources available on individual on-board computers and the differing specialisation required for the engineering of the control and communication functions.

The rising availability of more powerful processor technology for on-board computing, such as the Embedded Real-Time Computing Core (ERC32 for short), a 32-bit SPARC v7 based chipset recently developed by the European Space Agency [12, 23], now challenges the economic convenience of the federated approach and fosters the transition to single-computer platforms capable of integrating together the whole set of AOC and DHC functions. In fact, the reduction of the hardware and harness required for on-board computing is instrumental to the drastic reduction of the costs incurred for the development, qualification and integration of the spacecraft. New-generation systems more and more frequently adopt this novel architectural concept.

3.2. Computational Model. Our computational model, which originates from the definitions given in HRT-HOOD [4, 5] is based around the principles of fixed priority preemptive scheduling [1, 2].

HRT-HOOD extends the base HOOD design method [14] in use at the European Space Agency by incorporating the abstractions supported by the revised tasking model of Ada 95 in a fashion that matches the tasking profile identified at the 8th International Real-Time Ada Workshop as the preferred candidate for the support of time-critical applications, commonly referred to as the *Ravenscar profile* [3].

Our computational model contemplates: *periodic* objects, which denote threaded objects used to model time-triggered activities; *sporadic* objects, which denote threaded objects used to model event-triggered activities; and *protected* objects, which denote those objects that provide protected access to shared data structures.

The triggering event for sporadic objects may be external, i.e. an interrupt, or internal, i.e. on demand from another software object in the system. The object triggered by the former type of execution request is called *interrupt sporadic*; the object triggered by the latter, *software sporadic*.

Threads of control within periodic and sporadic objects may access shared data in a protected manner by means of mutually exclusive calls to dedicated *resource* servers, which are modelled as protected object. Threads of control may also synchronise with one another by means of mutually exclusive calls to dedicated *synchronisation* servers.

Resource servers may offer a variety of services, each denoted by one distinct execution request. The execution requests exported by a resource server must ensure mutual exclusion to concurrent callers and must be internally non-blocking.

Synchronisation servers enable selected threads to suspend on synchronisation calls and other threads to perform non-blocking triggering calls. The model requires that any thread that wishes to suspend on a synchronisation call be allowed to do so exclusively through the services of a dedicated synchronisation server. In other words, no two threads can suspend on one and the same synchronisation call so that no suspension queue be required for any synchronisation service.

As part of the technology demonstration activity of the European Space Agency, we had our computational model implemented on top of a compact, tailored and fully characterised Ada run-time system. The implementor redesigned all of the required tasking primitives so as to provide for optimised bounds to their worst-case execution time. As a result of that design, we now have a specific correspondence between the object abstractions in our computational model and a restricted set of fully characterised run-time primitives. In force of that correspondence, the notion of thread in our computational model maps to the notion of task in our Ada implementation, so that the two terms are synonym of one another.

3.3. Analysis Model. The static analysis model associated to our computational model aims at the prediction of worst-case response times (cf. e.g.: [2, 15]). The model stipulates that one task's worst-case response time be defined as the longest elapsed time it takes for that task to complete its most demanding set of activities in response to an activation occurring under maximum contention from the rest of the system. In practice, the worst-case response time of any task τ_i results from combination of the following three components:

(i) The *worst-case computation time* of task τ_i, denoted $\boldsymbol{C_i}$, which is defined as the sum of the time cost of all τ_i's sequential blocks of execution that lay in the statically determined worst-case execution path of the task, in addition to the time cost of the run-time system services required for the support of that execution.

(ii) The *interference* incurred by τ_i, which is caused by the occurrence of preemptive execution of higher-priority tasks and higher-priority run-time system services incurred during τ_i's ready period.

(iii) The *blocking* experienced by τ_i, denoted $\boldsymbol{B}_i$, which originates from the possibility that a due release of τ_i be delayed by other effects than those arising from preemptive interference; such effects occur when the run-time system protects the execution of internal critical sections by temporarily inhibiting (i.e. deferring) preemption as well as a consequence of using *priority ceiling emulation* [13] for the implementation of mutual exclusion in the communications between tasks and servers; use of priority ceiling emulation may, in fact, delay the release of tasks whose priority is higher than the caller but lower than the server's ceiling; response time analysis prescribes that worst-case blocking be determined as the largest possible delay effect incurred from any of the two sources.

For any task τ_i, component $\boldsymbol{C}_i$ is fully determined at compile time (e.g.: on the Ada closure of the program); component $\boldsymbol{B}_i$ is a function of the assigned priorities and the system's run-time operation; and the interference component is a function of the system load. Bounds to components $\boldsymbol{C}_i$ and $\boldsymbol{B}_i$ are determined by timing analysis of the functional code of the system. The interference component is bounded by assuming the worst-case release pattern for all tasks in the system. This assumption is normally referred to as the *critical instant* assumption, whereby tasks are assumed to arrive independently of one another at their maximum frequency. The critical instant assumption is sufficient for any arrival pattern as long as the effects of *release jitter* are taken into account.

DEFINITION 3.1. *We define release jitter, denoted* $\boldsymbol{J}_i$, *as the difference between the earliest and the latest release of a task* τ_i *for a given arrival.*

Release jitter takes a slightly different connotation according to the type of tasks under consideration. For periodic tasks, the release jitter is the delay with which the scheduler recognises their arrival. Conversely, for sporadic tasks, the release jitter also denotes the variability in their arrival pattern (i.e. in the arrival of their triggering event). In our implementation model, release jitter manifests itself as follows:

1. periodic tasks have no release jitter, as our interval-timer based implementation ensures immediate notification of the task invocation;
2. interrupt sporadic tasks have no release jitter, as we allow no interrupt masking during the immediate handling that results in the triggering of the task;
3. software sporadic tasks have release jitter equal to the *output jitter* of the releasing task (which, incidentally, shows that software sporadic tasks do not actually have an independent arrival pattern).

Output jitter can occur when the computation of a task is completed at irregular times. As described by Locke [18], there are two reasons for this to occur: (i) the actual computation time of the task may be inferior to the worst case; (ii) the amount of interference actually incurred between two successive arrivals of the task may be inferior to the worst case. It follows that, from the perspective of static analysis, the output jitter of a task can be as large as the response time of that task, which in turn gives us an upperbound for the release jitter of software sporadic tasks.

We can therefore conclude that the notional concept of critical instant implies the following conditions:

(i) all periodic tasks are assumed to be disjointly released at time $t_0 = 0$

(ii) all interrupt sporadic tasks are assumed to be disjointly triggered at time $t_0 = 0$ and arrive at their maximum frequency

(iii) all software sporadic tasks are assumed to be disjointly released off their synchronisation server's queue at time $t_0 = 0$ with a release jitter equal to the output jitter of their releasing task.

DEFINITION 3.2. *In accordance with [16], we define "level i busy period", denoted* $\boldsymbol{W}_i$*, as the time span during which a defined invocation of task* τ_i *is continuously in the notional ready (or running) state.*

By definition, the busy period extends to include all the interference effects caused by preemption. In our computational model, we recognise two sources of interference over the busy period of task τ_i:

(i) the interference caused by the preemptive execution of all tasks with higher priority than τ_i (captured by the notation $HP(i)$), which we denote $\boldsymbol{I}_i^{\mathbf{W}_i}$:

$$\boldsymbol{I}_i^{\mathbf{W}_i} = \sum_{j \epsilon HP(i)} \left\lceil \frac{\boldsymbol{W}_i + \boldsymbol{J}_j}{\boldsymbol{T}_j} \right\rceil \boldsymbol{C}_j \tag{3.1}$$

(ii) the interference caused by the run-time services associated with the handling of interrupts off the interval timer, which we denote $\boldsymbol{S}_i^{\mathbf{W}_i}$:

$$\boldsymbol{S}_i^{\mathbf{W}_i} = \boldsymbol{K}_i^{\mathbf{W}_i}(Timer\_Int + Ready + Select) \tag{3.2}$$

The terms in *italics* in equation 3.2 denote the worst-case execution time bound for the run-time primitives involved in the readying of periodic tasks off the delay queue. Term $\boldsymbol{K}_i^{\mathbf{W}_i}$ determines how many times the Interval Timer triggers over the level i busy period:

$$\boldsymbol{K}_i^{\mathbf{W}_i} = \sum_{j \epsilon HP_{PERIODIC}(i)} \left\lceil \frac{\boldsymbol{W}_i + \boldsymbol{J}_j}{\boldsymbol{T}_j} \right\rceil + \sum_{j \epsilon LP_{PERIODIC}(i)} 1 \tag{3.3}$$

where the bound needs to consider also the first invocation of all the periodic tasks with lower priority than τ_i, denoted $LP(i)$, which are assumed to disjointly occur around the critical instant.

Based on the work of Tindell et al. [26], we note that the width of $\boldsymbol{W}_i$ is determined by Eqn. 3.4:

$$\boldsymbol{W}_i^{n+1}(q) = \boldsymbol{B}_i + (q+1)\boldsymbol{C}_i + \boldsymbol{I}_i^{\mathbf{W}_i^n(q)} + \boldsymbol{S}_i^{\mathbf{W}_i^n(q)} \tag{3.4}$$

for $q, n \geq 0$; where q denotes the $(q+1)_{th}$ occurrence of the busy period, and:

$$\boldsymbol{W}_i^0(0) = \boldsymbol{B}_i + \boldsymbol{C}_i \tag{3.5}$$

The width of $\boldsymbol{B}_i$ is determined, for example, as prescribed in [30].

Knowledge about $\boldsymbol{W}_i$ enables the determination of the worst-case response time of task τ_i, denoted $\boldsymbol{R}_i$. This is obtained by 3.6:

$$\boldsymbol{R}_i = \max_{q \epsilon N}(\boldsymbol{W}_i^n(q) - q\boldsymbol{T}_i + \boldsymbol{J}_i) \tag{3.6}$$

where, for the deadline monotonic case, in which $\boldsymbol{D}_i \leq \boldsymbol{T}_i$, the solution space is limited to one single critical-instant arrival of the task, and hence:

$$N = \{q = 0\} \tag{3.7}$$

whereas, for the arbitrary deadline case, in which $\boldsymbol{D}_i$ and $\boldsymbol{T}_i$ are in arbitrary relationship, the solution space extends to multiple overlapping busy periods of the task, and hence:

$$N = \{q\} : \boldsymbol{W}_i^n(q) > (q+1)\boldsymbol{T}_i \tag{3.8}$$

4. Towards the Distribution of On-Board Functions.

4.1. Technical Approach. The technical approach we take in this paper has a strong evolutionary connotation in that we strive to construct a distributed solution that preserves the applicability of the centralised solution described in Section 3 to the maximum possible extent. To do so, we want to extend the core elements of our centralised computational model to a distributed system for which:

1. the incorporation of inter-node communications between tasks does not break the integrity of the originating computational model;
2. the analysis model we have proposed for task scheduling fully holds on each and every node of the system;
3. there exists a model for the analysis of the inter-node communications that derives from the same family as that of the analysis of task scheduling.

To this end, we first outline an application model that meets the requirements arising on new-generation distributed on-board systems; subsequently we determine the required extensions to the centralised computational model; and, finally, we construct one model that subsumes together in a tractable fashion the analysis of task scheduling and that of communications scheduling.

4.2. Extended Application Model. The European Space Agency's Packet Telemetry and Packet Telecommand Standards [9, 10] and the CCSDS[1] Recommendations from which they are derived [6, 7] address the end-to-end transport of telemetry and telecommand data between user applications on ground and *application processes* on board.

The European Space Agency's Packet Utilisation Standard (PUS) [11] complements and extends these packet standards by defining a standard packet-based interface for the execution of certain *services* by on-board application processes. The PUS defines those services by prescribing the *service model* (i.e.

[1] Consultative Committee for Space Data Systems.

how the application processes are to behave on arrival of a given service request) and the structures of the associated telemetry and telecommand packets.

In this context, an application process is an on-board entity capable of generating telemetry (TM) source packets and receiving telecommand (TC) packets. An application process is uniquely and statically identified for the entirety of a mission. No restrictions are placed on the mapping between application processes and the usual functional subdivision of a satellite into subsystems and payloads. We retain this basic definition and assume that several application processes may reside on the same processing node.

The original definition of the PUS addressed the requirements arising from the commissioning and operation phase of the satellite life cycle. Recent work [8], however, has shown the usefulness of applying the PUS service model to the communications between on-board application processes without any necessary involvement of the ground centre. An on-going revision of the PUS standard is presently addressing the implications of this extension [22]. New space projects looking into autonomous operation of the spacecraft (e.g.: [24]) are also considering exploiting this potential. We are particularly interested in the extended interpretation of the PUS, for it provides a very attractive abstraction of the distributed application model we wish to address in this paper. Figure 4.1 depicts this model.

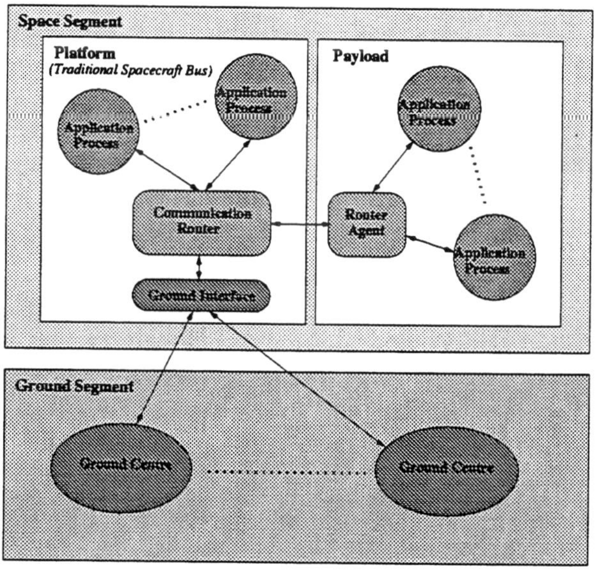

FIG. 4.1. *Distribution of on-board control functions.*

All communications to and from the ground segment take the form of standard TM and TC packets and are addressed to and from on-board application processes. In particular, the PUS standard prescribes that any communication to and from the spacecraft be comprised of exactly one packet. The header of a TC packet specifies the destination of the communication (the source being defaulted to ground), along with several other ancillary informations. Similarly, the header of a TM packet specifies the source of the communication (the destination being defaulted to ground). In the case of multiple control centres on ground, the TC packet header may also identify the specific source of the packet, and the TM packet header the specific destination. The actual length of the packet is specified in the header and can never exceed the maximum length prescribed by the standard.

In our vision, on acceptance at the telecommand receiver, incoming source TC packets are transformed into lighter-weight *internal packets* by a Ground Interface component and subsequently routed to the designated destination by a Communication Router component. Similarly, internal packets destined to ground are routed to the Ground Interface component and there transformed into outbound source TM packets. Internal packets differ from standard TM/TC packets in that the header of the former always includes a $[source, destination]$ pair that is used for the on-board routing of the communication.

The application model we consider in this paper is the one determined by the exchange of internal packets (i.e. messages) between application processes located on multiple nodes on-board the spacecraft and connected by a given communication device. We are not interested here in the physical communications to and from the ground and we abstract those in terms of an exchange of internal packets with the Ground Interface component (effectively, the local 'agent' of the ground centre concerned).

In our application model, the Communication Router implements a mailbox-based message passing scheme, whereby each application process possesses its own private mailbox. The Communication Router places the incoming packet in the mailbox corresponding to the application process specified in the header of the message. On arrival of the message in the mailbox, a dedicated interface object within the application process fetches the message, determines the service requested by the sender and dispatches the request to the designated service component within the process.

4.3. Extended Computational Model. Our distributed computational model configures as a natural extension of the centralised model described in Section 3. Accordingly, tasks allocation and communication paths in our distributed model are static and tasks on any node are scheduled with fixed priority preemptive scheduling. Tasks can send any number of messages as part of their current invocation. Receiver tasks can only receive and process one single message per invocation. Each processing node hosts a message dispatcher (i.e. the communication router shown in Fig. 4.1) in charge of forwarding incoming messages to their local or remote destination. In our model, the sending of a message is abstracted to posting the message in the mailbox of the message dispatcher. The combination of these prescriptions makes receiver tasks and the dispatcher itself fully equivalent to the software sporadic object of our centralised computational model, for which the arrival of the message represents the triggering event.

The communication device we assume for our model is a serial data bus complying with the European Space Agency's PSS-04-255 standard [20], denominated on-board data handling (OBDH) bus.

The OBDH bus is a shared broadcast medium with a single-master architecture and a small bandwidth. The OBDH communication protocol uses a classical time-division multiplexing scheme (typically referred to as TDMA) to guarantee each node deterministic access to the communication device. The protocol assumes the existence of a single central controller that operates as the master of the data bus and the executor of the TDMA scheme on behalf of each node in the system.

The central controller, denominated Central Terminal Unit (CTU), polls remote terminals in accord with a given polling scheme described in a polling sequence table. The OBDH polling scheme is naturally adaptive since, if a terminal does not have data to transfer when it is polled, the CTU may poll the next terminal in the sequence. The polling sequence table captures the priority relationship between the nodes in the system. In practice, we can assimilate the OBDH protocol to the timed token-passing protocol analysed in [27]. The polling frequency to a terminal determines the communication bandwidth availed to that terminal.

The CTU is physically connected to, but otherwise independent from, a specific processing node in the system. This node is denominated Central Data Management Unit (CDMU). Thanks to this independence, an application process resident on the CDMU accesses the bus in exactly the same manner as one resident on a remote terminal. Processing nodes connect to the OBDH bus via a dedicated remote bus interface (RBI). The CTU allows one remote terminal (as well as the CDMU) to communicate to another node across the bus by setting up the proper physical connections between the relevant RBIs.

Messages are transmitted on the bus in transfer units (each containing up to 24 bits of user data). On account of the negligible network propagation delays in our application environment, we assume ρ is the constant time to transmit one transfer unit from any source to any destination on the bus.

Each node N_i may globally transfer up to Q_i transfer units per poll. Hence, ρQ_i represents the OBDH equivalent of the 'token holding slot' for that node. Assuming ϕ as the time needed to set up a sending-mode connection between node N_i and the OBDH bus, there exists a characteristic 'poll time' of the system that is equal to:

$$T_{poll} = \sum_{i \epsilon Nodes} (\rho Q_i + \phi). \tag{4.1}$$

The message dispatcher resident on the node maintains a pair of FIFO message queue per local application process; one for the input and one for the output. Each queue is assigned the priority of the owner task. The RBI visits the output queues in priority order on the poll of the node and symmetrically writes the input queues at the destination node.

An application process that posts a message just after the poll to that node will have that message considered at the next poll. Consequently, we may assume that any outgoing message off any node in the system (except for the lowest-priority one) has a worst-case 'blocking' time:

$$B_{m_i} = T_{poll}. \tag{4.2}$$

4.4. Extended Analysis Model. For a system with the characteristics described in Section 4, it is crucial that any communication between a sending task on a node and a receiving task on another node complete in a bounded time. In accordance with [27], we regard the *end-to-end delay* of a communication as made up of four components:

1. the *generation delay*, i.e. the time taken for the sending task to generate and queue a message at the media access control of the local node (e.g.: the task's output buffer in the local Communication Router);
2. the *queuing delay*, i.e. the time taken by the message to gain access to the communications device (e.g.: the OBDH bus);
3. the *transmission delay*, i.e. the time taken by the message to be transmitted over the communications device; and
4. the *delivery delay*, i.e. the time taken by the message at the destination node prior to delivery to the receiving task.

In force of the computational model described in Section 3, we know that the *generation delay* is bounded by the worst-case response time of the sender task. The analysis devices associated to that computational model provide the means to determine this bound.

The *delivery delay* represents the distance in time between the arrival of the last transfer unit of the message at the hardware interface of the node and the arrival of the message at the private mailbox of the receiver. The width of this component, which is entirely local to the destination node, is bounded by the property of the centralised computational model described in Section 3. For the purposes of our analysis, we assume that this component, denoted θ, is a constant characteristic of the communications interface at all nodes in the system. Hence, the problem we are left with is the determination of the bound for the *queuing delay* and *transmission delay* for any outgoing message.

Tindell et al. [27] establish an interesting analogy between the problem of task scheduling on one processor and the problem of message scheduling on a communication device. We take on that analogy to transpose definition 3.2 into the following definition:

DEFINITION 4.1. *We define "busy period of message m_i", denoted W_{m_i}, as the sum of the queuing delay and transmission delay of a message m_i.*

Our extended computational model ensures that W_{m_i} is bounded for any message m_i. This property follows from the assurance of bounded response time for tasks provided by the centralised computational model (cf. Section 3) and the assurance of bounded delivery time for messages provided by the TDMA characteristics of the OBDH bus. We now want to transpose the application of response time analysis for task scheduling to bound the width of $\boldsymbol{W}_{m_i}$.

For this purpose, we overload the symbols used for task scheduling to express the corresponding notion for use in message scheduling. As an effect of this analogy, the term $\boldsymbol{C}_{m_i}$ now denotes the worst-case number of bus transfer units that a message m_i sent by task τ_i may contain.

Attribute Inheritance. If we are to build on the analogy between task scheduling and message scheduling, then we need a way to consistently capture the scheduling attributes of messages. The concept of *attribute inheritance* introduced by Tindell and Clark [28] is the key to consistently relating to one another the scheduling attributes of tasks and messages in a distributed system. In force of attribute inheritance, every message inherits priority, period and release jitter from the sender task. Messages off the same sender are assigned priority in an arbitrary order, providing that no two messages share the same priority level. (Obviously, the most natural priority order for these messages is determined by their order of arrival in the FIFO output queue of the sender task.)

Assuming a message m_i is queued at every e_i invocations of task τ_i, then message m_i inherits a period:

$$\boldsymbol{T}_{m_i} = e_i \boldsymbol{T}_i \tag{4.3}$$

and a release jitter:

$$\boldsymbol{J}_{m_i} = \boldsymbol{R}_i \tag{4.4}$$

from τ_i.

Similarly, the receiver task inherits period and release jitter from the incoming message: the former is equal to the period of the message; the latter is equal to the response time of the message. In order for these relationships to hold, it is crucial that the receiver receives (and processes) only one message per invocation. Hence, for the destination τ_j of message m_i, we have:

$$\boldsymbol{T}_j = \boldsymbol{T}_{m_i} \tag{4.5}$$

and

$$\boldsymbol{J}_j = \boldsymbol{R}_{m_i} \tag{4.6}$$

Derivation of Message Scheduling Equations. Having determined the basic scheduling attributes of a message, we now turn our attention to the derivation of the relevant scheduling equations. To do so, we once again build on the analogy between task scheduling and message scheduling.

Similarly to the case of task scheduling, the width of $\boldsymbol{W}_{m_i}$ extends to include all the interference effects incurred on queuing and transmission of the message.

Message m_i experiences interference at two levels:

(i) from other messages sent out by higher-priority tasks residing on the same node as the sender of message m_i:

$$I_{m_i}^{W_{m_i}} = \sum_{m_h \epsilon HP(m_i)} \lceil \frac{W_{m_i} + J_{m_h}}{T_{m_h}} \rceil C_{m_h} \tag{4.7}$$

(ii) from the use of the communication device made by other nodes in the system:

$$S_{m_i}^{W_{m_i}} = \lceil \frac{W_{m_i}}{T_{poll}} \rceil (T_{poll} - \rho Q_i) \tag{4.8}$$

On this basis, we transpose Eqn. 3.4 into Eqn. 4.9 and use the latter for the determination of W_{m_i} for the k_{th} transfer unit of message m_i $(0 < k \leq C_{m_i})$:

$$W_{m_{i.k}}^{n+1}(q) = B_{m_i} + (qC_{m_i} + k + I_{m_i}^{W_{m_{i.k}}^n(q)})\rho + S_{m_i}^{W_{m_{i.k}}^n(q)} \tag{4.9}$$

Similarly, we transpose Eqn. 3.6 into Eqn. 4.10 and use the latter for the determination of the worst-case response time of the k_{th} transfer unit of message m_i. In doing so, we must take due account of the *delivery delay*, denoted θ, experienced by the message at the destination node:

$$R_{m_{i.k}} = \max_{q \epsilon N}(W_{m_{i.k}}^n(q) - qT_{m_i} + J_{m_i} + \theta) \tag{4.10}$$

where Eqns. 3.7 and 3.8 determine the width of N; and $W_{m_{i.k}}^0(0) = 0$ is a suitable initial value for 4.9.

The values for the busy period and worst-case response time of message m_i are trivially obtained by substitution of k for C_{m_i}.

Holistic Scheduling. One obvious consequence of attribute inheritance is that the equations for task and message response time analysis become mutually dependent and, consequently, cannot be resolved in isolation. Tindell et al. [27] term this dependence *holistic*. The term denotes the fact that the schedulability of the components of a system with these characteristics of dependence can only be determined by addressing the schedulability of the system as a whole.

This dependence is overcome by forming a recurrence relation between the equations concerned (essentially, Eqns. 3.4 and 3.6 for task scheduling; and Eqns. 4.10 and 4.9 for message scheduling) and by relaxing the initial condition for task response time analysis set in Eqn. 3.5 to start from zero.

As Tindell et al. observe [27], those combined equations form a monotonic function. In fact, an increase in the term on which they are mutually dependent (i.e. J_i for task scheduling, determined by Eqn. 4.6; and J_{m_i} for message scheduling, determined by Eqn. 4.4) does not lead to a decrease in the relevant response time equation.

The solution space for both response time equations is thus explored by first computing an initial bound for message response time; then using that bound for the determination of task response time; and, finally, returning to the next iteration of the message response time equation. The solutions are determined by continuing this iteration until either both sets of equations converge or some predetermined threshold is reached.

We illustrate highlights of this process in the following simple example.

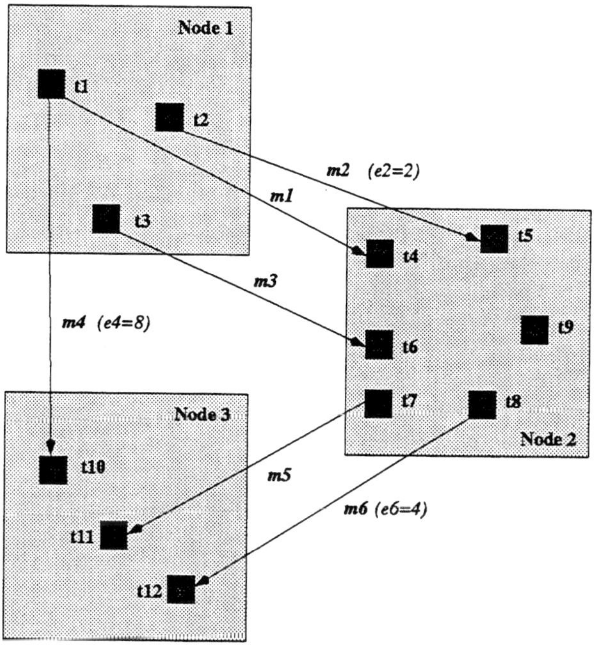

FIG. 4.2. *Example system.*

5. A Simple Example. The simple system we consider in this section is inspired by the example discussed in [27]. The system is depicted in Figure 4.2. Our goal is to show that the use of the equations established in sections 3 and 4 allows to determine the response time of all tasks and messages.

The system is made up of 3 nodes connected by an OBDH bus, with Node_1 as the bus master. Tasks on Node_1 are sender only and have known $\boldsymbol{J}$ and $\boldsymbol{T}$ attributes. For the other attributes, we assume: $\boldsymbol{B_i} = 0, \boldsymbol{S_i} = 0, \boldsymbol{C_i} = 100, \forall \tau_i$, for tasks; $\boldsymbol{C_{m_i}} = 100, \boldsymbol{B_{m_i}} = \boldsymbol{T_{poll}} = 10, \forall m_i, \rho = 1, \phi = \theta = 0$ for messages; and $Q_1 = 8, Q_2 = 2, Q_3 = 0$ for nodes. Normally, tasks and messages would also have deadline attributes, but those are not considered here as they do not serve the purpose of the example.

In this example, we progressively resolve all necessary equations in a *heuristic* manner so as to better reflect the progression in the resolution of holistic dependencies between tasks and messages in the system. In fact, the same progression could easily be automated, as shown, for example, by Tindell et al. in [27].

In order to illustrate the origin of the values determined in the example, we use the following convention: *assumed* attributes are boldfaced; *inherited* attributes are in italics; *computed* attributes are plainfaced.

The tasks on Node_i are defined to have no *holistic* dependence. Hence, the worst-case response times of these tasks can be directly determined using the equations shown in Section 3. The relevant results are shown in the first part of Table 5.1, where tasks are listed in decreasing priority order.

TABLE 5.1
Task Scheduling

task	J	B	T	C	R
			on Node$_1$		
τ_1	**0**	**0**	**700**	**100**	100
τ_2	**0**	**0**	**1,000**	**100**	200
τ_3	**0**	**0**	**10,000**	**100**	300
			on Node$_2$		
τ_4	*238*	**0**	*700*	**100**	338
τ_5	*588*	**0**	*2,000*	**100**	788
τ_6	*800*	**0**	*10,000*	**100**	1,100
τ_7	**0**	**0**	**5,000**	**100**	400
τ_8	**0**	**0**	**7,000**	**100**	600
τ_9	**0**	**0**	**11,000**	**100**	700
			on Node$_3$		
τ_{10}	*364*	**0**	*8*5,600*	**100**	464
τ_{11}	*950*	**0**	*5,000*	**100**	1,150
τ_{12}	*1,600*	**0**	*4*28,000*	**100**	1,900

The determination of the worst-case response time for the sender tasks on Node_1 enables us to approach the scheduling analysis of messages sent off this node. The results are shown in the first part of Table 5.2, where messages are listed in decreasing priority order. At this point, we have determined all the information we need to solve the worst-case response time equations for tasks on Node_2. The results are shown in the second part of Table 5.1.

The solution of the worst-case response time equations for sender tasks on Node_2 gives way to the determination of the relevant values for messages sent off this node. The results are shown in the second part of Table 5.2. At this point, having resolved all the holistic dependences in place between the tasks on Node_3 and the rest of the system, we can compute the response time of those tasks and conclude the process. The results are shown in the third part of Table 5.1.

6. Prospective. In this paper we have presented an engineering approach to the distribution of control functions to multiple processing nodes on-board new-generation satellite systems. The demand for the distribution of control functions emanates directly from the increasing criticality of the payload com-

TABLE 5.2
Scheduling of Messages

message	J_m	B_m	T_m	C_m	R_m
off $Node_1$					
m_1	*100*	10	*700*	100	238
m_4	*100*	10	*8*700*	100	364
m_2	*200*	10	*2*1,000*	100	588
m_3	*300*	0	*10,000*	100	800
off $Node_2$					
m_5	*400*	10	*5,000*	100	950
m_6	*600*	0	*4*7,000*	100	1,600

ponents embedded on-board the spacecraft. The approach we have taken extends upon the engineering solution we had presented in earlier work for the more conventional centralised version of new-generation on-board systems. The approach builds on the analogy between task scheduling and message scheduling discussed in [27] and delivers a set of equations for the determination of the worst-case response time of tasks and the worst-case end-to-end delivery time of messages. As a direct effect of the analogy, however, the resulting equations become mutually dependent. Tindell and Clark [28] name this dependence holistic. We have shown in this paper how this dependence can be resolved, thus leading to the determination of the timing attributes of all the system components. We believe this approach constitutes a suitable basis to initially explore the economical and technical convenience of distributed on-board control for new-generation systems.

The need to use release jitter to model the variability in the sending and receiving of messages across the system, however, may introduce considerable pessimism in the analysis. Due to the novelty of the distributed application model addressed in this paper, we lack solid quantitative data to assess the criticality of this phenomenon. Our future research work will nonetheless look into the attenuation of pessimism that may be obtained by the introduction of *offset relationships* between tasks in the system. Optimal offset analysis is known to be NP-complete [17], hence intractable for realistic systems. The work of Tindell et al. [25] and its excellent refinement by Palencia et al. in [21] shows that offset relationships can be handled, suboptimally, within the same family of analysis techniques discussed in this paper. This is a crucial prerequisite to maintain the integrity of our overall engineering approach. However, there exists an important trade-off to make between the reduction of pessimism obtainable by tractable offset analysis and the effort required to master the greater complexity of the analysis techniques.

Disclaimer. The views expressed in this paper are those of the author only and do not necessarily engage those of the European Space Agency.

REFERENCES

[1] N. AUDSLEY, A. BURNS, M. RICHARDSON, AND A. WELLINGS, *Hard Real-Time Scheduling: The Deadline Monotonic Approach*, Proc. Workshop on Real-Time Operating Systems and Software, Vol. 8, IEEE Computer Society, 1991, pp. 127–132.

[2] N. AUDSLEY, A. BURNS, AND A. WELLINGS, *Deadline Monotonic Scheduling Theory and Application*, Control Engineering Practice, 1 (1993), pp. 71–78.

[3] T. BAKER AND T. VARDANEGA, *Session Summary: Tasking Profiles*, Ada Letters, Vol. 17 (1997), pp. 5–7. Proc. 8th Int'l Real-Time Ada Workshop.

[4] A. BURNS AND A. WELLINGS, *HRT-HOOD: A Structured Design Method for Hard Real-Time Systems*, Real-Time Systems, 6 (1994), pp. 73–114.

[5] ——, *HRT-HOOD: A Structured Design Method for Hard Real-Time Systems*, Elsevier Science, Amsterdam, 1995.

[6] CCSDS, *Telecommand Summary of Concept and Service*, Consultative Committee for Space Data Systems, CCSDS 200.0-G-6: Issue 6, January 1987. (`http://www.ccsds.org/publications.html#telecommand`).

[7] ——, *Telemetry Summary of Concept and Rationale*, Consultative Committee for Space Data Systems, CCSDS 100.0-G-1: Issue 1, December 1987. (`http://www.ccsds.org/publications.html#telemetry`).

[8] CRI, *Onboard Operations Support Software - Modules Users Manual*, Deliverable CRI/OOSS/WP-2.1.3/001, ESTEC Contract No. 11277/94/NL-/FM(SC), European Space Agency, Noordwijk, The Netherlands, 1997. (`http://ftp.estec.esa.nl/pub/ws/wsd/oboss/www/oboss.html`).

[9] ESA, *Packet Telemetry Standard*, European Space Agency, Noordwijk, The Netherlands, PSS-04-106: Issue 1, January 1988. (`http://esapub.esrin.esa.it/pss/pss-cat1.htm`).

[10] ——, *Packet Telecommand Standard*, European Space Agency, Noordwijk, The Netherlands, PSS-04-107: Issue 2, April 1992. (`http://esapub.esrin.esa.it/pss/pss-cat1.htm`).

[11] ——, *Packet Utilisation Standard*, European Space Agency, Noordwijk, The Netherlands, ESA PSS-07-101 Issue 1, May 1994. (`http://esapub.esrin.esa.it/pss/pss-cat1.htm`).

[12] J. GAISLER, *Concurrent Error-Detection and Modular Fault Tolerance in a 32-bit Processing Core for Embedded Space Flight Applications*, Proc. Fault-Tolerant Computing Symposium, Vol. 24, IEEE Computer Society, 1994, pp. 128–130.

[13] J. GOODENOUGH AND L. SHA, *The Priority Ceiling Protocol: A Method for Minimising the Blocking of High-Priority Tasks*, Ada Letters, 8 (1988), pp. 35–38.

[14] HTG, *HOOD Reference Manual 3.1*, HOOD Technical Group, Prentice Hall, Englewood Clifs, NJ, 1993.

[15] M. JOSEPH AND P. PANDIA, *Finding Response Times in a Real-Time System*, The Computer Journal, 29 (1986), pp. 390–395.

[16] J. LEHOCZKY, *Fixed Priority Scheduling of Periodic Tasks Sets with Arbitrary Deadlines*, Proc. 1990 Real-Time Systems Symposium, IEEE Computer Society, 1990, pp. 201–209.

[17] J. LEUNG AND J. WHITEHEAD, *On the Complexity of Fixed-Priority Scheduling of Periodic, Real-Time Tasks*, Performance Evaluation, 2 (1982), pp. 237–250.

[18] C. LOCKE, *Software Architectures for Hard Real-Time Applications*, Real-Time Systems, 4 (1992), pp. 37–53.

[19] B. MILLER, *Satellites Free the Mobile Phone*, IEEE Spectrum, 35 (1998), pp. 26–35.

[20] OBDH WORKING GROUP, *Final Report on Spacecraft Data Handling Interface Definition*, WDI/DM/2156 Issue 1.0, European Space Agency, Noordwijk, The Netherlands, September 1994.

[21] J. PALENCIA AND M. GONZÁLEZ-HARBOUR, *Schedulability Analysis for Tasks with Static and Dynamic Offsets*, Proc. 1998 Real-Time Systems Symposium, IEEE Computer Society, 1998, pp. 26–37.

[22] A. PARKES, P. KAUFELER, M. MERRI, S. VALERA, AND T. VARDANEGA, *The Future of*

the Packet Utilisation Standard, Proc. 1st ESA Workshop on Tracking, Telemetry and Command Systems, European Space Agency, Noordwijk, The Netherlands, June 1998.

[23] SAAB ERICSSON SPACE, *32-bit Microprocessor and Computer System Development*, Final Report, ESTEC Contract No. 9848/92/NL/FM, European Space Agency, Noordwijk, The Netherlands, December 1996. (http://www.estec.esa.nl/wsmwww/erc32/erc32.html).

[24] F. TESTON, R. CREASEY, AND J. VAN DER HA, *PROBA: ESA's Autonomy and Technology Demonstration Mission*, Proc. Int'l Astronautical Congress, Vol. 48, International Aeronautical Federation, 1997.

[25] K. TINDELL, *Adding Time-Offsets to Schedulability Analysis*, Technical Report No. 221, Real-Time Systems Group, Department of Computer Science, University of York, York, UK, 1994.

[26] K. TINDELL, A. BURNS, AND A. WELLINGS, *An Extendible Approach for Analysing Fixed Priority Hard Real-Time Tasks*, Real-Time Systems, 6 (1994), pp. 133–152.

[27] ——, *Analysis of Hard Real-Time Communications*, Real-Time Systems, 9 (1995), pp. 147–171.

[28] K. TINDELL AND J. CLARK, *Holistic Schedulability Analysis for Distributed Real-Time Systems*, Microprocessing and Microprogramming, 40 (1994), pp. 117–134.

[29] T. VARDANEGA AND J. VAN KATWIJK, *Productive Engineering of Predictable Embedded Real-Time Systems: The Road to Maturity*, Information and Software Technology, 40 (1998), pp. 745–764.

[30] ——, *A Software Process for the Construction of Predictable On-Board Embedded Real-Time Systems*, Software - Practice and Experience, 29 (1999), pp. 1–32.

ARCHITECTURE OF A DISTRIBUTED REAL-TIME SYSTEM TO CONTROL LARGE HIGH-ENERGY PHYSICS EXPERIMENTS

C. GASPAR*, B. FRANEK†, AND J. J. SCHWARZ‡

Abstract. The control of a large high energy physics experiment involves multiple domains with different requirements (some parts have to work in real time, some are safety critical, others have to be user-friendly). Usually these domains are engineered separately. In order to increase the operating efficiency and the reliability and maintainability of the system, Delphi project at CERN took a global approach in the design of the complete experiment control. This approach allowed for the interconnection of the various domains and led to a high degree of automation and an homogeneous interface to the full control system. This paper describes an architecture and a development framework that can handle the different and sometimes contradictory requirements of the different parts of the experiment's online system.

Key words. control systems, object-oriented systems, finite state machines, asynchronous communication

1. Introduction. The Online System of a high-energy physics experiment deals with all aspects of the detector's operations at the experimental site, grouped in domains: data acquisition, detector survey (position, temperature, pressure, etc.) and control, supply of fluids (gas, water, electric power), communication with the outside world (accelerator system, data storage provider, offline analysis, etc.). In many respects, sub-detectors have their own independent systems which are then integrated in the framework of the experiment, as are also the various domains. The operation of the experiment is based on a control system which allows a limited team of operators to operate the detector in a safe and efficient manner.

This paper describes the approach that was used for the experiment control system in one of the four experiments at CERN's LEP collider - Delphi [1], and it shows how a common approach to the problem of controls has been used from the design phase up to the complete implementation in order to build an efficient and reliable system. The proposed approach is based on a framework in which the different components of the Online System can be described and implemented, providing built-in functionality like transparent communications, modelling tools and user interface capabilities and allowing the users to describe the behaviour of each subsystem and to manipulate specific hardware devices.

It is shown that this framework can be used to control and monitor all aspects of an experiment's Online System, and that it can easily be handled by

*CERN, European Organization for Nuclear Research, CH-1211 Geneva 23, Swizerland (clara.gaspar@cern.ch).

†Rutherford Appleton Laboratory, Chilton, Didcot, OX11 0QX, Great Britain (b.franek@rl.ac.uk).

‡INSA L3I, B502 IF, 20 av. A. Einstein, F-69621 Villeurbanne Cedex, France (jjs@if.insa-lyon.fr).

non-computing experts (both at implementation time and during operations). The experience gained with the development of this framework proves also that it can greatly improve the design, implementation, test, operation and maintenance of the complete Online System.

2. Experiment Online Systems. The Online System of the experiment is responsible for the control and monitoring of all parts of the experiment, involving many different fields, from safety concerns to real-time data read-out. Four main areas have been identified:

- The Slow Controls System (SCS) [2]. It controls and monitors slowly moving technical parameters and settings, like temperatures and high voltages. In Delphi the number of parameters to be constantly monitored and kept under control is of the order of a few hundred thousands for the full detector. The safety of the people and material are highly dependent on the reliability and availability of the SCS.
- The Data Acquisition System (DAS) [3]. It reads event data from the 20 sub-detectors composing Delphi and writes onto tape. In Delphi the event data read-out is done through a dedicated bus that connects around 3000 front-end electronics modules and 80 embedded processors. The size of a complete Delphi event is around 100 Kbytes.
- The Trigger System [4]. It provides the DAS system the information on whether or not the event is interesting and should be written to tape. In Delphi, the trigger system reduces the rate at which data are read-out from the detector to about 5 events per second, imposing a data rate of 500 Kbytes per second.
- The LEP Communication System [5]. It controls the exchange of data between the LEP control system and Delphi. The unavailability of the information coming from the accelerator can cause significant damage to the detector.

The design of the different parts of an Online System involves many different requirements and constraints:

- Real-time behaviour. The trigger and data acquisition systems impose response times of the order of hundreds of milliseconds (trigger rate). Missing a deadline results in loosing physics data but it does not endanger people or material. In the SCS, however, the response time can be of the order of several seconds or even minutes but it represents a hard real-time constraint since the safety of the people and the material can be involved.
- Fault-tolerance. In order to make sure that all the physics data are being stored and that the critical parameters are being monitored the system should be fault tolerant. A fault in the system should not prevent the monitoring of important quantities. Also in such a complex system a fault in one part of the detector should not prevent the rest of the system to continue functioning.
- Availability. During data-taking periods the experiments run 24 hours

a day, 7 days a week. The system should be robust and reliable and constantly available.

- Maintainability. Experiments normally run for about 10 years. During this time many things change, some sub-detectors are upgraded or replaced. Physics is not a static field, many new ideas involve changes in the experiment. The system has to be able to handle even radical changes.

In previous experiments the control of the different areas was normally designed separately by different experts, using different methodologies and tools resulting on a set of dedicated control systems that were difficult to operate, upgrade and maintain.

3. Building Online Systems. The approach used by Delphi, that can be proposed for future experiments, is to use wherever possible a common approach in the design and implementation of the various domains of an Online System. In order to make this integrated approach possible it is required to propose:

- An Architecture that can handle all aspects of the monitoring and control of a complete Online System.
- A Framework, that is a collection of tools and mechanisms that allow the implementation of the architecture.

3.1. The Architecture. In order to design and implement such a complex system several levels of abstraction are necessary. Therefore, a hierarchical architecture, with as many levels as necessary to represent the full experiment, has been adopted. This hierarchical structure will be composed of building blocks organised in a tree-like structure. At the leaves of the tree there are blocks which handle real devices and where users can insert their own code. Other blocks contain the description, model, of the system and of its dynamic behaviour (control blocks). Any other blocks can be inserted for data processing, monitoring and user interfacing at any level. All these blocks should be able to communicate with each other across processes and machines. Figure 3.1 shows the representation of such an architecture.

3.2. The Framework. In order to allow the implementation of such an architecture, the framework should provide:

- The reduction of complexity, a method allowing the decomposition of a particular system or subsystem into smaller, manageable, entities.
- Modeling tools to help describing and implementing the model and the behaviour of each entity.
- Distribution - transparent distributed communications among all entities.

The full control system should be built as a hierarchy of simpler control blocks where the behaviour of the different parts of the system are described. The framework should provide a uniform communication model, which can be used by all blocks for all types of data exchanges. Furthermore, each building block should at any time, "publish" the information it produces to the communication system so that it becomes available to the other blocks.

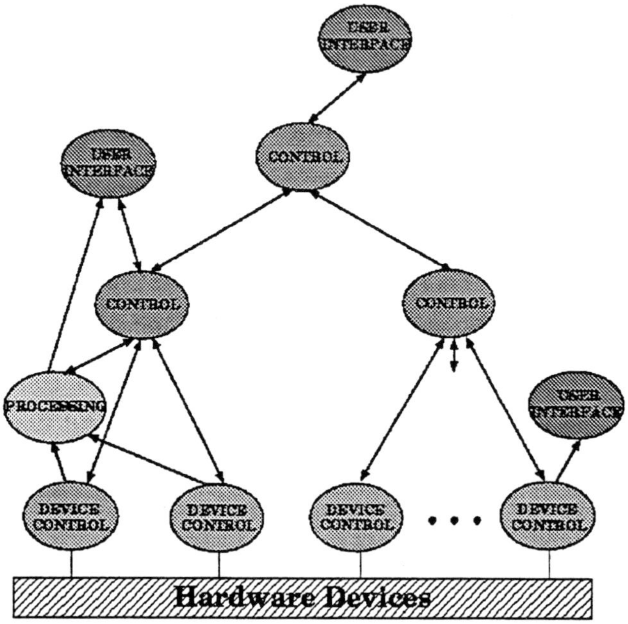

FIG. 3.1. : *"Brick" Architecture*

4. Control via SMI++. SMI++ is based on the original State Manager concept [6] which was developed by the Delphi experiment in collaboration with the DD/OC group of CERN. SMI (State Management Interface), the first implementation of this concept, was used in Delphi since 1990. Due to lack of flexibility in many areas SMI was completely re-designed using object-oriented technology and SMI++ implements significant extensions to the SMI concept and a more powerful set of tools. SMI++ is an Object Oriented Framework for Designing and Implementing Distributed Control Systems. It helps designing, implementing, testing and monitoring a control system by providing:

- A method for modelling the real-world system backed up by a simple language allowing the description of the real-world components and of the control logic.
- A set of tools to implement and test the control system.

The SMI++ method combines two concepts: objects and finite state machines (FSM). The real world to be controlled, being typically a set of hardware devices and software tasks, is decomposed into well defined entities (objects). The control system is equally conceived as a set of abstract (or logical) objects. These objects contain the control logic and can send commands to other objects. In order to reduce the complexity of large systems, logically related objects are grouped into SMI domains. In each domain, the objects are organised in a hierarchical structure and form a control subsystem. Usually only one object (top level object) in each domain is accessed by other domains. The final control system is then constructed as a hierarchy of SMI domains. Each of these objects' behaviour is described as an FSM, i.e., each object is always in a well-defined state, it can transit from one state to another on the reception of a command or when a logical condition on states of other objects becomes true.

These two concepts (objects and FSMs) work together perfectly. The object concept allows the reduction of a complicated system into a hierarchical set of small and manageable entities. The FSM approach allows the model and the dynamic behaviour of each of these entities to be described in simple terms of states and actions.

The SML language allows the specification of the objects and the description of their behaviour. Using this language the user can specify which objects belong to a certain domain, the set of states a particular object can be in and for each state the list of actions that can be executed. For abstract objects the actions are completely described, i.e., the sequence of instructions composing the action is specified (like send a command to another object or test the state of another one). For concrete objects the action is simply declared and its execution consists on sending a command out to the proxy that implements it.

Proxy processes provide the abstractions of the hardware components in the SMI world and implement the actual actions on the hardware. Proxies should not contain any logic, they should only implement basic actions and report back the status of the operation.

User Interfaces allow the control and visualisation of the system.

This framework allows an easy reconfiguration of the system: changes in the hardware can be easily integrated by modifying or replacing proxies and modifications in the control logic by changing the SML code. The de-coupling between the actual actions on the hardware (done by the proxy processes) and the control logic (residing in the SMI objects) makes the evolution of a system from its first test phase up to the final complexity a very smooth process. The basic concepts of the framework are graphically outlined in Figure 4.1.

4.1. State Manager Language - SML. The object model of the control system is described using State Manager Language. This language allows detailed specification of the objects such as their states, actions and associated conditions. The main characteristics of this language are:

- Finite State Logic. Objects are described as finite state machines. The only attribute of an object is its state. Commands sent to an object trigger actions that can bring about a change in its state.
- Sequencing. An action on an abstract object is specified by a sequence of instructions, mainly consisting of commands sent to other objects and logical tests on states of other objects. Actions on objects representing hardware components are sent off as messages to the proxy processes.
- Asynchronism. Several actions may proceed in parallel: a command sent by object-A to object-B does not suspend the instruction sequence of

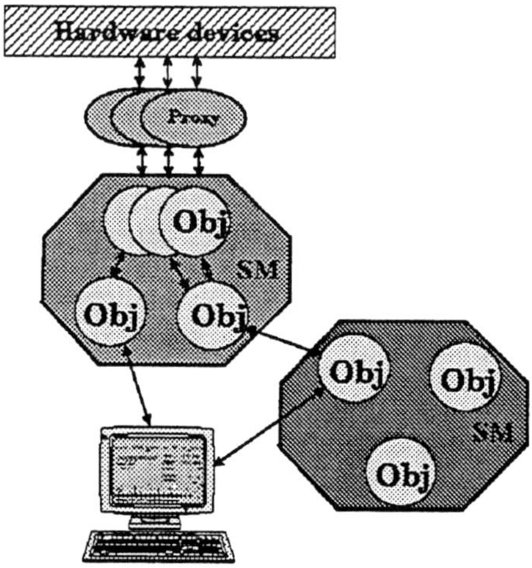

FIG. 4.1. : *Basic Concepts of SMI++*

object-A. Only a test by object-A on the state of object-B suspends the instruction sequence of object-A until object-B reaches a stable state.

- AI-like rules. Each object can specify logical conditions based on states of other objects. These conditions, when satisfied will trigger an action on the local object. This provides the mechanism for an object to respond to unsolicited state changes of its environment.

SML's instruction set is deliberately small and simple, since the design of a control system is not always done by a computer scientist. A system description done in SML can easily be understood and modified by a non-expert in computer programming. Figure 4.2 shows an example of a program written in SML language.

4.2. Tools. The SMI++ framework provides a set of tools to generate and implement the control system. Once the system and its desired behaviour are described using SML the control system is almost completely automatically generated by using the SMI++ tool set, as shown in Figure 4.3:

- SML Translator. The objects described in one SML file will at run-time correspond to an SMI domain. The SML translator parses, checks for internal consistency and translates the description and behaviour of the objects coded in SML into a Domain Description intermediate file. This intermediate file is then read at run-time by a generic Logic Engine in order to instantiate and drive the model of the domain.
- Generic Logic Engine. The Logic Engine is the key tool in the SMI framework. It is responsible for actually driving or implementing the model of a particular SMI domain. The Logic Engine is a generic package. At startup, it reads the Domain Description (translated from the SML code) and instantiates the various objects defined in the domain.

```
object : RUN_CONTROL
  state : READY
    action : START_RUN
      do MOUNT TAPE
      if ( not (TAPE in_state MOUNTED ) ) then
        do MOUNT_ERROR ERROR_OBJ
        terminate_action/state = ERROR
      endif
      do START_RUN READOUT_CONTROLLER
      if (READOUT_CONTROLLER in_state RUNNING) then
        terminate_action/state = RUN_IN_PROGRESS
      else
        ...
      endif

  state : RUN_IN_PROGRESS
    when (TAPE in_state FILE_FULL) do PAUSE_RUN
    when (READOUT_CONTROLLER in_state ERROR) do ABORT_RUN
    action : PAUSE_RUN
      ...
    action : ABORT_RUN
      ...

object : READOUT_CONTROLLER/proxy
  state : READY
    action : START_RUN
  state : RUNNING
    action : STOP_RUN
  state : ERROR
    ...
```

FIG. 4.2. : *Example of an SML Program*

It then provides the organisation of work and synchronisation between the different objects (internal logic objects, objects representing proxies and objects in other domains when necessary). The Logic Engine responds to external events and 'drives' the control system by following the coded control logic and sending the necessary commands to local objects, proxies and objects in other domains. The Logic Engine was designed by following the Object Oriented Analysis and Design Methodology [7], using the Booch notation [8] and a tool Rational Rose/C++ [9].

- Proxy Generator. In order to ease the task of the developer the Proxy Generator reads the SML code and generates skeletons for all the proxies in a given domain. The proxy skeleton contains the definition of all possible actions and of all possible states the proxy can set itself in. The user can then plug-in specific code to implement a particular action and choose in which state it terminates. The user can also decide

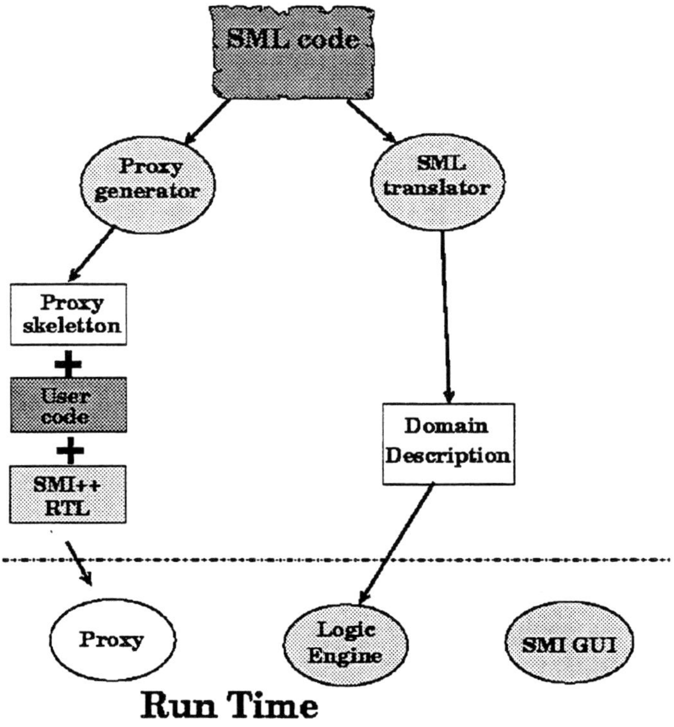

FIG. 4.3. : *SMI++ Tool Set*

to set the proxy to a given state without the reception of an action, asynchronously. The proxy composed of the generated skeleton plus the user routines is then linked with an SMI++ run time library to produce an executable.

- SMIRTL. The SMIRTL is a run-time library to be linked with proxies. It implements all communications with the SMI domain the proxy belongs to. That is, it connects to the domain and passes actions down to the proxy and states up to the Logic Engine implementing the domain.
- SMI GUI. A generic user interface is also provided. It allows the control and monitoring of the objects in a specific domain. The states of the objects can be visualised and commands can be sent to each object. The interface is configurable: the objects can be selectively displayed, moved around the display and different colours can be selected for different states of the objects. The generic user interface provided in the tool set is very useful during the implementation and test phase of a control system, but is not recommended as production user interface for the control system. Normally in the final interface the user would like to combine objects from different domains and also information on quan-

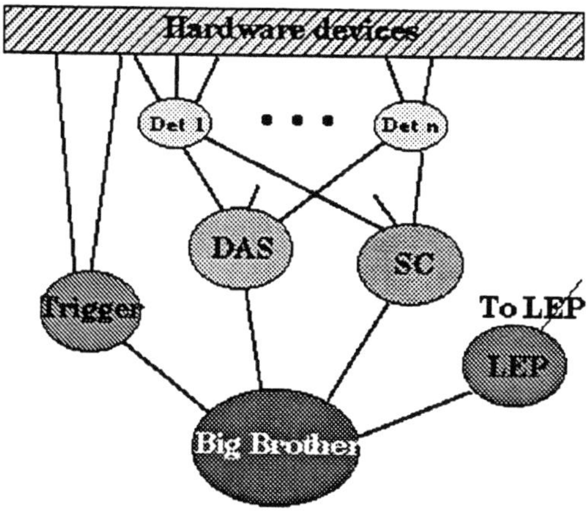

FIG. 4.4. : *Big Brother Control*

tities like RUN-NUMBER and TRIGGER-RATE that are not available as SMI object states. The SMI toolset contains a library that allows easy access to information on objects, states, and available or currently executing actions. In order to access these functions a user interface program should link with this library, the SMIUIRTL.

- SMIUIRTL. The SMI User Interface Run-Time Library allows user interfaces or any other processes to send commands to SMI objects and/or to inquire the state of a particular object somewhere in the system. Attention on particular objects can be requested so that whenever state changes happen a user routine can be called in order, for instance, to update the screen. The standard SMI GUI uses this library for object access.

4.3. SMI++ Application in Delphi. In Delphi the full Online System is controlled through this mechanism, the various areas of Delphi have been mapped into SMI domains: sub-detector domains, data acquisition (DAS) domain, slow controls (SC) domain, trigger domain, LEP machine domain, etc. The full system comprises about 1000 SMI objects in 50 different domains distributed over 40 machines.

A high level of automation of the experiment's control system is very important in order to avoid human mistakes and to speed up standard procedures. Using the SMI mechanism the creation of a top level domain - BIG BROTHER - containing the logic allowing the interconnection of the underlying domains (LEP, DAS, SCC, etc.) was a relatively easy task [10]. Under normal running conditions BIG BROTHER pilots the system with minimal operator intervention as shown in Figure 4.4. In other test and set-up periods the operator becomes the top-level object and using the user-interfaces he can send commands to any SMI domain.

5. Communications - DIM. Delphi's control system has a highly distributed architecture consisting of several workstations and embedded processors interconnected by a local area network. As mentioned before, SMI++ domains, proxies and user interfaces can be distributed over several different machines. Distribution is embedded in the SMI++ system, all co-operation between the different components of an SMI++ environment is transparently handled by an underlying communication system - the Distributed Information Management (DIM) package [11, 12].

DIM was designed to handle all data exchanges in the Delphi Online System. It should provide transparent distributed communications for all the different activities: control (SMI++), data acquisition read-out, data quality monitoring and processing, user-interfacing, etc.

5.1. Design Requirements. The main purpose of the DIM System is to make data available where and when it is necessary, independently of where it is produced. In order to accomplish its mission DIM was designed according to the following requirements:

- Uniformity. The DIM system should be capable of handling all exchanges within the Online System. All processes involved with control, monitoring, processing or display should use the same communication system. A homogeneous system is much easier to program and to maintain.
- Transparency. No matter where a process runs, it should be able to communicate with any other process in the system, using a single mechanism that is independent of where the processes are located. At run-time the DIM system should allow processes to move freely from one machine to another. All communications should be transparently re-established. This feature would allow for load balancing between machines, using either manual balancing for a static evaluation or dynamic balancing using automatic methods. At coding-time the programming interface should hide from the user all communication issues and reduce to the minimum the necessity for additional user code.
- Reliability and Robustness. In an environment with many processes, processors and networks, it often happens that a process, a processor or a network link breaks down. The loss of one of these items should not perturb the rest of the application. DIM should provide for automatic recovery from crash situations or the migration of processes.
- Wide-area Transparency. Since Delphi is an international collaboration, any necessary information should be available to the outside world, using the same system.

5.2. Communication Mechanism Considerations. When designing a communication system, the choice of the communication mechanism to be used is an important issue. Distributed applications are often based on remote procedure calls (RPC) [13]. In the RPC mechanism the client sends a message containing the name of a routine to be executed and its parameters to a server,

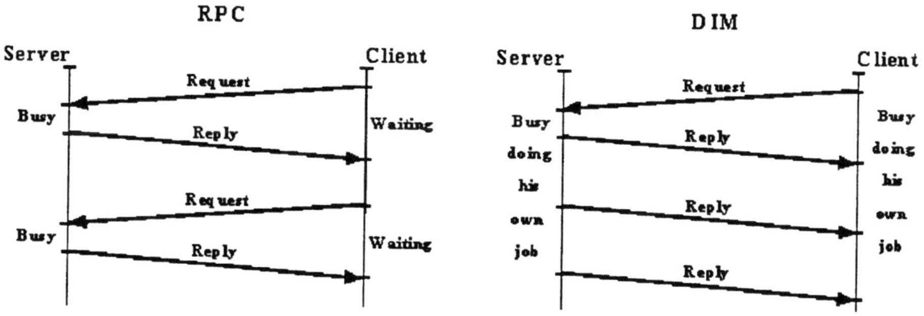

FIG. 5.1. : *RPC x DIM Mechanism*

the server executes the routine and sends a message back containing the result. This implies that the communication is point-to-point and synchronous, since the client always waits until the routine finishes execution, as shown in the diagram of Figure 5.1.

For an application like Delphi (but probably also for others such as industrial control or real-time applications) the RPC mechanism is very heavy and ill suited. In the Online System most of the processes should be able to react to asynchronous changes of conditions and the communication package should allow for this. Another important requirement is one-to-many communications, as in the case of change of conditions in many cases more than one process has to be notified. Furthermore most tasks are normally repetitive and have to be executed indefinitely.

The solution that seemed the best in this case is for clients to declare interest in a service provided by a server only once (at start-up), and then get updates at regular time intervals or when the conditions change. A protocol should allow asynchronous and one-to-many communications, as depicted in Figure 5.1.

This mechanism, interrupt-driven, as opposed to RPC's polling approach involves twice less messages sent over the network, i.e. it is faster and saves network bandwidth. It has also the advantages of allowing parallelism (since the client does not have to wait for the server to reply) and of allowing multiple clients to receive updates in parallel. This approach, together with the possibility of sending commands to servers (more RPC-like), are the main features of the DIM communication mechanism.

5.3. Design Philosophy. The basic concept in the DIM client/server approach is the concept of "service". Servers provide services to clients. A service is normally a set of data (of any type or size) and it is recognised by a name "named services". The name space for services is free. Four commonly used types of services have been identified:

- ONCE-ONLY: The client requests information.

- TIMED: The client requests the information to be updated at regular time intervals.
- MONITORED: The client requests the information to be updated whenever it changes (availability depends on whether the server can provide it).
- COMMAND: The client sends a command to the server.

The TIMED and MONITORED services are only requested once by the client (normally at start-up); the service will then be updated automatically by the server. When using MONITORED services, the server will update the information sent to all clients whenever it changes, thus making sure the data are coherent over all the clients of a certain service. The updating mechanism can be of two types, implemented either by executing a client call-back routine or by updating a client buffer with the new set of data, or both. In fact this last type works as if the clients maintain a copy of the server's data in cache, the cache coherence being assured by the server.

In order to allow for the required transparency (i.e., a client does not need to know where a server is running) as well as to allow for easy recovery from crashes and migration of servers, a name server was introduced. Servers "publish" their services by registering them with the name server (normally once, at start-up). Clients "subscribe" to services by asking the name server which server provides the service and then contacting the server directly, providing the type of service and the type of update as parameters.

The name server keeps an up-to-date directory of all the servers and services available in the system.

Whenever one of the processes (a server or even the name server) in the system crashes or dies all processes connected to it will be notified and will reconnect as soon as it comes back to life. This feature not only allows for easy recovery, but allows for the easy migration of a server from one machine to another (by stopping it in the first machine and starting it in the second one), and so for the possibility of balancing the machine load of the different workstations.

5.4. DIM Servers. DIM Servers are processes that have information to provide. In order to become a server a process has to declare any services it can provide to the name server. Servers also have to declare any commands they are willing to accept.

Each service is declared by calling a library routine specifying: the service name, the format of the service data (necessary only if running in mixed environments) and the mechanism by which the service will be provided. That is, the server can provide an address and a size where the service data can be found or a call-back routine that will gather the service data whenever the service is requested. Commands are declared using another routine specifying: the command name and a call-back routine that will handle the command. After declaring all services and commands provided, another routine has to be called in order to start serving client requests. This routine will send the full list of services and commands to the name server and set-up all necessary mechanisms in order for client requests to be handled transparently.

From then on the server can go back to its normal task, any client requests and service updates will be handled automatically by the DIM system. The server can however force the update of a certain service whenever necessary (a condition changed or an error was found) by calling a routine specifying the service identifier of the service to be updated.

5.5. DIM Clients. DIM clients are processes that need the available information to accomplish their tasks, that being display, monitoring or processing. A process becomes a client by calling one subroutine specifying:

- the service name it is interested in
- the update type - only once (ONCE-ONLY), at regular time intervals (TIMED) or whenever there is a change (MONITORED)
- a time parameter specifying either the time interval for TIMED services or a time-out after which the server is considered dead for the other types of service (for the TIMED services the time-out is computed internally based on the time interval requested)
- the update mechanism - storing the service data in a buffer and/or calling a call-back routine
- optionally, a constant buffer to be used as service data whenever the service is or becomes unavailable.

From then on the client can go on with its work, any service data will transparently be stored in the provided buffer and/or the call-back executed whenever a service is received according to the update type specified. A process can at any time send a command to a server by calling another subroutine specifying the command name and the command data.

The steps involved in becoming a client, either by requesting a service or sending a command are the following. First, the client asks the Name Server where is the service available, the name server replies the server's co-ordinates. The client contacts then directly the server and formulates its request (including the update type). The server will then take care of updating the service whenever necessary. If the service is not available, the Name Server will reply negatively. The constant data are put into the service data path and an update is triggered but the request stays queued in the Name Server. Whenever the service becomes available the client will be notified and the connection established. If the Name Server was not available the client will retry at random (between limits) intervals, until the Name Server is back up.

Any process can at the same time be a DIM Server and a DIM client.

6. Performance and Availability.

6.1. DIM. In order to measure DIM's performance it has been compared with the performance of raw TCP/IP, i.e., the fastest possible TCP/IP transfer. The machines used are 250 MHz Alpha workstations running the VMS operating system connected through 10 Mbps Ethernet.

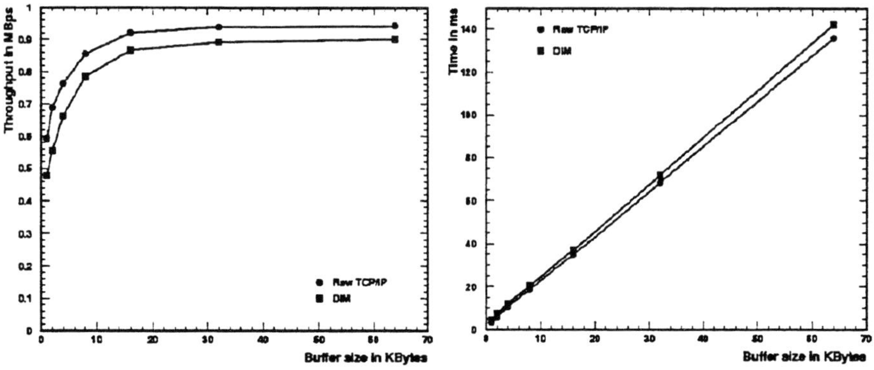

FIG. 6.1. : *Performance Results over Ethernet*

The test consists of sending a buffer from a client to a server and back to the client. In DIM's case the transfer is implemented using standard DIM calls, i.e., using the full functionality of DIM. What we call raw TCP/IP are two very simple programs containing a loop consisting of only read buffer and write buffer for the server, and write buffer and read buffer for the client.

Two quantities are measured: the throughput, i.e., the number of bytes transferred per second and the time of each transfer (both ways) for different sizes of the buffer transferred. As we see from the graphs in Figure 6.1, both DIM and raw TCP/IP curves saturate due to the Ethernet limited bandwidth. DIM is only about 1.05 times slower than raw TCP/IP and can be used to transfer data up to 900 Kbytes/second via Ethernet.

From the results of the performance tests we can conclude that DIM is well within the more severe time constraints expressed before. A data acquisition read-out (max. 500 Kbytes/second) deadline has been identified .

6.2. SMI++. The evaluation of the SMI's performance is based on the following test: an SMI domain contains an object "Top" and a proxy (Figure 6.2) implementing a simple ping-pong mechanism (change state - new state). One measure is the time SMI takes to react to an external change, send a command to a proxy (the proxy responds immediately) and for the new state to come back - "t" in Figure 6.3.

The other measure is t_{DIM} obtained by simulating the same transfer of data using directly the DIM package. Both quantities are measured when SMI and the proxy are running on the same machine, A, and when the SMI is running on machine A and the proxy on machine B across a slow Ethernet network. From this test it can be shown that SMI takes around 0.4 ms on an Alpha station to react to an external change and dispatch a command to the object concerned.

6.3. Availability. DIM is available in mixed environments comprising the operating systems: VMS (VAX and Alpha), Unix flavours (HP-UX, IBM AIX, SunOS, SUN Solaris, DEC OSF), Windows NT, Linux, OS9, LynxOS and Vx-

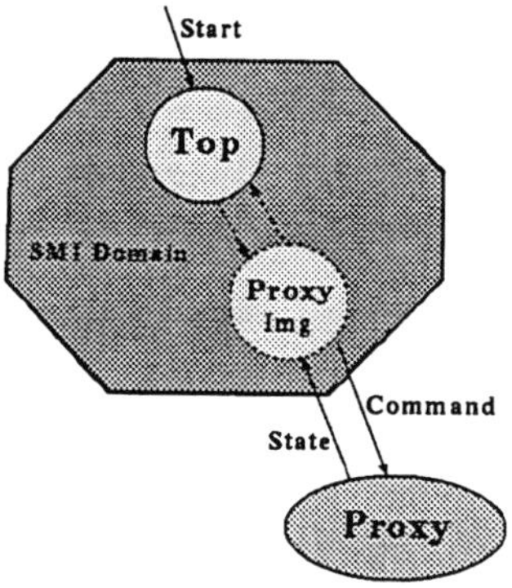

FIG. 6.2. : *SMI++ Test Set-up*

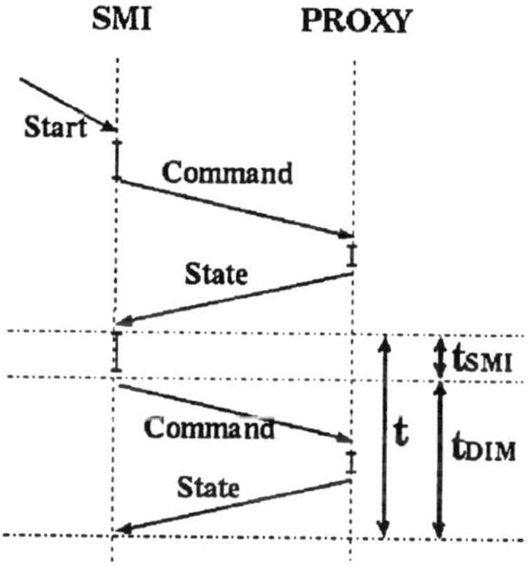

	A-A	A-B
t	1.2ms	6.6ms
t_{DIM}	800µs	6.2ms
$t_{SMI} = t - t_{DIM}$	400µs	400µs

A - ALPHA/VMS

B - VAX/VMS

FIG. 6.3. : *Time Measurements*

Works.

When exchanging data between these machines the data formats and data representation in the different machines have to be taken into account. All differences (byte ordering, structure alignment, floating point representation, etc.) are transparently handled by the DIM library. The full SMI++ tool set is also available on mixed environments comprising the platforms where DIM is available.

6.4. Monitoring and Debugging. The behaviour of complex distributed applications can be very difficult to understand without the help of a dedicated tool. A tool DID, the Distributed Information Display, allows the visualisation of the processes involved in the application. DID provides information on all the servers and services available in the system at a given moment and on the clients using them. The contents of a particular service can also be visualised.

The information available as DIM services can also be accessed through the World Wide Web, via a DIM-WWW gateway [14]. The WWW page can be written in HTML with specific DIM tags containing the service name. The DIM tags are translated when the page is loaded.

7. Conclusions. The control and monitoring of a modern physics experiment represents an important challenge. Unlike previous and "competitor" experiments, a generic architecture and a framework capable of handling the control and monitoring of all aspects of a physics experiment has been proposed and implemented. Our proposed architecture is to view the whole experiment as a collection of building blocks organised in a hierarchical tree-like structure.

Two main areas that should be inherent parts of such a generic framework corresponding to the proposed architecture for this kind of online distributed system have been identified: control and communications.

The control component of this framework is the State Management Interface - SMI++ Toolkit. SMI++ provides a method for describing the components of an Online System and to model their behaviour with the help of a simple language. It provides hooks for the implementer of a specific low-level component to insert the software that manipulates the hardware. SMI++ also provides tools to help running and testing the control system.

Any communications are transparently built into the framework. We proposed the DIM system as the lower layer in the framework. DIM provides efficient and reliable inter-process communications across different platforms. Its communication mechanism is based on the publish/subscribe method and allows for asynchronous communications and multiple destination updates.

Using such a framework throughout the Online System of an experiment can provide complete automation when possible, homegeneous operation and a better evolution and maintenance of the complete system.

REFERENCES

[1] P. Aarnio et al., *The Delphi Detector at LEP*, Nuclear Instruments and Methods in Physics Research, A303 (1991), pp. 233–276

[2] T. Adye et al., *The Slow Controls of the Delphi Experiment at LEP*, Proceedings of the International Conference on Computing in High Energy Physics '92, Annecy, France, September 1992.

[3] P. Charpentier et al., *Architecture and Performance of the Delphi Data Acquisition and Control System*, Proceedings of the International Conference on Computing in High Energy Physics '91, Tsukuba, Japan, March 1991.

[4] J. A. Fuster et al., *Architecture and Performance of the Delphi Trigger System*, Proceedings of the IEEE 1992 Nuclear Science Symposium, Orlando, Florida, October 1992.

[5] M. Dönszelmann and C. Gaspar, *The Delphi Distributed System for Exchanging LEP Machine Related Information*, Proceedings of the International Conference on Accelarator and Large Experimental Physics Control Systems, Berlin, Germany, October 1993.

[6] J. Barlow et al., *Run Control in MODEL: The State Manager*, IEEE Trans. Nucl. Sci., 36 (1989), pp. 1549-1553

[7] J. RUMBAUGH, M. BLAHA, W. PREMERLANI, F. EDDY, F. LORENSEN, *Object Oriented Modeling and Design*, Englewood Cliffs (NJ): Prentice Hall, 1991.
[8] G. BOOCH, *Object-Oriented Analysis and Design with Applications*, (2nd ed.). Redwood City (CA): Benjamin / Cummings, 1994.
[9] *Rational Rose/C++ User's Guide*, Rational Software Corporation, USA, 1995.
[10] B. FRANEK, PH. CHARPENTIER, M. DNSZELMANN, C. GASPAR, M. JONKER, R. SEKULIN, *Big Brother - A Fully Automated Control System for the Delphi Experiment*, Proceedings of the International Conference on Computing in High Energy Physics, San Francisco, USA, 1994, pp. 130-133.
[11] C. GASPAR AND M. DÖNSZELMANN, *DIM - A Distributed Information Management System for the Delphi Experiment at CERN*, Proceedings of the 8th Conference on Real-Time Computer Applications in Nuclear, Particle and Plasma Physics, Vancouver, Canada, June 1993.
[12] C. GASPAR, J. J. SCHWARZ, *Controlling a Large Physics Experiment: A Communication Issue*, Control Engineering Practice, Vol. 4, No. 2 (1996), pp. 257-264.
[13] A. D. BIRRELL AND B. J. NELSON, *Implementing Remote Procedure Calls*, ACM Trans. Comp. Syst., Vol. 2, No. 1 (1984), pp. 39-59
[14] M. DÖNSZELMANN, K. RODDEN, *Gateways for the World-Wide Web in the 'Online' Data Acquisition System of the Delphi Experiment at CERN*, Proceedings of the Second International World Wide Web (WWW) Conference, Chicago, Illinois, USA, 1994, p. 985-992.

INDEX

N

O

P

Q

R